Study Guide

Business

Seventh Edition

Study Guide

Kathryn W. Hegar, Ph.D.
Mountain View College

Business

Seventh Edition

William M. Pride
Texas A & M University

Robert J. Hughes
Dallas County Community Colleges

Jack R. Kapoor
College of DuPage

HOUGHTON MIFFLIN COMPANY   BOSTON   NEW YORK

Executive Editor: **George T. Hoffman**
Senior Development Editor: **Susan M. Kahn**
Senior Manufacturing Coordinator: **Marie Barnes**
Marketing Manager: **Steven W. Mikels**

Printed in the U.S.A.

ISBN: 0-618-11967-1

123456789-VGI-05 04 03 02 01

CONTENTS

Contents

TO THE STUDENT

Purpose

This study guide will help you learn the information found in the seventh edition of *Business* by Pride, Hughes, and Kapoor.

Objectives

This study guide will assist you in

- assessing your knowledge of business terms.
- checking your understanding of business concepts.
- identifying business topics that need further study.

Design of the Study Guide

The design of this study guide is based on the premise that new information must be reviewed up to seven times before it becomes part of one's understanding and knowledge. That is why it is important to follow the steps to successful learning found on the next page. After reading the textbook chapter assignment, outlining key ideas, and participating in class activities, use this study guide to:

- write definitions of terms and give examples.
- practice by taking three examinations.
- review the information missed on the examinations.

Key Terms. Space is provided to write the definition and give an example for each key term. Use the textbook page reference to check the accuracy of your answer.

Examinations. Three practice examinations will assess your comprehension of the information presented in the textbook. The results from the practice examinations will help you identify topics that need further study.

Layout of the Examinations

Each practice examination contains four types of objective questions:

1. *Matching questions.* The matching exercises focus on key business terms defined and used in the chapter.
2. *True-False questions.* The true-false questions assess basic knowledge discussed in the chapter.

3. *Multiple-choice questions.* The multiple-choice questions test for understanding of business terminology, concepts, and business practices. Application questions are included.

4. *Short-answer questions.* The short-answer questions examine your understanding of the learning objectives.

Steps to Successful Learning Using this Study Guide

1. *Read the information in the textbook chapter.* You may find it helpful to outline the information in the chapter.

2. *Write definitions and give examples for key terms.* Examples can help you remember the term.

3. *Attend class, participate in class discussions, take notes, and organize your notes.*

4. *Study the business terms and review the information in the textbook chapter before taking the first practice examination in this study guide.*

5. *Take Practice Examination A and check the results.* If you miss a lot of questions, you should review the textbook material before taking the second exam.

6. *Take Practice Examination B and check the results.* If you miss a number of questions on this examination, you still do not know the information and have not spent enough time studying the material. Spend more time studying. Go to your instructor for help.

7. *Take Practice Examination C and check the results.* You should make a good score on this examination.

After completing these exercises, you should know the information. Good luck in this course and best wishes for success in your career!

CHAPTER 1

EXPLORING THE WORLD OF BUSINESS

Key Terms

Define each term briefly. Writing down the definition and giving an example will help you learn the term.

free enterprise (p. 4)

e-commerce (p. 7)

business (p. 9)

consumers (p. 10)

profit (p. 11)

economics (p. 11)

economy (p. 11)

factors of production (p. 11)

entrepreneur (p. 13)

capitalism (p. 13)

market economy (p. 13)

mixed economy (p. 13)

consumer products (p. 14)

command economy (p. 15)

productivity (p. 16)

gross domestic product (GDP) (p. 16)

inflation (p. 16)

business cycle (p. 17)

recession (p. 18)

depression (p. 18)

monetary policies (p. 18)

fiscal policy (p. 18)

federal deficit (p. 18)

national debt (p. 18)

competition (p. 18)

pure competition (p. 19)

supply (p. 19)

demand (p. 19)

market price (p. 20)

monopolistic competition (p. 20)

product differentiation (p. 20)

oligopoly (p. 20)

monopoly (p. 21)

natural monopoly (p. 21)

barter (p. 23)

domestic system (p. 23)

factory system (p. 23)

specialization (p. 23)

standard of living (p. 24)

PRACTICE EXAMINATION A

Matching Questions (A)

Match each term with a statement.

a. free enterprise
b. competition
c. business
d. entrepreneur
e. e-commerce
f. economy

g. gross domestic product
h. consumers
i. profit
j. economics
k. monetary policies
l. fiscal policy

_____ 1. A motivating factor for starting a business.
_____ 2. A study of how goods are produced and distributed.
_____ 3. An organized effort to produce and sell goods and services for a profit.
_____ 4. A system that determines how wealth is created.

_____ 5. Describes the American economic system.
_____ 6. The process of rivalry to attract potential customers.
_____ 7. It uses the Internet to sell products.
_____ 8. Individuals who buy goods for their personal use.
_____ 9. A person who takes the risks and invests in a business.
_____ 10. Value of all goods and services produced within a country for a given period of time.
_____ 11. The levels of government spending are changed.
_____ 12. It determines the level of interest rates.

True-False Questions (A)

Select the correct answer.

T   F   13. Free enterprise is a system in which individuals decide what to produce and how to produce it.
T   F   14. Consumers are individuals who purchase goods to be resold.
T   F   15. Money is an information resource that entrepreneurs use effectively to keep a business operating.
T   F   16. Adam Smith, in his book, *The Wealth of Nations,* advocated capitalism as a way to serve society.
T   F   17. Economists recognize four categories of resources: workers, natural resources, capital, and ownership.
T   F   18. The equilibrium price means that the supply and demand for a product are in balance.
T   F   19. Under communism, individual consumers determine what will be produced.
T   F   20. Many buyers and sellers of products create a pure competitive market situation.
T   F   21. The Industrial Revolution in America started with the textile industry.
T   F   22. The barter system requires a well-established monetary system.

Multiple-Choice Questions (A)

Circle the letter before the most accurate answer.

23. The resources required to organize a business include _____ resources.
    a. material, human, financial, and information
    b. material, abilities, skills, and financial
    c. work output, quality control, and data
    d. wages, human, service, and production
    e. planning

24. A risk that an entrepreneur takes when starting a business involves
    a. being able to pay all the bills.
    b. earning a profit.
    c. expanding the business.
    d. losing whatever investments are in the business.
    e. losing economic freedom.

25. _____ is a necessary and extremely important by-product of free enterprise.
    a. Monopoly
    b. Competition
    c. Socialism
    d. Poverty
    e. Communism

26. The state of the economy when the level of prices are generally rising is called
    a. prosperity.
    b. recession.
    c. depression.
    d. recovery.
    e. inflation.

27. The total value of all goods and services produced in a nation reflects a country's
    a. stabilization.
    b. standard of living.
    c. progress.
    d. government.
    e. specialization.

28. Specialization
    a. combines tasks to make complete units.
    b. increases training requirements.
    c. increases the efficiency of industrial workers.
    d. occurred between 1870 and 1900.
    e. relieves boredom.

29. When consumers buy multimedia computers instead of notebook computers, they are telling the manufacturers
    a. to avoid faddish products.
    b. when to produce.
    c. how to produce.
    d. for whom to produce.
    e. what to produce.

30. A limited monopoly is created when
    a. the federal government issues a copyright.
    b. a customer purchases all items of a certain product.
    c. the Clayton Antitrust Act is repealed.
    d. an entrepreneur opens a sole proprietorship.
    e. None of the above.

Short-Answer Questions (A)

Complete each question.

31. Discuss four reasons why it is **important** to **study business**.

    a. _____

    b. _____

    c. _____

    d. _____

32. For a business to be **successful**, it must combine four types of **resources**. Identify the resources and give an example of each type.

RESOURCE	EXAMPLE

33. Business owners assume **two basic risks** in operating a business. Explain how business profits play a key role in minimizing these risks.

34. How does an **economic system** operating under capitalism differ from one operating as a command economy?

35. How a society answers **four basic economic questions** determines its economic system. What are the questions?

a. _____

b. _____

c. _____

d. _____

PRACTICE EXAMINATION B

Matching Questions (B)

Match each term with a statement.

a. market economy
b. capitalism
c. consumer products
d. command economy
e. mixed economy
f. communism
g. pure competition

h. supply
i. demand
j. market price
k. monopolistic competition
l. oligopoly
m. monopoly
n. productivity

_____ 1. The type of economy under which America operates.
_____ 2. Refers to the quantity of products available for sale.
_____ 3. Sellers attempt to provide similar products in a different way.
_____ 4. The market determines prices and quantities sold.
_____ 5. A market situation in which a firm has complete control over price.
_____ 6. Individuals buy and sell for personal consumption.
_____ 7. Refers to the quantity of products buyers are willing to purchase at various prices.
_____ 8. System of government used by Cuba.
_____ 9. The value at which supply and demand are exactly equal.
_____ 10. A market situation in which no single business affects price.
_____ 11. The market in which the American automobile industry operates.
_____ 12. Communism is an example.
_____ 13. A term describing the American economic system.
_____ 14. The average level of output per worker per hour.

True-False Questions (B)

Select the correct answer.

T F 15. People who invest their time, effort, and money to start a business are called middlemen.

T F 16. Ford Motor Company and Chrysler Corporation are monopolistic competitors in the marketplace.

T F 17. Consumers will always buy what manufacturers produce.

T F 18. Economic freedom ensures that buyers and sellers can enter markets as they choose.

T F 19. Sweden operates its markets in a command economy.

T F 20. The three basic questions critical to a capitalistic economy are what natural resources are available, how labor will be used, and who will run the business.

T F 21. In a monopoly market, the price of each product is determined by the actions of all buyers and sellers together.

T F 22. Sellers have little control over prices in an oligopoly market situation.

T F 23. If a firm's sales revenue exceeds its expenses, the firm has earned a profit.

T F 24. Fiscal policy determines the level of interest rates.

Multiple-Choice Questions (B)

Circle the letter before the most accurate answer.

25. The total of all federal deficits is called
   a. depression.
   b. fiscal policy.
   c. gross national product.
   d. national debt.
   e. business cycle.

26. Required questions for determining the type of economic plan a country will follow include
   a. what to produce, how to produce, and for whom to produce.
   b. which resources to import and which resources to export.
   c. who will be the president and who will run for Congress.
   d. what to produce and how much will be used as foreign aid.
   e. how much money will be allocated to social services.

27. When key industries are owned and controlled by the government and individuals can own and produce goods, the economy is called
   a. capitalism.
   b. communism.
   c. a planned economy.
   d. socialism.
   e. free enterprise.

28. The U.S. government provides an array of services to its citizens, which include
   a. education, national defense, and police protection.
   b. disaster relief, highways, and welfare payments.
   c. police protection, state parks, and standards for food.
   d. business loans and research and development funds.
   e. All of the above.

29. When businesses trade electrical services for plumbing services, they are engaging in
   a. the factory system.
   b. an unequal exchange of goods.
   c. ancient trading.
   d. bartering.
   e. fair trade.

30. Travis Henry recently started a small retail business offering specialty items from China. He realizes that economic freedom includes all of the following *except* the right to
   a. reject worker's demands.
   b. set the price of a product.
   c. guarantee economic success.
   d. use his own success formula.
   e. buy goods others produce.

31. Which of the following are characteristic of a socialist economy?
   a. The government owns and controls key industries.
   b. Key industries are owned and controlled by private businesses.
   c. The distribution of goods and services are controlled by the state.
   d. The government owns all land and raw materials.
   e. People may not choose their own occupations.

32. When a company sets its product apart from its competitors, by packaging the product in a unique manner, it is achieving price control in a manner known as
    a. oligopoly.
    b. advertising.
    c. marketing.
    d. distribution efficiency.
    e. product differentiation.

Short-Answer Questions (B)

Complete each question.

33. What is the role of each **factor of production** in producing goods and services? Identify the factors and explain their roles.

FACTOR OF PRODUCTION	ROLES

34. To determine the economic status of a nation, the following **measures** are used. How do they differ?

    a. Productivity _____

    b. Gross domestic product (GDP) _____

35. In each state of **fluctuation**, describe what happens in a nation's economy.

    a. Inflation _____

    b. Recession _____

    c. Depression _____

36. Describe the characteristics for each **type of competition**:

    a. Pure competition _____

    b. Monopolistic competition _____

    c. Oligopoly _____

    d. Monopoly _____

PRACTICE EXAMINATION C

Matching Questions (C)

Match each term with a statement.

a.	natural monopoly	g.	barter
b.	depression	h.	business cycle
c.	factory system	i.	recession
d.	specialization	j.	factors of production
e.	standard of living	k.	federal deficit
f.	inflation	l.	national debt

_____   1. Determines the level of individual satisfaction in terms of goods.
_____   2. When workers manufacture products in a central plan.
_____   3. Natural resources, labor, capital, and entrepreneurship.
_____   4. Reflects an increase in the level of prices.
_____   5. The market in which public utilities operate.
_____   6. Aimed at increasing the efficiency of industrial workers.
_____   7. System of exchange.
_____   8. Characterized by extremely high unemployment rates.
_____   9. The total of all federal deficits.
_____ 10. The government spends more than it receives.

True-False Questions (C)

Select the correct answer.

T F 11. Adam Smith argues in *The Wealth of Nations* that the government should control the economy.

T F 12. The main objective of every firm is to satisfy the needs of its customers.

T F 13. Profits provide business owners with the incentive to produce.

T F 14. Under capitalism, the central government plays a major role in the planning of the economy.

T F 15. Adam Smith is the father of communism and advocated a classless society.

T F 16. The factory system of production started with the beginning of the colonial period.

T F 17. A business cycle consists of four states: prosperity, recession, depression, and recovery.

T F 18. Most of the American work force is involved in manufacturing industries.

T F 19. The economy of the United States can best be classified as a mixed economy.

T F 20. The gross domestic product is the total value of all goods and services produced by all the citizens of a country for a one-year period of time.

Multiple-Choice Questions (C)

Circle the letter before the most accurate answer.

21. When goods are purchased for personal use, they are bought by
    a. consumers.
    b. manufacturers.
    c. middlemen.
    d. retailers.
    e. wholesalers.

22. Private ownership of property is a component of
    a. communism.
    b. a planned economy.
    c. Karl Marx's theory.
    d. capitalism.
    e. a dictatorship.

23. Demand is a
    a. relationship between prices and the quantities purchased by buyers.
    b. relationship between prices and the quantities offered by producers.
    c. quantity of goods available for purchase.
    d. price the consumer is willing to pay.
    e. by-product of communism.

24. Key issues challenging the business system over the next few decades include
    a. decreased inflation.
    b. the amount of government involvement.
    c. fewer monopolies being approved.
    d. low unemployment.
    e. the United States isolating itself from global markets.

25. Material resources include
    a. interpreting data files.
    b. paying employees a good wage.
    c. communication systems and networks.
    d. satisfying customers.
    e. raw materials, buildings, and machinery.

26. The process of separating work into distinct tasks is called
    a. bartering.
    b. networking.
    c. specialization.
    d. a factory system.
    e. a domestic system.

27. The economic freedom of a company to abandon its primary market and begin focusing on an entirely new type of business is typical of
    a. socialism.
    b. a free-market economy.
    c. a controlled economy.
    d. a mixed economy.
    e. communism.

28. To compare the economic growth of the United States with that of Mexico, one should examine the
    a. productivity rates.
    b. gross domestic product.
    c. types of competition.
    d. economic systems.
    e. consumer price indexes.

29. Which term best describes how public utilities operate in the United States?
    a. Monopolies
    b. Partners in barter
    c. Limited monopolies
    d. Natural monopolies
    e. Oligopolies

30. The U.S. government is deeply involved in business life. It collects a variety of taxes from households and businesses to support its programs and services. The services it offers to the public include
    a. apartment locators.
    b. car rentals.
    c. hair and nail care.
    d. investment brokerages.
    e. education.

31. Which statement characterizes the New Millennium environment?
    a. The stock market collapses.
    b. The steel, oil, and chemical industries expand.
    c. Information technology fuels the economy.
    d. Specialization increases workers' efficiency.
    e. Government intervenes in business operations for the first time.

Short-Answer Questions (C)

Complete each question.

32. How can the **supply** and **demand** of a product affect the price of the product in the marketplace?

33. How is the **domestic system** different from the **barter system**? Why did the change occur?

34. Explain how **specialization** helped promote the Industrial Revolution.

35. What are **five key issues** that will challenge our economic system in the next decade or two?

    a. _____

    b. _____

    c. _____

    d. _____

    e. _____

CHAPTER 2

BEING ETHICAL AND SOCIALLY RESPONSIBLE

Key Terms

Define each term briefly. Writing down the definition and giving an example will help you learn the term.

ethics (p. 37)

business ethics (p. 37)

code of ethics (p. 41)

whistle blowing (p. 43)

social responsibility (p. 44)

caveat emptor (p. 46)

economic model of social responsibility (p. 47)

socioeconomic model of social responsibility (p. 48)

consumerism (p. 50)

minority (p. 52)

affirmative action program (p. 54)

Equal Employment Opportunity Commission (EEOC) (p. 54)

hard-core unemployed (p. 54)

National Alliance of Business (NAB) (p. 55)

pollution (p. 56)

social audit (p. 61)

PRACTICE EXAMINATION A

Matching Questions (A)

Match the term with the statement.

a. social responsibility
b. caveat emptor
c. economic model

d. socioeconomic model
e. consumerism
f. minority

_____ 1. Protecting the rights of consumers is its focus.
_____ 2. People who have experienced discrimination make up this group.
_____ 3. According to this view, social responsibility is someone else's job.
_____ 4. It reflects how businesses deal with societal issues.
_____ 5. The belief that businesses have a responsibility to society is a premise.
_____ 6. "What you see is what you get" is its essence.

True-False Questions (A)

Select the correct answer.

T F   7. Social responsibility is concerned with business activities that have an impact on society.

T F   8. "What you see is what you get" is the equivalent to the Latin phrase "caveat emptor" meaning "let the buyer beware."

T F   9. Stockholders today minimize the need for ethical behavior from business managers in making profits for a firm.

T F 10. The socioeconomic model of social responsibility holds that making a profit is the firm's only responsibility.

T F 11. In consumerism, the right to safety means that products have been tested by the manufacturer to ensure quality and reliability.

T F 12. The Fair Debt Collection Practices Act (1977) outlaws abusive collection practices by third parties.

T F 13. The Clean Air Act of 1977 has been abolished.

T F 14. Government and businesses are spending at least $72 billion each year to reduce pollution.

T F 15. Employees practice whistle blowing when they schedule business trips by train.

T F 16. Factors that influence ethical behavior in an organization include an individual's knowledge level regarding an issue, cultural norms, and the amount of freedom an organization gives an employee.

T F 17. The consumer's "right to choose" legislation has forced prices to increase on most products.

Multiple-Choice Questions (A)

Circle the letter before the most accurate answer.

18. The first federal act to regulate business practices was the _____ Act.
    a. Federal Trade Commission
    b. Clayton
    c. Interstate Commerce
    d. Sherman Antitrust
    e. Meat Inspection

19. The traditional concept that businesses are responsible to their investors and that social responsibility is someone else's job is the core of the
    a. economic model of social responsibility.
    b. socioeconomic model of social responsibility.
    c. corporate model of social responsibility.
    d. corporate code of ethics.
    e. doctrine of caveat emptor.

20. The act that requires warning labels on household chemicals if they are highly toxic is the
    a. Kefauver-Harris Drug Amendment.
    b. Fair Packaging and Labeling Act.
    c. Pure Food and Drug Act.
    d. Federal Hazardous Substances Labeling Act.
    e. Flammable Fabrics Act.

21. Minority groups have been discriminated against on the basis of
    a. race.
    b. age and sex.
    c. national origin.
    d. religion.
    e. All of the above.

22. Standards for cleaning navigable streams and lakes and eliminating all harmful waste disposal by 1985 were established by the
    a. Water Quality Improvement Act (1970).
    b. Resource Recovery Act (1970).
    c. Water Pollution Control Act Amendment (1972).
    d. National Environmental Policy Act.
    e. Magnuson-Moss Warranty Federal Trade Commission Act (1975).

23. The application of moral standards to business situations is called
    a. business ethics.
    b. ethics.
    c. code of conduct.
    d. doing the right thing.
    e. freedom of choice.

24. If a company wants to encourage a more ethical climate, it should
    a. add an officer who constantly monitors employee behavior.
    b. make certain that the company has a code of ethics that is enforced.
    c. install security cameras and one-way mirrors.
    d. avoid the topic, since people can be trusted.
    e. do nothing, as values take too much time to develop in employees.

25. Which practice could have averted the *Challenger* disaster?
    a. Trusting members in the team
    b. Whistle blowing
    c. Developing a more cohesive team
    d. Disregarding the code of ethics
    e. Tightening the communication network

26. "Our purpose is to provide the best products and services to our customers and to earn a return on our stockholder's investment, not to provide day-care centers and counseling for drug abusers." What concept does this attitude reflect?
    a. Socioeconomic model of social responsibility
    b. Code of ethical behavior
    c. Economic model of social responsibility
    d. Consumerism
    e. Equal employment opportunity

27. The Food and Drug Administration and the Consumer Product Safety Commission, by ensuring that products are safe and reliable, are taking part in a movement known as
    a. protectionism.
    b. socialism.
    c. product liability management.
    d. product activism.
    e. consumerism.

28. A major consumer advocate who has devoted time to protecting the rights of consumers is
    a. George Bush.
    b. Bill Clinton.
    c. Henry Ford.
    d. Bill Gates.
    e. Ralph Nader.

29. John Ameron has no marketable skills, a chronic record of unemployment, and did not complete high school. Which organization could best help him?
    a. National Alliance of Business
    b. American Federation of Labor
    c. Chamber of Commerce
    d. Equal Employment Opportunity Commission
    e. Consumer Product Safety Commission

30. When Maytag provides customers with a booklet describing how to use a washing machine, the company is satisfying the consumer bill of rights to
    a. choose.
    b. be informed.
    c. safety.
    d. be heard.
    e. consume.

Short-Answer Questions (A)

Complete each question.

31. **Business ethics** is the application of what is "right" or "wrong" to business situations. Identify which of the following business activities are ethically *right* or *wrong*. Place an **"R"** before the activities that are ethically acceptable and a **"W"** before the activities you feel are ethically wrong.

    _____ The Joe Camel advertising campaign for cigarettes.
    _____ Supervisors taking credit for work completed by employees in their department.
    _____ A supervisor refuses to accept a gift from a vendor for signing a contract in a timely manner.
    _____ Employees making personal phone calls at work.
    _____ A vice president fails to approve the marketing of non-tested drugs in a third-world country.
    _____ An employee notifies a government official about activities that are not in compliance with the government contract.

32. **Add two business activities you feel are ethically wrong, and tell why they are wrong.**

    a. _____

    b. _____

33. For each **ethical issue**, describe the **type of behavior** in the workplace that would be ethically acceptable.

ETHICAL ISSUES	ACCEPTABLE WORKPLACE BEHAVIORS
Fairness and Honesty	
Organizational Relationships	
Conflict of Interest	
Communications	

34. Explain why all **bribes** are **unethical** in America.

35. Describe the **characteristics** of each factor and tell how it **affects the level of ethical behavior** in an organization.

FACTOR	CHARACTERISTICS OF THE FACTOR	HOW THE FACTOR AFFECTS ETHICAL BEHAVIOR
Individual Factor		
Social Factor		
Opportunity Factor		

36. Explain how **diversity** in today's workplace is affecting business ethics.

PRACTICE EXAMINATION B

Matching Questions (B)

Match the term with the statement.

a. affirmative action program
b. reverse discrimination
c. EEOC

d. hard-core unemployed
e. NAB
f. pollution

_____ 1. Complaints of discrimination are investigated.
_____ 2. The result is deterioration of the natural environment.
_____ 3. It occurs when only minorities are considered for a job opening.
_____ 4. People who have little education or training.
_____ 5. A joint business-government program designed to train the hard-core unemployed.
_____ 6. The purpose is to ensure that minorities are represented throughout a firm.

True-False Questions (B)

Select the correct answer.

T F 7. Demands for social responsibility are a direct result of the United States involvement in the Vietnam War.

T F 8. Before the 1930s, competition and market activities were expected to correct most abuses.

T F 9. An internal business force that affects decisions concerning social responsibility is government regulation.

T F 10. By helping resolve social issues, businesses can create a more stable environment for long-term profitability.

T F 11. The NAB has the power to police firms that produce defective products.

T F 12. Quotas requiring firms to hire minorities have caused problems in affirmative action programs.

T F 13. Carbon monoxide and hydrocarbons are two major causes of air pollution.

T F 14. Business ethics is no longer a major concern in our society.

T F 15. Employees generally find it easy to assess ethical issues.

T F 16. The ethics director coordinates ethical behavior, conducts open meetings on specific employee behaviors, and reports these actions to the public.

Multiple-Choice Questions (B)

Circle the letter before the most accurate answer.

17. This act prevents mergers where competition is endangered.
   a. Interstate Commerce Act
   b. Sherman Antitrust Act
   c. Federal Trade Commission Act
   d. Clayton Act
   e. Truth in Lending Act

18. An argument for increased social responsibility includes the idea that
   a. corporate talent should be used to maximize profits.
   b. social issues are the responsibility of elected officials.
   c. business managers are primarily responsible to business owners.
   d. businesses have the resources to tackle complex social issues.
   e. business managers are primarily responsible to stockholders.

19. Lenders and credit merchants are required to disclose the full cost of finance charges in both dollars and annual percentage rates under the _____ Act.
   a. Truth in Lending
   b. Credit Card Liability
   c. Fair Credit Reporting
   d. Fair Credit Billing
   e. Land Sales Disclosure

20. The following program ensures that minorities are represented within the organization in approximately the same proportion as in the surrounding community:
    a. National Alliance of Business
    b. Affirmative Action Program
    c. Equal Employment Opportunity Program
    d. Hard-Core Unemployment Program
    e. All of the above

21. It requires motor vehicles to be equipped with onboard systems to control about 90 percent of refueling vapors.
    a. Clean Air Act Amendments (1990)
    b. National Environmental Policy Act (1970)
    c. Clean Air Amendment (1970)
    d. Oil Pollution Act (1990)
    e. Resource Recovery Act (1970)

22. When advertisers of health-related foods use descriptive terms such as "low fat," "fat free," or "lite," they may be engaging in a(n)
    a. conflict of interest.
    b. moral issue.
    c. example of social responsibility.
    d. need for better communications.
    e. ethical problem by deception.

23. The human resource manager has recently become aware that many employees in the company are taking long lunch breaks, using their computers to prepare personal correspondence, and not coming in on time. The *best* way to proceed would be to
    a. suspend all those who fail to arrive at work on time and take extended lunch breaks.
    b. change the code of ethics to prohibit these practices.
    c. change the corporate environment to encourage more ethical behavior.
    d. let the union handle the problems through their grievances policy.
    e. hire more security personnel to monitor employee behaviors.

24. Major advances in consumerism have come through
    a. increased competition.
    b. consumer advocates.
    c. educating consumers.
    d. federal legislation.
    e. employment practices.

25. A local bank just completed its social audit for the past year. Which statement indicates a valid attempt at responding to social responsibility by the bank?
    a. This year marked an increase of 100 percent in the number of depositors.
    b. Each employee completed at least 200 hours of service to community functions.
    c. The loan department expanded services to large businesses.
    d. One white female was promoted to an officer's position.
    e. A reward system encourages all employees to market the bank's products and services.

26. To cover the costs of social responsibility activities, management can
    a. pass the costs on to consumers in higher prices.
    b. absorb the costs of the program.
    c. let the government pay for all of it through special incentive programs.
    d. let tax reduction programs pay for it.
    e. All of the above ways are acceptable.

27. John Brown, a local entertainment store manager, carried a few items of merchandise that did not meet with approval of parents in the community. Police were called several times to inform the store manager to remove the items. John failed to do anything about it. Eventually, the parents in the community forced him out of business. John might be in business today had he
    a. asked the police to stop bothering him.
    b. added more items to increase his sales.
    c. read the complaints.
    d. worked more with the community to solve the problem.
    e. been more concerned with the economic model of social responsibility.

28. The Cran-Apple Corporation decided to set up a program for social responsibility. Its top managers developed a policy statement outlining key areas of concern. This statement will serve as a guide for employees. Now
    a. a committee of managers should be appointed to plan the program.
    b. employees should be appointed to submit suggestions to management.
    c. a top-level executive should be appointed to direct implementation of the program.
    d. employees should evaluate the program.
    e. the program director should prepare a social audit for the firm at specified intervals.

29. Which of the following is *not* one of the steps a business takes in initiating a social responsibility program?
    a. Development of a plan
    b. Commitment of top executives
    c. Recognizing the existence of a problem
    d. Appointment of a program director
    e. Conducting a social audit

Short-Answer Questions (B)

Complete each question.

30. The purpose of a **code of ethics** is to encourage ethical behavior in the workplace. Describe four things that should be included in every code of ethics.

    a. _____

    b. _____

c. _____

d. _____

31. Describe **whistle blowing.** What are both the pros and the cons for an employee who may engage in whistle blowing?

32. Describe how two businesses are attempting to be **socially responsible**. First, think of the company where you work. Is the company practicing social responsibility? If so, how? Second, give an example from another company.

a. _____

b. _____

33. List the **characteristics** for each **model** for social responsibility:

ECONOMIC MODEL	SOCIOECONOMIC MODEL

34. Business owners, managers, customers, and government officials have debated the pros and cons of **increased social responsibility** for years. What are some arguments for and against increasing social responsibility?

ARGUMENTS FOR (PROS)	ARGUMENTS AGAINST (CONS)

PRACTICE EXAMINATION C

Matching Questions (C)

Match the term with the statement.

a. economic model
b. ethics
c. business ethics
d. code of ethics

e. whistle blowing
f. social audit
g. socioeconomic model

_____ 1. Moral standards are applied to business.
_____ 2. The social responsibility program is evaluated.
_____ 3. Employees' expected behavior on the job is described.
_____ 4. It guides an individual's behavior in dealing with others.
_____ 5. Employees tell government officials about unethical practices in their workplace.
_____ 6. The primary emphasis is on production.
_____ 7. Quality of life is important.

True-False Questions (C)

Select the correct answer.

T   F   8. "Significant others" is a term used to indicate the person to whom an employee reports in the office.

T F   9. In the early days, employees joined labor unions in an effort to improve working conditions.

T F   10. Franklin D. Roosevelt was instrumental in initiating programs to curb monopolistic abuses by big business.

T F   11. The economic model of social responsibility is used exclusively by IBM and Johnson & Johnson.

T F   12. An argument against increased social responsibility is that corporate time, money, and talent should be used to maximize profits, not to solve society's problems.

T F   13. The Fair Packaging and Labeling Act of 1966 calls for all products sold across state lines to be labeled with net weight, ingredients, and the manufacturer's name and address.

T F   14. The National Alliance of Business is a locally sponsored program that offers scholarships to academically successful students.

T F   15. A Superfund was established in 1980 to finance the cleanup of hazardous waste sites across the nation.

T F   16. A corporate code of ethics provides guidelines for acceptable and ethical behavior in business operations.

T F   17. The economic model of social responsibility emphasizes the effect of business decisions on society.

T F   18. A shortage of landfills, stricter regulations, strip mining, and housing developments are examples of causes of increased land pollution problems.

Multiple-Choice Questions (C)

Circle the letter before the most accurate answer.

19. The act that eliminated many forms of price discrimination that gave large businesses a competitive advantage over smaller firms was the _____ Act.
    a. Clayton Antitrust
    b. Sherman Antitrust
    c. Fair Packaging and Labeling
    d. Pure Food and Drug
    e. Federal Trade Commission

20. John F. Kennedy's consumer bill of rights includes the right to
    a. waste.   d. freedom.
    b. safety.   e. religion.
    c. national origin.

21. The first federal act to regulate business practices and provide regulation of railroads and shipping rates was the
    a. Federal Trade Commission Act (1914).
    b. Clayton Antitrust Act (1914).
    c. Interstate Commerce Act (1887).
    d. Sherman Antitrust Act (1890).
    e. Truth in Lending Act (1968).

22. A corporate code of ethics is a guide to acceptable behavior in business operations and should reflect relationships with
    a. suppliers.
    b. customers.
    c. coworkers.
    d. competitors.
    e. All of the above.

23. You are the executive vice president for Cooper Tire, the sixth largest U.S. tire maker. You have the responsibility to locate land for a new distribution center in Mississippi, and you personally own over 1,000 acres of land near one site in Tupelo. This could create for you
    a. a code of ethics.
    b. the usual decision-making problems of cost versus benefit to Cooper Tire.
    c. a conflict of interest.
    d. a wonderful, ethical opportunity to make a lot of money.
    e. an ethical opportunity to move the distribution center to your hometown.

24. The primary emphasis of the economic model of social responsibility is
    a. quality of life.
    b. conservation of natural resources.
    c. the interests of the firm and the community.
    d. active government involvement.
    e. production.

25. Working conditions have changed over the years. Since the 1930s, what has been government's role in social responsibility? Government has
    a. allowed businesses to operate as they chose.
    b. increased the workweek to 60 hours by law.
    c. discouraged unions from forming.
    d. decreased its role.
    e. increased protection of workers and consumers.

26. Proponents of the socioeconomic model of social responsibility argue that
    a. corporate time, money, and talent should be used to maximize profits, not to solve society's problems.
    b. by helping to resolve social issues, businesses can create a more stable environment for long-term profitability.
    c. social issues are the responsibility of government officials elected by the people.
    d. individual businesses are not equipped to solve social problems that affect society in general.
    e. business managers are primarily responsible to stockholders.

27. Which factor *least* affects the level of ethical behavior in an organization?
    a. Employee's knowledge about an issue
    b. Passage of federal laws
    c. Cultural background of employees
    d. "Significant others" in employees' lives
    e. Firm's code of ethics

28. Carol Randal has the educational requirements, experience, and skills required to be promoted to the next management level in an insurance company. Overhearing a conversation between two other employees, she learns that the person who was promoted to the position had been with the firm less than a year, was currently working on completing his degree in the next semester, and lacks skills in several areas. She should file a complaint with the
    a. Equal Employment Opportunity Commission.
    b. National Alliance of Business.
    c. union.
    d. National Organization for Women.
    e. Federal Trade Commission.

29. The first step in developing a social responsibility program is
    a. appointing a director.
    b. preparing a plan.
    c. getting support from top executives.
    d. preparing a social audit.
    e. reviewing the external programs.

Short-Answer Questions (C)

Complete each question.

30. Identify the four **basic rights of consumers** and give an example for each.

BASIC RIGHTS OF CONSUMERS	EXAMPLE

31. Describe an **affirmative action plan.** What should it include?

32. What is the purpose of the **National Alliance of Business (NAB)**?

33. **Pollution** is the contamination of water, air, land, or noise. For each type of pollution describe legislation designed to clean up the environment.

POLLUTION	LEGISLATION	MAJOR PROVISIONS
Water		
Air		
Land		
Noise		

34. Who should **pay** for a **clean environment** and why?

35. Developing and implementing a **social responsibility program** requires four steps:

   a. _____

   b. _____

   c. _____

   d. _____

36. What is a **social audit**? Identify typical subject areas covered in the audit.

CHAPTER 3

EXPLORING GLOBAL BUSINESS

Key Terms

Define each term briefly. Writing down the definition and giving an example will help you learn the term.

international business (p. 69)

absolute advantage (p. 70)

comparative advantage (p. 70)

exporting (p. 71)

importing (p. 71)

balance of trade (p. 71)

trade deficit (p. 71)

balance of payments (p. 72)

import duty (tariff) (p. 74)

dumping (p. 74)

nontariff barrier (p. 74)

import quota (p. 74)

embargo (p. 74)

foreign-exchange control (p. 74)

currency devaluation (p. 74)

General Agreement on Tariffs and Trade (GATT) (p. 82)

World Trade Organization (WTO) (p. 82)

economic community (p. 83)

licensing (p. 86)

letter of credit (p. 87)

bill of lading (p. 87)

draft (p. 87)

strategic alliance (p. 89)

trading company (p. 89)

countertrade (p. 89)

multinational enterprise (p. 90)

Export-Import Bank of the United States (Eximbank) (p. 94)

multilateral development bank (MDB) (p. 94)

International Monetary Fund (IMF) (p. 95)

PRACTICE EXAMINATION A

Matching Questions (A)

Match each term with a statement.

a. international business
b. absolute advantage
c. comparative advantage
d. exporting

e. importing
f. balance of trade
g. trade deficit
h. balance of payments

_____ 1. A country produces a specific product more efficiently than any other product.
_____ 2. It is the total value of exports less the total value of imports.
_____ 3. Goods and services are exchanged across national boundaries.
_____ 4. It is the process of selling goods to foreign nations.
_____ 5. It is a measure of the total flow of money into a country less the total flow of money out of a country.
_____ 6. A country has the ability to produce a specific product more efficiently than any other nation.
_____ 7. It is the process of buying goods from foreign countries.
_____ 8. An unfavorable balance of trade is created.

True-False Questions (A)

Select the correct answer.

T F 9. South Africa has an absolute advantage in diamonds.
T F 10. Importing and exporting are the principal activities involved in a nation's balance of trade.
T F 11. The last trade deficit of the United States occurred in 1990.
T F 12. The United States presently has an import embargo against Iraq.
T F 13. Dumping drives up the price of the domestic item.
T F 14. The Uruguay Round widened the GATT to include intellectual-property rights.
T F 15. OPEC was founded in 1960 to provide some control over oil prices.
T F 16. Licensing is a way to distribute goods internationally.
T F 17. Under the direct-investment approach, domestic firms are not allowed to purchase foreign firms.
T F 18. Research and development give the United States a comparative advantage.
T F 19. The World Bank provides assistance to developing nations.
T F 20. When a country imports $582.3 billion in goods and exports $395.2 billion, it has a trade deficit.
T F 21. South Korea is the largest emerging Asian market.

Multiple-Choice Questions (A)

Circle the letter before the most accurate answer.

22. When a business firm in Dallas, Texas, sells goods to a company in France, it is engaging in
    a. absolute advantage.
    b. comparative advantage.
    c. importing.
    d. international business.
    e. dumping.

23. A tax levied on a foreign product entering this country is called a(n)
    a. tariff.
    b. quota.
    c. control.
    d. embargo.
    e. export.

24. Arguments against imposing trade restrictions include
    a. protecting new or weak industries.
    b. protecting national security.
    c. protecting the health of citizens.
    d. the loss of jobs.
    e. protecting domestic jobs.

25. The joining of Mexico, United States, and Canada on January 1, 1994, into an agreement is called
    a. Canadian Free Trade Agreement (FTA).
    b. Pacific Rim.
    c. North American Free Trade Agreement (NAFTA).
    d. Organization for Economic Cooperation and Development (OECD).
    e. Commonwealth of Independent States (CIS).

26. An internationally supported bank that provides loans to developing countries for growth is the
    a. Eximbank.
    b. World Bank.
    c. African Development Bank.
    d. European Bank for Reconstruction and Development.
    e. Inter-American Development Bank.

27. Outside the United States seven out of ten of the largest multinational companies in the world are in
    a. America.
    b. France.
    c. Japan.
    d. Germany.
    e. Canada.

28. A small manufacturer wants to launch a well-known brand internationally. Which method is the *most* advantageous for the manufacturer?
    a. Joint venture
    b. Licensing
    c. Exporting
    d. Totally owned facilities
    e. Multinational firm

29. What is the *most* basic level of exporting to foreign markets?
    a. Export/import merchant
    b. Export/import agent
    c. Establishing a sales office
    d. Establishing a branch office
    e. Using a sales force

30. The uniting of Toyota and General Motors to make Chevrolet Novas and Toyota Tercels created an international business structure called a(n)
    a. strategic alliance.
    b. international partnership.
    c. trading company.
    d. joint venture.
    e. countertrade.

31. Recently Saudi Arabia traded crude oil for ten 747 jets from Boeing. This international barter transaction is called a
    a. multinational transaction.
    b. financing partnership.
    c. countertrade.
    d. venture.
    e. protective tariff.

32. Why might a country want to impose trade restrictions on the import of specific products? A good reason to restrict trade is to
    a. lower prices for consumers.
    b. protect weak industries.
    c. increase consumers' choices.
    d. use international resources more efficiently.
    e. increase jobs in the trading country.

33. An example of a nontariff barrier that creates obstacles to the marketing of foreign goods in a country and increases costs for exporters is
    a. an import quota.
    b. an embargo.
    c. a foreign-exchange control.
    d. currency devaluation.
    e. All of the above are examples.

34. A United States company wants to team up with an established Chinese firm to manufacture and market its products. The U.S. firm also wants to reduce its risk and have control over product quality. What is the *best* choice for the U.S. firm?
    a. Joint venture
    b. Licensing
    c. Direct investments
    d. Export/import merchant
    e. Export/import agent

35. When a firm has plants located in several foreign countries, it is called a(n)
    a. joint venture.
    b. multinational enterprise.
    c. international trading company.
    d. licensed firm.
    e. countertrade.

36. The National Trade Data Bank (NTDB)
   a. is a nationwide group of attorneys with experience in international trade.
   b. is a network of trade specialists who provide information on foreign markets.
   c. contains international economic and export promotion information supplied by over twenty United States agencies.
   d. provides export marketing and trade finance assistance.
   e. helps American firms compete in foreign markets and creates new jobs in the United States.

Short-Answer Questions (A)

Complete each question.

37. Explain why you are not engaging in **international trade** when you purchase foreign products in a local store.

38. How does a country with an **absolute advantage** differ from one with a **comparative advantage**? Give an example.

39. What is the difference between a nation's **balance of trade** and its **balance of payments**?

40. Describe how each **nontariff barrier** restricts trade.

BARRIER	HOW DOES EACH BARRIER AFFECT TRADE?
Import quota	
Embargo	
Foreign-exchange control	
Currency devaluation	
Bureaucratic red tape	

41. Compare the reasons for **imposing trade restrictions** to those reasons against imposing trade restrictions.

REASONS FOR TRADE RESTRICTIONS	REASONS AGAINST TRADE RESTRICTIONS

PRACTICE EXAMINATION B

Matching Questions (B)

Match each term with a statement.

a. embargo
b. foreign-exchange control
c. currency devaluation
d. import duty
e. tariff

f. economic community
g. licensing
h. multinational enterprise
i. import quota
j. multilateral development banks

_____ 1. The term is synonymous with import duty.
_____ 2. A contractual agreement is usually involved.
_____ 3. They provide loans to developing countries to assist in their growth.
_____ 4. It can be used as a political weapon.
_____ 5. A tax that is levied on foreign products entering a country.
_____ 6. An organization of nations formed to promote the free movement of products.
_____ 7. A limit imposed on a particular imported good.

_____ 8. Restrictions that are placed on the buying and selling of foreign currency.
_____ 9. A firm that operates on a worldwide scale.
_____ 10. The process reduces the value of a nation's currency.

True-False Questions (B)

Select the correct answer.

T F 11. The Boeing Corporation in the United States imports airplanes to England.
T F 12. A favorable balance of trade occurs when a nation imports more than it exports.
T F 13. When the cost of foreign goods increases and the cost of domestic goods to foreign firms decreases, the result could be caused by currency devaluation.
T F 14. A tariff has the effect of raising the price of the product in the exporting nation.
T F 15. ASEAN promotes exports to seven member countries of Southeast Asia.
T F 16. The Kennedy Round negotiations increased tariffs by 35 percent.
T F 17. An advantage of using licensing is that expansion can occur with very little investment.
T F 18. A joint venture is a partnership between firms.
T F 19. NAFTA will gradually eliminate all tariffs on goods produced and traded between Canada, Mexico, and the United States.
T F 20. Countertrade is a technique for financing world trade.
T F 21. The IMF makes long-term loans to fund international trade.
T F 22. If a country imports more than it exports, its balance of trade is said to be favorable.
T F 23. The European Free Trade Association is known as the Common Market.

Multiple-Choice Questions (B)

Circle the letter before the most accurate answer.

24. When Saudi Arabia specializes in the production of crude oil and petroleum products, it is practicing the concept of
    a. international business.
    b. comparative advantage.
    c. restricting trade.
    d. absolute advantage.
    e. licensing.

25. A complete halt to trading with a particular nation is known as
    a. an unfavorable balance of trade.
    b. a favorable balance of trade.
    c. an embargo.
    d. dumping.
    e. a dissolution of trading.

26. An important function of a trading company is
    a. providing loans to Pacific Rim countries.
    b. performing activities to move products into a foreign country.
    c. advising small business owners on trading internationally.
    d. increasing imports to the domestic country.
    e. All of the above are important functions.

27. A goal of OPEC is to
    a. increase the supply of oil.
    b. control the prices of crude oil.
    c. reduce the oversupply of oil.
    d. deregulate the oil industry.
    e. provide loans to oil-producing countries.

28. The *best* known United States trading company is
    a. the World Bank.
    b. NAFTA.
    c. Coca-Cola, Inc.
    d. General Motors.
    e. Sears World Trade.

29. When Sony decided to enter the motion picture business in the United States, it purchased Columbia Pictures Entertainment, Inc. What is this method of entering international business called?
    a. Direct investment
    b. Licensing
    c. Joint venture
    d. Strategic alliances
    e. Trading partnership

30. When Michelle from Texas flies to Mexico on a Mexican airline and buys silver jewelry to bring home, she is
    a. decreasing the trade deficit.
    b. being disloyal and unpatriotic.
    c. contributing to the negative balance of payments.
    d. buying American-made goods.
    e. buying American-produced services.

31. When the United States levies a tax on luxury cars from Japan, this tax is a type of
    a. export duty.
    b. tariff.
    c. barter.
    d. import.
    e. responsibility.

32. Pacific Rim refers to countries and economies of
    a. Canada.
    b. East Asia.
    c. Japan.
    d. China.
    e. All of the above.

33. The Commonwealth of Independent States (CIS) was established in 1991 as an association of
    a. countries bordering the Pacific Ocean.
    b. six countries in Europe.
    c. eleven republics of the former Soviet Union.
    d. Caribbean and Central American countries.
    e. South American countries.

34. Between 1973 and 1979, the Tokyo Round negotiations
    a. increased nontariff barriers such as import quotas.
    b. resulted in 50 percent tariff cuts.
    c. were implemented over a fifteen-year period.
    d. increased nontariff barriers.
    e. eased unrealistic quality standards for imports.

35. When South America produces coffee and exports it to the rest of the world, what advantage does it have?
    a. Absolute advantage
    b. Comparative advantage
    c. Economic advantage
    d. No advantage
    e. Some advantage

36. Which statement is *not* true about joint ventures. A joint venture
    a. may be used to produce an existing product in a foreign country.
    b. requires a low level of commitment from all parties involved.
    c. provides immediate market knowledge and access.
    d. reduces the risk element.
    e. allows greater control over product quality.

37. An embargo is
    a. a complete halt to trading with a particular country.
    b. used as a political weapon.
    c. a halt to the trading of a particular product from a country.
    d. imposed on Iraq by the United States.
    e. All of the above are true about embargoes.

38. When a limit is set on the amount of a particular good that can be imported into a country, what type of barrier has been imposed?
    a. Embargo
    b. Foreign-exchange control
    c. Currency devaluation
    d. Import quota
    e. Import duty

Short-Answer Questions (B)

Complete each question.

39. Why is **GATT** important to international trade?

40. Compare the **key negotiation points** in each Round. List the key points for each.

KENNEDY ROUND 1964-1967	TOKYO ROUND 1973-1979	URUGUAY ROUND 1986-1993

41. For the following countries, what is their **projected economic outlook** into the next millenium?

COUNTRIES	PROJECTED ECONOMIC OUTLOOK
Canada and Western Europe	
Mexico and South America	
Asia	
Central and Eastern Europe and Russia	
United States	

42. What is the purpose of each **international economic community**? Identify the countries that belong to the community.

ECONOMIC COMMUNITY	PURPOSE (Identify the countries involved)
European Union (EU)	
European Economic Area (EEA)	
North American Free Trade Agreement (NAFTA)	
Association of Southeast Asian Nations (ASEAN)	
Pacific Rim	
Commonwealth of Independent States (CIS)	
Caribbean Basin Initiative (CBI)	
Organization of Petroleum Exporting Countries (OPEC)	
Organization for Economic Cooperation and Development (OECD)	

43. How does each **method** for entering international business work?

METHOD OF ENTERING INTERNATIONAL TRADE	HOW DOES THE METHOD WORK?
Licensing	
Exporting	
Joint Ventures	
Totally Owned Facilities (Direct Investment)	
Strategic Alliances	
Trading Companies	
Countertrade	
Multinational Firms	

PRACTICE EXAMINATION C

Matching Questions (C)

Match each term with a statement.

a. General Agreement on Tariffs and Trade (GATT)
b. European Union (EU)
c. Export-Import Bank of the United States
d. International Monetary Fund (IMF)
e. Trade Expansion Act
f. Multilateral Development Bank (MDB)
g. Pacific Rim
h. Organization of Petroleum Exporting Countries (OPEC)
i. World Trade Organization (WTO)
j. European Economic Area (EEA)
k. North American Free Trade Agreement (NAFTA)
l. Kennedy Round
m. dumping
n. non-tariff barrier
o. letter of credit
p. bill of lading
q. draft
r. strategic alliance
s. trading company
t. countertrade

_____ 1. It was created to assist in financing the exports of American firms.
_____ 2. The Common Market is an example.
_____ 3. It allows for the free movement of goods throughout seventeen countries in Europe.
_____ 4. Countries with a balance of payments deficit can be assisted by this entity.
_____ 5. East Asia, Canada, and the United States all bordering the Pacific Ocean.
_____ 6. The organization focuses on reducing or eliminating tariffs.
_____ 7. The United States, Mexico, and Canada negotiate trade agreements.
_____ 8. The World Bank is an example.
_____ 9. It resolves trade disputes.
_____ 10. Authority is given for the United States to negotiate reciprocal trade agreements with other countries.
_____ 11. The organization was founded in 1960 to provide oil-producing nations with some control over oil prices.
_____ 12. Authorized by Congress in 1962 for a period of five years, these negotiations took place between 1964 and 1967 and involved reciprocal trade agreements that could reduce U.S. tariffs by 50 percent.
_____ 13. An international barter transaction occurs.
_____ 14. It is how the transporting carrier provides evidence of a shipment.

_____ 15. It takes title to products that move between countries.
_____ 16. The process drives down the price of a product sold domestically.
_____ 17. The document orders the importer's bank to pay for the merchandise.
_____ 18. An embargo is an example.
_____ 19. A partnership formed to create a global competitive advantage.
_____ 20. It is issued by a bank "in favor of the exporter."

True-False Questions (C)

Select the correct answer.

T F 21. Macy's department stores import rugs from India.
T F 22. Investment monies are also counted in the balance of payments.
T F 23. Import quotas may be stated in terms of either the quantity or the value of a product.
T F 24. Trade restrictions increase consumer choices.
T F 25. Trade restrictions cause people to lose their jobs.
T F 26. Revenue tariffs are imposed solely to generate income for people on unemployment.
T F 27. The primary objective of the Common Market was to remove barriers to trade on a worldwide basis.
T F 28. The direct investment approach to international trade provides complete control of operations.
T F 29. The volume of countertrade is decreasing and is expected to be eliminated.
T F 30. The Eximbank discounts negotiable instruments that arise from export transactions.
T F 31. *Balance of payments* is a much broader concept than *balance of trade*.
T F 32. The Eximbank makes short-term loans to countries experiencing balance-of-payment deficits.
T F 33. Import quotas limit the number of product units that can be imported into a country.

Multiple-Choice Questions (C)

Circle the letter before the most accurate answer.

34. An unfavorable trade balance is called
    a. a balance of trade.
    b. a trade deficit.
    c. dumping.
    d. a balance of payments.
    e. currency devaluation.

35. When a country imposes trade restrictions, it can
    a. equalize a nation's balance of payments.
    b. restrict consumers' choices.
    c. increase prices for consumers.
    d. misallocate international resources.
    e. cause the loss of jobs.

36. The organization responsible for sponsoring rounds of negotiations to reduce trade restrictions is the
    a. European Free Trade Association.
    b. European Community.
    c. General Agreement on Tariffs and Trade.
    d. Latin American Free Trade Association.
    e. Organization of Petroleum Exporting Countries.

37. When a firm establishes a subsidiary in a foreign country, it is entering the global market by
    a. partnership.
    b. joint venture.
    c. forming a license.
    d. direct investment.
    e. an agent.

38. An independent agency of the United States government that assists in financing American exports is
    a. the Export-Import Bank.
    b. a multilateral development bank.
    c. the International Monetary Fund.
    d. the World Bank.
    e. the United Nations.

39. When the United States buys automobiles from Japan and Germany, coffee from Brazil, and oil from Iran, it is engaging in
    a. dumping.
    b. exporting.
    c. tariffing.
    d. importing.
    e. deficit trading.

40. If the United States exports $100 worth of diamonds to the Kingdom of Mocha and imports $80 worth of bows and arrows, it has a(n)
    a. unfavorable balance of trade.
    b. trade deficit.
    c. trade surplus.
    d. negative cash flow.
    e. export slide.

41. On January 1, 1995, it was established by GATT to oversee the provisions of the Uruguay Round.
    a. North American Free Trade Agreement (NAFTA)
    b. United Nations
    c. Commonwealth of Independent States (CIS)
    d. World Trade Organization (WTO)
    e. Organization for Economic Cooperation and Development (OECD)

42. The **best** way to limit the amount of dollars another country can obtain is to
    a. impose an import duty.
    b. establish a foreign-exchange control.
    c. declare an embargo.
    d. set an import quota.
    e. impose an export duty.

43. Balance of payments includes
   a. investments.
   b. money spent by foreign tourists.
   c. payments by foreign governments.
   d. aid to foreign governments.
   e. All of the above are included.

44. Coca-Cola, Inc., wants to expand its international presence in a fast-growing international region. Coca-Cola probably should go to the _____ Region.
   a. Pacific Rim
   b. Japanese
   c. Eastern-European
   d. Chinese
   e. Middle East

45. Published daily by the Department of Commerce, it lists foreign business opportunities and information on federal programs and activities that support U.S. exports.
   a. Advocacy Center
   b. Commerce Business Daily
   c. National Trade Data Bank
   d. TRADESTATS
   e. STATUSA/Internet

46. If Mexico is experiencing balance-of-payments deficits, it can seek assistance from
   a. the Export-Import Bank.
   b. a multilateral development bank.
   c. the Eximbank.
   d. the IMF.
   e. the World Bank.

Short-Answer Questions (C)

Complete each question.

47. What does the **Trade Promotion Coordinating Committee (TPCC)** do?

48. How can each of the following **export assistance programs** help businesses trade internationally?

EXPORT ASSISTANCE PROGRAMS	PURPOSE OF EACH PROGRAM
U.S. Export Assistance Centers (USEACs)	
International Trade Adm. (ITA) U.S. Department of Commerce	
U. S. And Foreign Commercial Services (US&FCS)	
Export Legal Assistance Network (ELAN)	
The Advocacy Center	
Commerce Business Daily (CBD)	
Economic Bulletin Board (EBB)	
TRADESTATS	
National Trade Data Bank (NTDB)	

49. What is the role of each bank?

a. **The Export-Import Bank of the United States**

b. **World Bank**

50. What is the function of the **International Monetary Fund (IMF)**?

CHAPTER 4

NAVIGATING THE WORLD OF E-BUSINESS

Key Terms

Define each term briefly. Writing down the definition and giving an example will help you learn the term.

e-business (electronic business) (p. 104)

e-commerce (p. 104)

revenue stream (p. 106)

World Wide Web (the web) (p. 108)

digitized (p. 108)

e-zines (p. 110)

business model (p. 111)

business-to-business (B2B) model (p. 111)

business-to-consumer (B2C) model (p. 112)

cookie (p. 114)

computer viruses (p. 114)

copyright (p. 114)

convergence of technologies (p. 118)

online communities (p. 118)

PRACTICE EXAMINATION A

Matching Questions (A)

Match each term with a statement.

a. e-business
b. e-commerce
c. revenue stream

d. World Wide Web
e. digitized
f. e-zines

_____ 1.   Advertising placed on web pages is an example.
_____ 2.   Refers only to buying and selling activities.
_____ 3.   Signals the Internet understands.
_____ 4.   It is a multimedia environment of audio, visual, and text data.
_____ 5.   The Internet is the medium for individuals to make a profit through sales.
_____ 6.   Small online magazines bring customers a wide selection of information.

True-False Questions (A)

Select the correct answer.

T   F   7.   When an individual business conducts transactions on the Internet, it is called e-business.
T   F   8.   Internet human resources include web site designers and programmers.
T   F   9.   Informational resources for e-business include computers and high-speed Internet connection lines.
T   F   10. Electronic payment from customers is an example of financial resources for e-business.
T   F   11. Chat rooms help meet customers' needs online.
T   F   12. Interaction between the online program and the viewer is expected to be available beginning in 2005.
T   F   13. The Internet allows viewers to custom design content.
T   F   14. Customers who move their purchases from traditional stores to the Internet help increase the revenue stream for the business.
T   F   15. Companies, like SprintPCS, reduce their expenses by offering product information online.
T   F   16. The Internet was originally conceived as an elaborate military communications network that would allow vital messages to be transmitted in the event of war.

Multiple-Choice Questions (A)

Circle the letter before the most accurate answer.

17. Some e-commerce activities include
    a. identifying suppliers.
    b. selecting products or services.
    c. making purchase commitments.
    d. completing financial transactions.
    e. All of the above.

18. A customer tracking system is an example of e-business _____ resources.
    a. human
    b. informational
    c. material
    d. financial
    e. specialized

19. Which is *not* considered an e-business material resource?
    a. Specialized computers
    b. Software
    c. Web masters
    d. High-speed Internet connection lines
    e. Equipment

20. A college web site providing course information is a(n)
    a. value-added service for college students.
    b. browser for student e-mail.
    c. revenue stream for the college.
    d. access for web-based businesses.
    e. interaction students require for graduation.

21. Typically, e-business revenue streams are created by
    a. the sale of products online.
    b. advertising placed on web pages.
    c. subscription fees charged for access to online services.
    d. the sale of services over the Internet.
    e. All of the above.

22. A fundamental concern for online firms
    a. are the governmental restrictions placed on transactions.
    b. is how to select, develop, and nurture sources of revenue.
    c. is the speed at which Internet technology is growing.
    d. is the lack of opportunity for interaction between retailer and customer.
    e. are the intelligent informational resource systems.

23. Sponsors
    a. design web pages for online business.
    b. interact online with customers.
    c. monitor the web site for ethical issues.
    d. advertise their products and services on businesses' web sites.
    e. provide support when sales are low.

24. A major way in which e-business can increase profitability is
    a. through expense reduction.
    b. to reduce web space on the Internet.
    c. to demand that customers pay by cash.
    d. to shift revenues earned inside a real store to online revenues.
    e. to focus on the short-term value of the business.

Short-Answer Questions (A)

Complete each question.

25. Compare **e-business** with **e-commerce**. What is the difference?

E-BUSINESS	E-COMMERCE

26. An e-business combines **four types of resources**. Give examples for each type of resource.

E-BUSINESS RESOURCES	EXAMPLES OF EACH TYPE OF RESOURCE
Human resources	a. b. c.
Material resources	a. b. c.
Informational resources	a. b. c.
Financial resources	a. b. c.

27. What **types of services** does AOL offer its customers?

a. _____

b. _____

c. _____

d. _____

e. _____

28. Give examples of how an e-business can create a **profit** by increasing revenue and reducing expenses.

WAYS TO CREATE A PROFIT	EXAMPLES OF EACH SOURCE
Revenue Growth	
Expense Reduction	

PRACTICE EXAMINATION B

Matching Questions (B)

Match each term with a statement.

a. business model
b. business-to-business model
c. business-to-consumer model
d. cookie

e. computer viruses
f. copyright
g. convergence of technologies
h. online communities

_____ 1. The *LoveBug* is an example.
_____ 2. The essence of Napster's problems was control of ownership of the music it allowed customers to download.
_____ 3. It represents a group of shared characteristics and behaviors in a business situation.
_____ 4. The activities of Internet users can be tracked by a piece of software.
_____ 5. The focus is to facilitate sales transactions between businesses.
_____ 6. An example is iVillage.com.
_____ 7. Amazon.com makes a special effort to build long-term relationships with customers.
_____ 8. It involves an integrated interactive system.

True-False Questions (B)

Select the correct answer.

T F   9. The Internet is a large network of computers connected by cables and satellites.

T F 10. Internet service providers (ISPs) provide customers with the necessary technology to connect to the Internet through various phone plugs and cables.

T F 11. Netscape Communicator was the dominant browser in 2000.

T F 12. Some firms, like e-Bay, feel the Internet is not appropriate for them.

T F 13. The ability to customize content for individual customer's needs makes the Internet an adaptable tool for global enterprise.

T F 14. Access Markets International predicts that small business online purchases will be $118 billion in 2001.

T F 15. Customer focus is what designates the e-business model a firm will use.

T F 16. Research has identified online consumer behavior that is critical for an Internet retailer to be successful.

T F 17. Tracking and analyzing customer data has allowed Amazon.com to provide individualized service to its customers.

T F 18. Computerized tracking of users connected to the Internet is a commonly accepted social responsibility activity of an Internet retailer.

Multiple-Choice Questions (B)

Circle the letter before the most accurate answer

19. Before 1994, the U.S. National Science Foundation restricted the use of the Internet to
    a. commercial activities.
    b. noncommercial activities.
    c. Federal employees.
    d. the World Wide Web.
    e. communication networks.

20. Which group is typically involved in e-business activities?
    a. Online sellers and content providers
    b. Internet software producers
    c. Telecommunications and computer hardware manufacturers
    d. Internet service providers
    e. All of the above are involved.

21. Which company manufactures computers used by consumers?
    a. Cisco Systems
    b. Lucent Technologies
    c. Dell
    d. AOL
    e. General Electric

22. Which statement is *not* true?
    a. Fiber-optic connections will improve Internet delivery speed.
    b. AOL is the largest and best-known ISP.
    c. Browser software is the product for user interaction online.
    d. Penetrating online markets is restricted and difficult to master.
    e. Some products and services are only offered online.

23. Six out of ten small firms, according to Bose, stated their reluctance to sell products online because
    a. of security concerns.
    b. of technological challenges.
    c. their products were unsuited for online selling.
    d. All of the above are reasons.
    e. None of the above reasons are valid.

24. A reason why the Internet is accessible to small businesses is the
    a. low cost of going online.
    b. security it gives a small business.
    c. expertise gained from trading online.
    d. revenue streaming that is allowed.
    e. partnership created with another small firm.

25. When Dell sells a special-order computer directly to a customer, it is using
    a. the business-to-business model.
    b. the business-to-consumer model.
    c. an economic model
    d. specialized representatives.
    e. the revenue reduction plan.

26. B2C firms
    a. make a special effort to build long-term relationships with customers.
    b. focus on short-term relationships with customers.
    c. feel that analyzing customer data is a waste of money.
    d. place more emphasis on making a sale than on building customer trust.
    e. base inventory decisions on customer behavior.

Short-Answer Questions (B)

Complete each question.

27. Identify the three **primary user groups** of e-business.

    a. _____

    b. _____

    c. _____

28. Define the **role** of each e-business user group.

USER GROUP	ROLE OF EACH GROUP
Telecommunications and Computer Hardware Manufacturers and Internet Service Providers	
Internet Software Producers	
Online Sellers and Content Providers	

29. Identify three reasons why small businesses are **reluctant to sell online**.

a. _____

b. _____

c. _____

30. Discuss reasons why many small businesses are seeking **opportunities** online.

31. What are the major **characteristics** of each model?

BUSINESS-TO-BUSINESS MODEL (B2B)	BUSINESS-TO-CONSUMER MODEL (B2C)

32. For some people the online **social environment** encourages a false sense of privacy and security, which tends to change an individual's behavior. Why is this so?

PRACTICE EXAMINATION C

Matching Questions (C)

Match each term with a statement.

a. electronic business
b. e-commerce
c. revenue stream
d. the web
e. digitized
f. e-zines
g. business model

h. B2B model
i. B2C model
j. cookie
k. computer viruses
l. copyright
m. convergence of technologies
n. online communities

_____ 1. It protects ownership of content.
_____ 2. The software codes that disrupt normal computer operations.
_____ 3. It satisfies society's needs through the facilities on the Internet.
_____ 4. Subscription fees charged for access to online services and content are a source.
_____ 5. When Dell fills its corporate clients' orders for computers, it uses this environment.
_____ 6. It represents a descriptive characteristic for many e-businesses.
_____ 7. Its activities may include identifying suppliers, selecting products or services, making purchase commitments, completing financial transactions, and obtaining service.
_____ 8. It simplifies the use of the Internet.
_____ 9. Data requires this process to be transmitted over the Internet.
_____ 10. It allows people who share an interest or concern to communicate with each other.
_____ 11. It is predicted this technology will lead to interactive television programs.
_____ 12. Some people view it as an invasion of privacy.
_____ 13. Businesses selling toys on the Internet are engaged in this model.
_____ 14. Online publishing is growing.

True-False Questions (C)

Select the correct answer.

T F 15. The music and publishing industries are most affected on the Internet by copyright issues.
T F 16. Special government rules and regulations apply to business activities conducted online versus traditional business activities.
T F 17. The U.S. Government Electronic Commerce Policy site provides current information about regulations related to online business both within the United States and internationally.
T F 18. Women outnumber the men who use the Internet.
T F 19. U.S. home users spent an average of 7.2 hours a week online while the global Internet users spent an average of 7.6 hours online.

T F 20. The most exciting prospect for businesses and customers is not the creation of new and unique products and services, but the conversion of existing processes to e-business processes.

T F 21. The convergence of technologies is expected to lead to interactive television programs.

T F 22. OnVia.com is an online community site for women.

T F 23. Geocities.com is a portal to a huge selection of online communities.

T F 24. Many Internet firms have found it unprofitable to partnership with smaller firms.

Multiple-Choice Questions (C)

Circle the letter before the most accurate answer.

25. If a business wants to learn more about its online customers, it can use
    a. an e-zine.
    b. a business model.
    c. e-business.
    d. a cookie
    e. a telephone survey.

26. Computer viruses
    a. can originate anywhere in the world.
    b. are software codes designed to disrupt normal computer operations.
    c. provide online risks and dangers to e-business retailers.
    d. are a major concern to e-business firms.
    e. All of the above are true.

27. A copyright
    a. protects the design of a product.
    b. controls content ownership.
    c. allows tracking online.
    d. is a social concern.
    e. is an ethical problem.

28. Forrester Research, Inc. predicts that global Internet commerce will
    a. soar to $6.8 trillion by 2004.
    b. soar to $10 trillion by 2002.
    c. decrease in the eastern countries.
    d. stay about the same for the next three years.
    e. result in 40 percent failures.

29. In 2000 which Internet service provider was top in terms of unique visitors?
    a. Lycos
    b. Yahoo!
    c. AOL
    d. Excite@home
    e. Microsoft

30. Which firms will dominant the development on the Internet?
    a. Firms that create new products and services
    b. New firms entering the marketplace
    c. Firms that offer advice
    d. Firms that adapt existing business models to an online environment
    e. Firms that use a cookie

31. Groups of individuals or firms that want to exchange information, products, or services over the internet are
    a. partnerships.
    b. online communities.
    c. cookies.
    d. e-zines.
    e. business models.

32. When large firms allow small firms to link to their site, it is called
    a. partnering online.
    b. bartering.
    c. transacting.
    d. sharing.
    e. linking.

Short-Answer Questions (C)

Complete each question.

33. Discuss ways **government regulation** impacts online business activities by

    a. Imposing sales tax

    b. Restricting products

    c. Monitoring illegal activity

34. Describe the purpose of the **U.S. Government Electronic Commerce Policy** site.

35. U.S. users spent _____ hours online in 1998. Global Internet users spent an average of _____ hours online in March 2000. _____ Internet users spent the most time on the Internet in March 2000.

36. Which **segment** of the economy does each online community serve?

ONLINE COMMUNITY	WHO BENEFITS
iVillage.com	
OnVia.com	
Geocities.com	

37. Describe how **partnering** online works, and give an example.

CHAPTER 5

CHOOSING A FORM OF BUSINESS OWNERSHIP

Key Terms

Define each term briefly. Writing down the definition and giving an example will help you learn the term.

sole proprietorship (p. 127)

unlimited liability (p. 129)

partnership (p. 131)

general partner (p. 131)

general partnership (p. 131)

limited partner (p. 131)

limited partnership (p. 131)

master limited partnership (MLP) (p. 132)

articles of partnership (p. 133)

corporation (p. 135)

stock (p. 135)

stockholder/shareholder (p. 135)

close corporation (p. 136)

open corporation (p. 136)

incorporation (p. 136)

domestic corporation (p. 137)

foreign corporation (p. 137)

alien corporation (p. 137)

corporate charter (p. 137)

common stock (p. 138)

preferred stock (p. 138)

dividend (p. 138)

proxy (p. 138)

board of directors (p. 138)

corporate officers (p. 138)

limited liability (p. 139)

S-corporation (p. 142)

limited liability company (p. 142)

government-owned corporation (p. 142)

quasi-government corporation (p. 142)

not-for-profit corporation (p. 143)

cooperative (p. 143)

joint venture (p. 144)

syndicate (p. 144)

merger (p. 145)

hostile takeover (p. 145)

tender offer (p. 145)

proxy fight (p. 145)

divestiture (p. 149)

leveraged buyout (LBO) (p. 149)

PRACTICE EXAMINATION A

Matching Questions (A)

Match each term with a statement.

a. sole proprietorship
b. unlimited liability
c. partnership
d. general partner
e. limited partner

f. articles of partnership
g. corporation
h. stockholder
i. close corporation
j. open corporation

_____ 1. A written agreement.
_____ 2. A corporation that does not trade stock on the market.

_____ 3. An association of two or more business owners.
_____ 4. A person responsible for operating a partnership.
_____ 5. AT&T is an example of this type of corporation.
_____ 6. Easiest type of business to start.
_____ 7. A person who invests only capital in a partnership.
_____ 8. Owns part of a corporation.
_____ 9. Personal liability for all debts of a business.
_____ 10. An artificial being with most legal rights of a person.

True-False Questions (A)

Select the correct answer.

T F 11. Approximately 73 percent of the country's business firms are organized as sole proprietorships.
T F 12. Unlimited liability is an advantage of a sole proprietorship.
T F 13. All general partners are active in the day-to-day operations of the business.
T F 14. It is generally easier to withdraw funds from a partnership than from a corporation.
T F 15. Limited partners participate in management decisions of the firm.
T F 16. Corporations exist only on paper.
T F 17. Many businesses incorporate in the state of Delaware because it has a lenient tax structure.
T F 18. The president of a company is appointed by the board of directors.
T F 19. Not-for-profit corporations issue stock certificates and pay dividends from surplus funds.
T F 20. The Federal Deposit Insurance Corporation (FDIC) is an example of a quasi-government corporation.
T F 21. Cooperatives are owned by their members.
T F 22. Syndicates are formed to underwrite large loans for business expansions.

Multiple-Choice Questions (A)

Circle the letter before the most accurate answer.

23. An advantage of the sole proprietorship is its
    a. cost of formation.
    b. unlimited liability.
    c. lack of continuity.
    d. ability to borrow money.
    e. charter.

24. During college, Elyssa Wood earned extra money by using her computer skills to prepare papers for students. After graduation, she decided to turn her part-time job into a full-time business that she plans to expand in the future. In the meantime, she wants to maintain complete control of the business. She will *most likely* organize the business as a
    a. limited partnership.
    b. corporation.
    c. general partnership.
    d. sole proprietorship.
    e. cooperative.

25. Profits of corporations are
    a. exempted from taxes.
    b. taxed at a lower rate than individual profits.
    c. taxed twice.
    d. taxed at a rate equal to limited partnerships.
    e. taxed the same as individual profits.

26. General partners are responsible for all debts of the business. They run the risk of using their personal assets to pay creditors. This disadvantage is known as
    a. double taxation.
    b. frozen investment.
    c. lack of continuity.
    d. unlimited liability.
    e. limited liability.

27. Articles of partnership should describe
    a. the duties of each partner.
    b. how the business will be dissolved.
    c. the investment each partner will make.
    d. the length of the partnership.
    e. All of the above.

28. Which type of business ownership suffers the most when its owners disagree about how to operate the business?
    a. Cooperatives
    b. S-corporations
    c. Partnerships
    d. Sole proprietorships
    e. Corporations

29. Corporations
    a. are visible according to the law.
    b. are tangible in the eyes of the law.
    c. exist only in contemplation of the law.
    d. are the owners.
    e. are federal entities.

30. The KDS Hardware Company is incorporated in Texas and recently opened a store in Colorado. In Colorado the company is called a(n) _____ corporation.
    a. domestic
    b. foreign
    c. alien
    d. open
    e. close

31. Which of the following is *not* an advantage of a corporate form of ownership?
    a. It is easier to raise capital.
    b. Ownership can be transferred easily and quickly.
    c. The death of an owner does not terminate the corporation.
    d. Profits are taxed twice.
    e. The liability of the owners is limited.

32. A corporation incorporated in Texas doing business in New York is known
    a. in New York as a domestic corporation.
    b. in Texas as a foreign corporation.
    c. in Texas as a domestic corporation.
    d. in New York as an alien corporation.
    e. as all of the above.

33. Most government regulation of business is directed at
    a. partnerships.
    b. sole proprietorships.
    c. corporations.
    d. cooperatives.
    e. joint ventures.

34. Several years ago, Xerox purchased an insurance company. This merger of unrelated companies is known as a
    a. conglomerate merger.
    b. vertical merger.
    c. horizontal merger.
    d. corporate merger.
    e. joint venture.

35. Which technique might management use to avoid a hostile takeover?
    a. Give "golden parachute" contracts to top executives.
    b. Use leveraged recapitalization to make the company less attractive.
    c. Issue a new class of preferred stock.
    d. All of the above.
    e. None of the above.

36. PepsiCo acquired Pizza Hut. What type of merger was this?
    a. Conglomerate
    b. Syndicate
    c. Joint venture
    d. Horizontal
    e. Vertical

Short-Answer Questions (A)

Complete each question.

37. A **sole proprietorship** is a business that is owned and usually operated by one person. What are the advantages and disadvantages of owning and operating a business alone?

ADVANTAGES OF SOLE PROPRIETORSHIPS	DISADVANTAGES OF SOLE PROPRIETORSHIPS

38. What is the major difference between having **unlimited liability** and having **limited liability**?

39. A **partnership** is a voluntary association of two or more persons to act as co-owners of a business for profit. Partnerships are comprised of two types of partners: **general** or **limited**. What is the role of each type of partner?

ROLE OF A GENERAL PARTNER	ROLE OF A LIMITED PARTNER

40. List two advantages of a **master limited partnership (MLP)**.

    a. _____

    b. _____

41. **Partnerships** have many advantages and disadvantages. List several examples.

ADVANTAGES OF PARTNERSHIPS	DISADVANTAGES OF PARTNERSHIPS

42. What **advantages** does a partnership have over a sole proprietorship?

43. Discuss the effects of management **disagreements** in partnerships. How can partners effectively deal with this issue?

44. Describe the **characteristics** of a general partnership and a limited partnership.

GENERAL PARTNERSHIP	LIMITED PARTNERSHIP

PRACTICE EXAMINATION B

Matching Questions (B)

Match each term with a statement.

a. master limited partnership
b. domestic corporation
c. foreign corporation
d. corporate charter
e. common stock

f. preferred stock
g. proxy
h. board of directors
i. limited liability
j. government-owned corporation

_____ 1. Investors have first claim on profits.
_____ 2. A corporation doing business in the state where chartered.
_____ 3. Carries voting privileges.
_____ 4. Lists the purpose of the corporation.
_____ 5. A corporation doing business outside the state where chartered.
_____ 6. Units of ownership are traded on the exchange.
_____ 7. Transfers voting rights of stockholders to a second party.
_____ 8. Responsible for overall operations and setting company goals.
_____ 9. Financial liability that is limited to the investment.
_____ 10. The National Aeronautics and Space Administration (NASA) is an example.

True-False Questions (B)

Select the correct answer.

T F 11. Organizing a sole proprietorship requires an attorney to prepare the papers.
T F 12. When market conditions change quickly, sole proprietorships have more flexibility than other ownership forms.

T F 13. It is often difficult for sole owners to borrow large amounts of money.

T F 14. The articles of partnership are a written contract describing the terms of a partnership.

T F 15. To form a general partnership, an attorney is required to file the papers.

T F 16. Corporations generate almost 90 percent of all sales revenue in the United States.

T F 17. Preferred stockholders have voting rights.

T F 18. In comparison with other forms of ownership, forming a corporation is an easy and inexpensive process.

T F 19. Under corporations, the owner's financial liability is limited to the amount of money invested in the corporation's stock.

T F 20. The S-corporation form of organization allows a corporation to avoid double taxation.

T F 21. A limited liability company (LLO) combines the benefits of a corporation and a partnership.

T F 22. Cooperatives are more prevalent in the banking industry.

Multiple-Choice Questions (B)

Circle the letter before the most accurate answer.

23. The *most* important disadvantage of a sole proprietorship is its
    a. double taxation.
    b. flexibility.
    c. unlimited liability.
    d. perpetual life.
    e. limited liability.

24. Mergers in the next decade will
    a. involve more foreign investors.
    b. involve less borrowed money.
    c. focus on enhancing their position in the marketplace.
    d. include all of the above
    e. decrease in number.

25. Which of the following is *not* an advantage of a sole proprietorship?
    a. It has unlimited liability.
    b. It is easy to form and dissolve.
    c. Profits are taxed as personal income.
    d. There is no legal requirement to reveal vital facts about the business.
    e. The owner keeps all profits.

26. An advantage of a general partnership is its
    a. unlimited liability.
    b. frozen investments.
    c. ability to combine skills and knowledge.
    d. transferability of stock.
    e. ability to borrow money easily.

27. Even though Mary Lee's Restaurant sells stock, it is taxed like a partnership. What is the ownership called?
    a. General partnership
    b. Master limited partnership
    c. S-corporation
    d. Close corporation
    e. None of the above

28. A technique used to gather enough stockholder votes to control a company is called a
    a. tender offer.
    b. hostile takeover.
    c. merger.
    d. acquisition.
    e. proxy fight.

29. Shareholders
    a. appoint the corporate officers.
    b. appoint the board of directors.
    c. run the company.
    d. elect the board of directors.
    e. hire the staff.

30. Government-owned corporations operate to
    a. make a profit.
    b. provide a service.
    c. provide employment.
    d. generate revenue.
    e. control products.

31. A corporation whose stock is owned by relatively few people is called a(n)
    a. close corporation.
    b. public corporation.
    c. open corporation.
    d. joint venture.
    e. syndicate.

32. An arrangement that allows employees to purchase their company is called a
    a. vertical merger.
    b. divestiture.
    c. leveraged buyout.
    d. tender offer.
    e. hostile takeover.

33. The Tennessee Valley Authority is an example of a(n)
    a. S-corporation.
    b. not-for-profit corporation.
    c. open corporation.
    d. government-owned corporation.
    e. quasi-government corporation.

34. Businesses use horizontal mergers to
    a. increase growth.
    b. accomplish goals versus growth.
    c. increase the number of firms in the industry.
    d. increase competition.
    e. gain control over more levels of the operation.

35. Which type of business ownership is more prevalent in agriculture?
    a. Syndicate
    b. S-corporation
    c. Corporation
    d. Joint venture
    e. Cooperative

36. When groups of individuals need to acquire large sums of money for a job, they are likely to establish a(n)
    a. syndicate.
    b. cooperative.
    c. joint venture.
    d. alliance.
    e. horizontal merger.

Short-Answer Questions (B)

Complete each question.

37. A corporation is an artificial person created by law, with most of the legal rights of a real person, such as:

    a. _____   b. _____

    c. _____   d. _____

38. Explain the difference between each of the following types of corporations:

CLOSE CORPORATION	OPEN CORPORATION

DOMESTIC CORPORATION	FOREIGN CORPORATION	ALIEN CORPORATION

GOVERNMENT-OWNED CORPORATION	QUASI-GOVERNMENT CORPORATION	NOT-FOR-PROFIT CORPORATION

39. What is the process for **incorporating** a business?

40. The **articles of incorporation** should include the following information:

    a. _____   b. _____

    c. _____   d. _____

    e. _____   f. _____

41. The **Board of Directors** is the top governing body of a corporation, and the stockholders elect the members. What are the major responsibilities of the Board of Directors?

    a. _____

    b. _____

42. Corporations have definite advantages and disadvantages compared to other forms of ownership. Some of them stem from the corporation's legal definition as an artificial person or legal entity. List the advantages and disadvantages of corporations.

ADVANTAGES OF CORPORATIONS	DISADVANTAGES OF CORPORATIONS

PRACTICE EXAMINATION C

Matching Questions (C)

Match each term with a statement.

a. quasi-government corporation
b. S-corporation
c. not-for-profit corporation
d. merger
e. horizontal merger
f. vertical merger
g. conglomerate merger
h. cooperative
i. joint venture
j. syndicate

_____ 1. A business owned partly by government and partly by individuals.
_____ 2. The merger of two department stores.
_____ 3. Credit unions are an example.
_____ 4. A business whose income is taxed only as the personal income of its shareholders.
_____ 5. Organized to undertake large capital ventures.
_____ 6. The process of purchasing another firm.
_____ 7. A merger between a soft drink firm and an auto assembly plant.
_____ 8. Formed to provide a service rather than to make a profit.
_____ 9. Formed to fulfill a specific purpose.
_____ 10. A merger between a flour mill and a grain silo.

True-False Questions (C)

Select the correct answer.

T F 11. The profits of a sole proprietorship are taxed as the personal income of the owner.
T F 12. The partnership form of ownership is more prevalent than the corporate form of ownership.
T F 13. Under the Uniform Partnership Act, every partnership requires at least one general partner.
T F 14. Partnerships must pay a special federal income tax on their business profits.
T F 15. The owners of corporations are called stockholders.
T F 16. Stock represents shares of ownership in a corporation.
T F 17. Double taxation is a disadvantage of the corporate form of business ownership.
T F 18. The stock of a close corporation is listed on the New York Stock Exchange.
T F 19. The board of directors is elected by the shareholders.
T F 20. The joining of two firms in unrelated industries is a conglomerate merger.
T F 21. Corporations are prohibited by law from entering into joint ventures.
T F 22. A major objective of buying cooperatives is to reduce the unit price of goods to the members by buying in bulk and distributing to all members.

Multiple-Choice Questions (C)

Circle the letter before the most accurate answer.

23. Which type of business ownership would you recommend for people who want the most flexibility and control in their business operations?
    a. Joint venture
    b. Partnership
    c. Cooperative
    d. Sole proprietorship
    e. Corporation

24. Retention of profits and combining skills are advantages of which type of business ownership?
    a. Sole proprietorship
    b. Conglomerate
    c. Syndicate
    d. Partnership
    e. Joint venture

25. A person who contributes money to a business but is not interested in actively working in the firm is called a(n)
    a. incorporator.
    b. limited partner.
    c. general partner.
    d. director.
    e. secret partner.

26. Management disagreement can have its most detrimental effect on
    a. sole proprietorships.
    b. partnerships.
    c. corporations.
    d. S-corporations.
    e. syndicates.

27. The process of selling off part of a recently acquired target company is called
    a. diversification.
    b. differentiation.
    c. divestiture.
    d. diversion.
    e. digression.

28. Limited partners receive
    a. income.
    b. profits.
    c. tax benefits.
    d. All of the above.
    e. None of the above.

29. An attractive feature of corporate ownership is its
    a. secrecy.
    b. taxation.
    c. formation.
    d. liability.
    e. partners.

30. S-corporations must
    a. have more than one hundred shareholders.
    b. have two classes of stock.
    c. have several corporate stockholders.
    d. be a domestic corporation.
    e. have income from interest that exceeds 25 percent of gross income.

31. A corporation whose stock can be purchased by anyone and is traded on stock markets is known as a(n)
    a. government-owned corporation.
    b. open corporation.
    c. close corporation.
    d. S-corporation.
    e. not-for-profit corporation.

32. When stockholders cannot attend an annual meeting, they can vote by
    a. registered mail.
    b. pre-emptive right.
    c. proxy.
    d. power of attorney.
    e. preferred stock.

33. The Federal National Mortgage Association (Fannie Mae) is an example of a
    a. quasi-government corporation.
    b. close corporation.
    c. not-for-profit corporation.
    d. S-corporation.
    e. government-owned corporation

34. A distribution of earnings to the stockholders of a corporation is called
    a. interest.
    b. profit sharing.
    c. dividends.
    d. ownership.
    e. shares.

35. After approval by the secretary of state, the articles of incorporation become a corporation's
    a. bylaws.
    b. procedural manual.
    c. policy guide.
    d. corporate charter.
    e. proxy.

36. Two or more persons acting as co-owners of a business for profit are known as a
    a. syndicate.
    b. joint venture.
    c. corporation.
    d. cooperative.
    e. partnership.

Short-Answer Questions (C)

Complete each question.

37. Compare an **S-corporation** with a **limited liability company (LLC)**. What are the advantages of each form of ownership? What are some restrictions of each?

S-CORPORATION	LIMITED LIABILITY COMPANY
Advantages	Advantages
Restrictions	Restrictions

38. How are **joint ventures** and **syndicates** alike, and how are they different?

    a. Similarities between joint ventures and syndicates include:

    b. Differences between joint ventures and syndicates include:

39. Compare three types of **mergers**. Give a definition and an example for each.

HORIZONTAL MERGER	VERTICAL MERGER	CONGLOMERATE MERGER
Definition	Definition	Definition
Example	Example	Example

40. Why are **cooperatives** formed? Explain how they operate.

41. What is a **hostile takeover**?

42. How do the following **processes** work in a hostile takeover?

    a.   Tender offer

    b.   Proxy fight

43. Identify three basic **reasons for mergers** to occur in the twenty-first century.

    a.   _____

    b.   _____

    c.   _____

44. Describe how a **divestiture** and a **leveraged buyout** work.

DIVESTITURE	LEVERAGED BUYOUT (LBO)

CHAPTER 6

SMALL BUSINESS, ENTREPRENEURSHIP, AND FRANCHISES

Key Terms

Define each term briefly. Writing down the definition and giving an example will help you learn the term.

small business (p. 157)

business plan (p. 167)

Small Business Administration (SBA) (p. 168)

Service Corps of Retired Executives (SCORE) (p. 169)

Minority Business Development Agency (p. 170)

Small Business Institute (SBI) (p. 170)

Small Business Development Center (SBDC) (p. 170)

venture capital (p. 171)

Small Business Investment Company (SBIC) (p. 171)

franchise (p. 171)

franchising (p. 171)

franchisor (p. 171)

franchisee (p. 171)

PRACTICE EXAMINATION A

Matching Questions (A)

Match each term with a statement.

a. Small Business Administration
b. small business
c. Service Corps of Retired Executives
d. Minority Business Development Agency

e. Small Business Institutes
f. Small Business Development Centers
g. Small Business Investment Companies
h. business plan

_____ 1. A group of seniors and graduate students who counsel small businesses.
_____ 2. Created by Congress in 1953 to assist small businesses.
_____ 3. University-based groups that provide training to small-business owners.
_____ 4. A manufacturing plant with twenty employees is an example.
_____ 5. A group of retired businesspeople who counsel small businesses.
_____ 6. Evaluates the weaknesses of a business.
_____ 7. Awards grants to develop and increase business opportunities.
_____ 8. Privately owned firms that provide venture capital.

True-False Questions (A)

Select the correct answer.

T F   9. Approximately 33 percent of all small businesses in the United States are found in distribution industries.
T F 10. Service industries account for only 68 percent of all small businesses.
T F 11. Small businesses tend to be more successful when they have owners with previous experience in their fields.
T F 12. The main reason small businesses fail is poor management skills of the owners.
T F 13. Difficulty in developing working relationships between the owner-manager and customers is one of the main disadvantages of small businesses.
T F 14. The Small Business Administration was created by Congress in 1983.
T F 15. SBA loans are made by private banks for a duration of approximately 25 years.
T F 16. SCORE counselors analyze problems for small businesses and offer plans for resolution.
T F 17. Franchisees grant franchise licenses to franchisors.
T F 18. Businesses in the fast-food industry are the major users of franchise licensing in the United States.

Multiple-Choice Questions (A)

Circle the letter before the most accurate answer.

19. The maximum number of employees in a small manufacturing firm ranges from _____ according to the SBA.
    a. 250 to 1,500
    b. 500 to 1,500
    c. 800 to 1,800
    d. 1,000 to 2,000
    e. 1,500 to 2,500

20. People go into business for themselves because of
    a. an entrepreneurial spirit.
    b. independence.
    c. a willingness to accept a challenge.
    d. a desire to determine one's own destiny.
    e. All of the above.

21. In a small service business the maximum annual receipts ranges from
    a. $0.5 million to $9 million.
    b. $2 million to $5 million.
    c. $5 million to $21 million.
    d. $2.5 million to $21.5 million.
    e. $13.5 million to $17 million.

22. An advantage of operating a small business is
    a. the personal relationships with customers.
    b. the limited potential for failure.
    c. the ability to borrow vast amounts of money.
    d. opportunities for employees.
    e. All of the above.

23. Which firm is in the service industry?
    a. Neiman Marcus
    b. Sam's Club
    c. Alpha Dental Center
    d. AT&T
    e. Fleetline Trucking

24. Which type of business is in the production industry?
    a. Dry cleaners
    b. Construction company
    c. Restaurants
    d. Medical office
    e. Cable company

25. Which of the following statements is *not* true about women? Women
    a. make up more than half of America's population.
    b. owned 50 percent of all small businesses in 2000.
    c. are receiving services from the SBA.
    d. owned-businesses have a higher than average risk of failure.
    e. owned-businesses provide 15.5 million jobs in the United States.

26. Andrea Wood's franchise license provides her with a brand name, techniques, methods, marketing strategies, and other important services necessary for succeeding in business. This type of license allows her to
    a. authorize a retail store to sell her national brand product.
    b. open a typical fast-food store, such as McDonald's or Kentucky Fried Chicken.
    c. sell cars and trucks.
    d. manage a retail service station.
    e. manufacture soft-drink syrups for the Coca-Cola Company.

27. Small businesses are important to the economy of the United States. Which contribution is provided by small business?
    a. Creates jobs
    b. Provides technical innovations
    c. Responds efficiently and effectively to consumer needs
    d. Meets the needs of small groups of consumers
    e. All of the above are contributed by small businesses.

28. You have decided to open a carpet-cleaning business and have engaged in a contract with Chem-Dry. You and the company have drawn up an agreement that allows you to use the company's name and its proven method of doing business, to receive training, and to use its advertising materials. In this agreement, Chem-Dry is the _____ and you are the _____.
    a. franchisor; franchisee
    b. entrepreneur; corporation
    c. entrepreneur; local chain
    d. employee; employer
    e. corporation; manager

Short-Answer Questions (A)

Complete each question.

29. According to the SBA Guidelines, what information determines whether a firm is classified as a **small business**? Identify the indicators and record the amounts for each industry.

INDUSTRY	NO. OF EMPLOYEES	YEARLY SALES	ANNUAL RECEIPTS	ANNUAL SALES
Manufacturing				
Wholesaling				
Retailing				
General Construction				
Special trade Construction				
Agriculture				
Services				

30. Over 70 percent of new businesses fail within their first five years. What are the primary reasons for the failures? Explain.

31. Distinguish among three types of industries. Give examples of businesses in each type of industry.

DISTRIBUTION INDUSTRIES	SERVICE INDUSTRIES	PRODUCTION INDUSTRIES
33% of all small business	48% of all small businesses	19% of all small businesses

32. Identify four personal reasons why people go into business for themselves.

a. _____

b. _____

c. _____

d. _____

33. Capital, management, and planning are three key ingredients in the survival of small businesses. Why are these also reasons for failure?

KEY INGREDIENTS FOR SURVIVAL	REASONS FOR FAILURE
Capital	
Management	
Planning	

34. Small businesses are important in our economy. Discuss how small businesses make a difference in each area of our economy.

a. Providing technical innovation:

   b. Providing employment:

   c. Providing competition:

   d. Filling needs of society and other businesses:

PRACTICE EXAMINATION B

Matching Questions (B)

Match the term with the statement.

a. venture capital
b. franchises
c. franchising

d. franchisor
e. franchisee
f. business plan

_____ 1. The one who opens a franchise business.
_____ 2. Subway and Arby's are examples.
_____ 3. Investment that has a potential for rapid growth.
_____ 4. A method of doing business.
_____ 5. It grants the operating license.
_____ 6. It serves as a guide for the business.

True-False Questions (B)

Select the correct answer.

T   F   7.   A small business must be independently owned, operated for profit, and not dominant in its field.

T   F   8.   Statistically, over 95 percent of new businesses can be expected to fail within their first five years of operations.

T   F   9.   People younger than 25 and older than 44 are less likely to start their own business.

T   F   10. Owners of small businesses usually find it difficult to adjust to change.

T   F   11. The primary reason for failures of new businesses is mismanagement that results from a lack of business know-how.

T   F   12. Businesses generally fall into three broad categories of industries: distribution, service, and production.

T   F   13. The SBA provides small-business owners with free counseling, courses, conferences, workshops, and a wide range of publications.

T   F   14. The SBA loan-guarantee program guarantees loans up to 95 percent of the loan.

T   F   15. For a small business to survive, it must manage money, time, personnel, and inventory effectively.

T   F   16. A disadvantage of franchising is that the franchisee retains a great deal of control over the operations of the franchisor.

Multiple-Choice Questions (B)

Circle the letter before the most accurate answer.

17. The SBA defines a small retailing business as one that has maximum yearly sales or receipts ranging from
    a. $2 million to $10 million.
    b. $3 million to $7.5 million.
    c. $5 million to $21 million.
    d. $4 million to $20 million.
    e. $8 million to $25 million.

18. There are approximately _____ businesses operating in the United States.
    a. 25 million
    b. 35.5 million
    c. 48 million
    d. 78 million
    e. a billion

19. A document critical to the success of any business is called a
    a. franchise contract.
    b. business plan.
    c. will.
    d. record.
    e. venture.

20. Business administration students on approximately 520 college campuses provide management counseling to small businesses through the
    a. Small Business Institutes.
    b. Service Corps of Retired Executives.
    c. Active Corps of Executives.
    d. SBA management courses.
    e. Small Business Investment Company.

21. Which firm provides venture capital to small business?
    a. Active Corps of Executives
    b. Small Business Institutes
    c. Small Business Investment Companies
    d. Service Corps of Retired Executives
    e. The International Franchise Association

22. There are only 19 percent of small businesses in production industries. The main reason is that
    a. production is done mainly offshore.
    b. labor costs are too high in the United States.
    c. there is little chance for profit in production industries.
    d. production industries need a large initial investment.
    e. few people have the skills to work in production industries.

23. It takes an entrepreneurial spirit to succeed in a small business. Which phrase is *not* characteristic of an entrepreneurial spirit?
    a. Have the desire to create a new business
    b. Depend on others to make good decisions
    c. Be willing to accept a challenge
    d. Be independent
    e. Be highly motivated

24. The average size of an SBA-guaranteed business loan is
    a. $50,000.
    b. $100,000.
    c. $120,000.
    d. $180,000.
    e. $208,000.

25. Under a typical franchise license, the franchisee is furnished all of the following *except*
    a. a known business name.
    b. land to locate the business.
    c. the methods of doing business.
    d. all required training and materials.
    e. management skills.

26. Which statement reflects the main advantage for opening a small business?
    a. Financing can be obtained easily.
    b. Operating a small business is risky but offers challenge.
    c. Managing a small business offers flexibility and independence.
    d. Help is readily available from many sources.
    e. Record keeping is not complicated.

Short-Answer Questions (B)

Complete each question.

27. What are the pros and cons of a business remaining small? List several advantages and several disadvantages.

ADVANTAGES OF SMALL BUSINESSES	DISADVANTAGES OF SMALL BUSINESSES

28. What are four questions a **business plan** must answer?

    a. _____

    b. _____

    c. _____

    d. _____

29. How does the SBA help small businesses obtain **venture capital**?

30. Describe each component of a **business plan**.

COMPONENTS OF A BUSINESS PLAN	DESCRIPTION OF EACH COMPONENT
Introduction	
Executive Summary	
Industry Analysis	
Detailed Description of the Business	
Production Plan	
Marketing Plan	
Organizational Plan	
Assessment of Risk	
Financial Plan	
Appendix	

31. The **Small Business Administration (SBA)** provides two types of assistance: management and financial. Describe each type of assistance.

MANAGEMENT ASSISTANCE	DESCRIPTION
Counseling	
Courses, workshops, and publications	
Service Corps of Retired Executives (SCORE)	
Minority Business Development Agency	
Small Business Institutes	
Small Business Development Center (SBDC)	
FINANCIAL ASSISTANCE	**DESCRIPTION**
Regular guaranteed loans	
Small Business Investment Company (SBIC)	

PRACTICE EXAMINATION C

Matching Questions (C)

Match the term with the statement.

a. small business
b. business plan
c. Small Business Administration (SBA)
d. Service Corps of Retired Executives (SCORE)
e. Dual-branded franchises
f. Small Business Institute (SBI)
g. Small Business Development Center (SBDC)
h. venture capital
i. Small Business Investment Company (SBIC)
j. franchise
k. franchisor
l. franchisee

_____ 1. Graduate students, faculty advisors, and SBA experts provide management counseling.

_____ 2. Independently owned.

_____ 3. Business experienced volunteers.

_____ 4. Summarizes investment needs for a business.

_____ 5. Provides venture capital.

_____ 6. A new small business trend.

_____ 7. Purchaser of a proven business method.

_____ 8. License to operate.

_____ 9. Provides financial resources.

_____ 10. Grantor allows business operator to use his/her idea.

_____ 11. Agency of the government.

_____ 12. University-based group provides technical training.

True-False Questions (C)

Select the correct answer.

T F 13. Small businesses provide jobs for more than 50 percent of the employed.

T F 14. Most business failures are caused by too much planning.

T F 15. A disadvantage of operating a small business is its limited ability to obtain capital.

T F 16. Service industries make up about 48 percent of all small businesses.

T F 17. Small business competition causes larger companies to be more efficient and responsive to consumer needs.

T F 18. Over 70 percent of new businesses close their doors within the first five years.

T F 19. SCORE is the university graduate program that provides counseling to small-business owners.

T F 20. Franchising is a method of doing business.

T F 21. The franchisor pays the franchisee a royalty on gross revenue.

T F 22. In a recent survey 94 percent of franchisees indicated they were very or somewhat successful.

Multiple-Choice Questions (C)

Circle the letter before the most accurate answer.

23. Which of the following is *not* a major advantage of franchising?
    a. Franchisor establishes a well-controlled distribution of products.
    b. Franchisor has a minimal capital outlay.
    c. Franchisor pays royalties to the franchisee.
    d. Franchisee makes use of the business experience of others.
    e. Franchisee can sell to an existing clientele.

24. Which group of businesspeople visits small business establishments, analyzes their business situations, and offers a plan for solving their problems?
    a. SBI
    b. SBDC
    c. SBA
    d. SBIC
    e. SCORE

25. Most businesses fail because of
    a. too strict credit-granting practices.
    b. slow growth in planned expansions.
    c. lack of experience.
    d. a large credit line required.
    e. the high cost of advertising.

26. Which question should *not* be answered in a successfully written business plan?
    a. What exactly is the nature and mission of the new venture?
    b. How does the businessperson spend vacation time?
    c. Why is this new enterprise a good idea?
    d. What are the businessperson's goals?
    e. How much will the new venture cost?

27. It settles contract disputes between franchisors and franchisees.
    a. The Small Business Administration
    b. National Franchise Mediation Program
    c. Minority Business Development Agency
    d. National Franchising Association
    e. U.S. Civil Courts

28. Do you have what it takes to be an entrepreneur? Which statement correctly describes entrepreneurs?
    a. Entrepreneurs are poor spectators.
    b. There is a low correlation between immigrants and entrepreneurs.
    c. Inventors make good entrepreneurs.
    d. The ideal age to start a business is between 24 and 28.
    e. Entrepreneurs generally come from large companies.

29. SBA-guaranteed business loans have an average life duration of _____ years.
    a. eight
    b. twelve
    c. fifteen
    d. eighteen
    e. twenty-five

30. A business plan should contain a(n)
    a. introduction and executive summary.
    b. industry analysis and a detailed description of the business.
    c. production plan and marketing plan.
    d. organization plan and an assessment of risk.
    e. financial plan and all the above items.

31. The process of granting a license to an individual to operate an outlet or store under the company name is called
    a. planning.
    b. licensing.
    c. franchising.
    d. merging.
    e. profiteering

32. Which company failed to make the list of the top ten franchises for 2000 as ranked by *Entrepreneur* magazine?
    a. McDonald's
    b. Holiday Inn
    c. Subway
    d. Snap-On Tools
    e. Mail Boxes Etc.

33. An advantage for the franchisee includes which of the following?
    a. Provides an opportunity to start a business with limited capital
    b. Can take part in national promotional campaigns
    c. Offers the ability to minimize the cost of supplies
    d. Receives guidance and advice concerning problems
    e. All of the above are advantages.

Short-Answer Questions (C)

Complete each question.

34. **Franchising** is a method of doing business. How is it different from opening a sole proprietorship?

35. Describe three types of **franchising arrangements**.

FRANCHISING ARRANGEMENTS	DESCRIPTION
Retail Stores sell a certain brand-name item:	Examples:
Producer licenses distributors to sell a given product:	Examples:
Franchisor supplies brand name, techniques, or other services instead of a complete product:	Examples:

36. What is the projected **growth in franchising** for the next decade and into the twenty-first century?

37. Compare the **advantages of franchising** for the franchisor with those of the franchisee.

FRANCHISOR	FRANCHISEE

38. Cite one major benefit of franchising for the **franchisor**.

39. Cite one major benefit of franchising for the **franchisee**.

40. How has the Internet **impacted** small business operations?

CHAPTER 7

UNDERSTANDING THE MANAGEMENT PROCESS

Key Terms

Define each term briefly. Writing down the definition and giving an example will help you learn the term.

management (p. 186)

planning (p. 188)

mission (p. 188)

strategic planning (p. 188)

goal (p. 188)

objective (p. 188)

plan (p. 189)

strategy (p. 189)

tactical plan (p. 189)

operational plan (p. 189)

contingency plan (p. 189)

organizing (p. 190)

leading (p. 190)

motivating (p. 190)

directing (p. 190)

controlling (p. 190)

top manager (p. 192)

middle manager (p. 192)

first-line manager (p. 192)

financial manager (p. 193)

operations manager (p. 194)

marketing manager (p. 194)

human resources manager (p. 194)

administrative manager (p. 194)

technical skill (p. 195)

conceptual skill (p. 195)

interpersonal skill (p. 195)

decisional role (p. 196)

interpersonal role (p. 196)

informational role (p. 196)

leadership (p. 196)

authoritarian leader (p. 197)

laissez-faire leader (p. 198)

democratic leader (p. 197)

decision making (p. 197)

problem (p. 198)

total quality management (TQM) (p. 200)

PRACTICE EXAMINATION A

Matching Questions (A)

Match each term with a statement.

a. management
b. goal
c. leading
d. motivating
e. mission

f. objectives
g. strategic planning
h. plan
i. planning
j. strategy

k. tactical plan
l. operational plan
m. contingency plan
n. directing
o. leadership

_____ 1. The process of deciding what to do and how to do it.
_____ 2. Needs and desires are at the core of the process.
_____ 3. It describes activities that will help increase sales.
_____ 4. The process of accomplishing objectives through people.
_____ 5. Plans set by the board of directors.
_____ 6. The "manufacturing of computers" is an example.
_____ 7. A general statement of the end results of an activity.
_____ 8. A road map for achieving results.
_____ 9. It implements a strategy.
_____ 10. Measurable statements of organizational activities.

     11. The process of influencing people.
     12. Process of establishing an organization's goals and objectives.
     13. It outlines alternative courses of action.
     14. The ability to influence others.
     15. A combination of leading and motivating.

True-False Questions (A)

Select the correct answer.

T   F   16. Management is the process of coordinating the resources of an organization.
T   F   17. Developing self-managed work teams is a way to increase employee participation and to improve quality in the workplace.
T   F   18. As managers carry out their functions, the first step is to control, the second to organize, and the third to plan.
T   F   19. A goal is a general statement about what is expected to be achieved.
T   F   20. CEOs supervise activities of operating employees.
T   F   21. The directing function includes both leading and motivating activities.
T   F   22. Tactical plans are long-range plans developed to implement a strategy.
T   F   23. Operational plans aimed at increasing sales would include specific advertising activities.
T   F   24. Controlling involves influencing people to work toward a common goal.
T   F   25. Measuring actual performance is the first step in the control process.
T   F   26. The job of an administrative manager is to fill positions within a firm.
T   F   27. As entrepreneur, the manager is the voluntary initiator of change.

Multiple-Choice Questions (A)

Circle the letter before the most accurate answer.

28. Which resource helps an organization meet its obligations to investors and creditors?
    a. Material   d. Human
    b. Financial   e. Market
    c. Informational

29. The process of developing a set of goals and committing an organization to them is called
    a. organizing.   d. controlling.
    b. planning.   e. directing.
    c. optimizing.

30. Who is responsible for developing a firm's mission?
    a. Top managers   d. Middle managers
    b. First-level managers   e. Supervisors
    c. Operations managers

31. Which statement is true about administrative managers?
    a. In some firms, they are called general managers.
    b. They provide overall guidance and leadership.
    c. They are not associated with any particular functional area of the firm.
    d. They coordinate the activities of specialized managers.
    e. Administrative managers do all of the above.

32. It outlines actions for accomplishing goals.
    a. Mission
    b. Goal
    c. Plan
    d. Strategy
    e. Motivations

33. Acme Houseware established a goal to increase its sales by 20 percent in the next year. To ensure that the firm reaches its goal, the sales reports are monitored on a weekly basis. When sales show a slight decline, the sales manager takes actions to correct the problem. Which management function is the manager using?
    a. Leading
    b. Controlling
    c. Directing
    d. Organizing
    e. Planning

34. The chief executive officer of Southwest Airlines provides the company with leadership and overall guidance and is responsible for developing its mission and establishing its goals. Which area of management is being used?
    a. Human resources
    b. Operations
    c. Financial
    d. Administrative
    e. Marketing

35. Plans that are developed by the board of directors and top management are called _____ plans.
    a. tactical
    b. operational
    c. contingency
    d. general
    e. strategic

36. Under an authoritarian leader, communication
    a. usually moves from bottom to top.
    b. flows horizontally at the top only.
    c. usually moves from top to bottom.
    d. flows horizontally among group members.
    e. does not occur.

37. For a total quality management program to be effective, it must be treated as a top priority by
    a. line management.
    b. lower-level management.
    c. workers.
    d. middle management.
    e. top management.

Short-Answer Questions (A)

Complete each question.

38. Using the following key words, prepare a statement that defines **management**.

organization	management	achieve
process	people	resources
goals	coordinating	

Definition of management: _____

_____

39. List four kinds of **resources** that firms use to reach their goals and give examples for each resource.

RESOURCES	EXAMPLES

40. Explain how an organization's **mission** impacts its **strategic planning process**.

41. List the basic **management functions** and tell what each function entails.

MANAGEMENT FUNCTION	DESCRIPTION OF THE FUNCTION

42. Explain how an **objective** is different from a goal.

43. A **plan** outlines the actions required to accomplish a firm's goals and objectives. Describe how each type of plan helps a firm to be successful.

TYPE OF PLAN	PURPOSE FOR EACH PLAN
Strategic Plan	
Tactical Plan	
Operational Plan	
Contingency Plan	

44. **Leading** and **motivating** are concerned with the human resources within an organization. How do they differ?

45. **Controlling** is a process of evaluating and regulating ongoing activities to ensure that goals are achieved. What are the steps in the controlling process?

a. _____

b. _____

c. _____

46. What are the major responsibilities for each **level of management**? Give examples of titles at each level.

LEVEL OF MANAGEMENT	RESPONSIBILITIES OF THE MANAGERS	EXAMPLES OF TITLES WITHIN THE LEVEL OF MANAGEMENT
Top Managers		
Middle Managers		
First-Line Managers		

47. What are the responsibilities of managers in each **specialized area** within a firm?

SPECIALIZED MANAGERS	RESPONSIBILITIES
Financial Managers	
Operations Managers	
Marketing Managers	
Human Resources Managers	
Administrative Managers	

PRACTICE EXAMINATION B

Matching Questions (B)

Match each term with a statement.

a. organizing
b. leading
c. motivating
d. controlling
e. decisional role
f. interpersonal role

g. informational role
h. problem
i. laissez-faire leader
j. total quality management
k. decision making
l. authoritarian leader

_____ 1. Process of evaluating plans and personnel.
_____ 2. Process of providing reasons for people to work.
_____ 3. Process of influencing people to work.
_____ 4. Process of grouping resources and activities.
_____ 5. Identifying causes are at the core of the process.
_____ 6. Strives to improve customer satisfaction.
_____ 7. Manager transmits key information.
_____ 8. One who delegates authority.

_____ 9. The manager takes an important client to dinner.
_____ 10. It involves a discrepancy.
_____ 11. Assigns all tasks and expects precise results.
_____ 12. A negotiator settles a dispute.

True-False Questions (B)

Select the correct answer.

T F 13. Steel, glass, and fiberglass are material resources of the automobile industry.
T F 14. Informational resources require knowing what is changing in the external environment and how it is changing.
T F 15. Tactical plans are long-range global plans for the organization.
T F 16. The board of directors is responsible for setting all goals in a firm.
T F 17. An organization's mission is the means by which it fulfills its purpose.
T F 18. A plan is an outline for accomplishing goals.
T F 19. Common titles for middle managers are office manager and supervisor.
T F 20. Policies are specific guidelines that give the steps for carrying out strategies.
T F 21. Operations managers are concerned strictly with the production of goods, not of services.
T F 22. A democratic leader makes all the decisions and tells subordinates what to do.
T F 23. Middle managers develop tactical plans.
T F 24. Technical skills involve the ability to think in the abstract.

Multiple-Choice Questions (B)

Circle the letter before the most accurate answer.

25. The most important resources in an organization are its _____ resources.
   a. human
   b. financial
   c. informational
   d. material
   e. inventory

26. Establishing a structure in which to carry out plans is called
   a. organizing.
   b. directing.
   c. leading.
   d. planning.
   e. influencing.

27. Who manages the production system?
   a. Financial managers
   b. Administrative managers
   c. Operations managers
   d. Marketing managers
   e. First-level managers

28. A spokesperson is an example of a(n)
   a. decisional role.
   b. informational role.
   c. middle manager.
   d. interpersonal role.
   e. entrepreneur.

29. When a manager in a local bank attends a dedication ceremony at the local library, which role is the manager performing?
    a. Informational
    b. Decisional
    c. Spokesperson
    d. Interpersonal
    e. Liaison

30. The first step in the managerial decision-making process is
    a. generating alternatives.
    b. analyzing the alternatives.
    c. identifying an opportunity.
    d. preparing a plan of action.
    e. evaluating the solution.

31. Bill Powell is in charge of designing the production layout for a new Ford factory and also for implementing just-in-time inventory control at the plant. What type of manager is Bill?
    a. Industrial
    b. Operations
    c. Logistics
    d. Materials
    e. Administrative

32. In carrying out her managerial duties, Susan may tip off the appropriate marketing manager about a business opportunity and warn the human resources manager about a possible strike. In doing so, what type of role is Susan performing?
    a. Decisional
    b. Conceptual
    c. Interpersonal
    d. Analytic
    e. Informational

33. Which statement *incorrectly* reflects the concept of total quality management?
    a. The importance of managing a firm's environment decreases.
    b. The firm's coordination efforts are directed at improving customer satisfaction.
    c. Employees are encouraged to make decisions and assume responsibility.
    d. Improving relationships with suppliers is important.
    e. Self-managed work teams are accountable for improving the quality of their work.

34. Which of the following is *not* considered a personal skill required for success in a competitive business environment?
    a. Has the ability to communicate clear ideas
    b. Possesses technical knowledge
    c. Can use a computer
    d. Can critically analyze problems
    e. Can write clear instructions

35. TQM programs provide benefits. Which of the following is *not* a benefit?
    a. Lower operating costs
    b. Lower levels of customer retention
    c. Higher levels of customer retention
    d. Improved access to global markets
    e. Higher return on investment

Short-Answer Questions (B)

Complete each question.

36. Contrast a **formal leader** with an **informal leader**. What are the characteristics of each?

FORMAL LEADER	INFORMAL LEADER

37. Effective managers possess key **management skills** and use these skills to carry out several **managerial roles**. Explain each type of skill and what is involved in each role.

MANAGEMENT SKILL	MANAGERIAL ROLES
Technical Skills	Decisional Roles
Conceptual Skills	Interpersonal Roles
Interpersonal Skills	Informational Roles

38. How do the following **styles of leadership** compare? Describe each style and give an example for each type of leader.

STYLE OF LEADERSHIP	DESCRIPTION	EXAMPLES
Authoritarian Leader		
Laissez-faire Leader		
Democratic Leader		

39. Discuss the **leadership style** you believe to be the best and why.

PRACTICE EXAMINATION C

Matching Questions (C)

Match each term with a statement.

a. top manager
b. middle managers
c. first-line manager
d. financial manager
e. operations manager
f. marketing manager
g. human resources manager

h. administrative manager
i. technical skills
j. conceptual skills
k. interpersonal skills
l. democratic leader
m. negotiator

_____ 1. One who delegates authority.
_____ 2. Responsible for coordinating activities of managers.
_____ 3. Spends a vast amount of time motivating employees.
_____ 4. Skills needed to work a computer.
_____ 5. The president of the company is an example.
_____ 6. Responsible for the production process.
_____ 7. The ability to deal effectively with people.
_____ 8. Managers who develop tactical plans.
_____ 9. Promotes goods or services for a firm.
_____ 10. Allow a manager to see the "big picture."
_____ 11. One who settles disputes.
_____ 12. Responsible for accounting and investments in a firm.
_____ 13. Designs systems for hiring, training, and evaluating employees.

True-False Questions (C)

Select the correct answer.

T F 14. Doctors, nurses, and orderlies are considered financial resources for hospitals.
T F 15. The primary functions of managers include planning, organizing, directing, and controlling.
T F 16. Organizations plan first, then set goals.
T F 17. Objectives should be established for every level in the firm.
T F 18. Technical skills require thinking in abstract terms to perform technical tasks.
T F 19. A strategy defines how the firm will accomplish its long-term goals.

T F 20. The organizing function involves decisions about the resources that are needed to do a job and who will do the job.

T F 21. A laissez-faire leader allows subordinates to make decisions about their job.

T F 22. Employee commitment is higher under an authoritarian leader than under other types of leaders.

T F 23. Marketing managers are responsible for the distribution of products.

T F 24. Interpersonal skills involve the ability to work effectively with people.

T F 25. A problem can be defined as "what is happening at the moment."

Multiple-Choice Questions (C)

Circle the letter before the most accurate answer.

26. Planning involves
    a. organizing the activities.
    b. setting objectives.
    c. developing plans.
    d. motivating employees.
    e. evaluating activities.

27. "To transport people from one location to another location" is an example of a firm's
    a. goal.
    b. strategy.
    c. plan.
    d. mission.
    e. objective.

28. The control process includes which step?
    a. Deciding how to do the job
    b. Measuring actual performance and comparing with a standard
    c. Logistically organizing raw resources
    d. Rewarding the supervisor for achieving the highest results
    e. Motivating customers to buy more

29. A leader who delegates authority and also participates in determining work assignments for subordinates is known as a(n) _____ leader.
    a. laissez-faire
    b. autocratic
    c. top-level
    d. democratic
    e. first-level

30. Skills that reflect the know-how and knowledge required to do a job are called _____ skills.
    a. human
    b. technical
    c. analytic
    d. conceptual
    e. diagnostic

31. Which skill involves visualizing an idea and turning it into a profitable business?
    a. Technical
    b. Diagnostic
    c. Analytic
    d. Interpersonal
    e. Conceptual

32. Which manager is responsible for training employees and ensuring that the organization follows government regulations?
    a. Administrative
    b. Marketing
    c. Human resources
    d. Operations
    e. Finance

33. Managers who allow subordinates to work as they choose are referred to as _____ leaders.
    a. democratic
    b. reactive
    c. proactive
    d. laissez-faire
    e. ineffective

34. As head of marketing, Sonya Mitchell's objective is to increase the customer base and reduce complaints. She begins by researching ideas on the topic in the library. Next, she calls meetings of salespeople, chats with experts in the field, and works in the service department for a week. These activities represent which step in the managerial decision-making process?
    a. Identifying the problems
    b. Generating alternatives
    c. Selecting an alternative
    d. Implementing the solution
    e. Performance measurement

35. Both _____ and _____ make up the process of directing.
    a. organizing; controlling
    b. networking; segmenting
    c. goal setting; planning
    d. hiring; firing
    e. leading; motivating

Short-Answer Questions (C)

Complete each question.

36. Identify the steps in the **decision-making process**.

    a. _____

    b. _____

    c. _____

    d. _____

37. Distinguish between a **symptom** and an **underlying cause** of a problem.

38. How can **TQM programs** address each of the following components? Give examples.

    a. Customer satisfaction

b. Employee participation

c. Strengthening supplier partnerships

d. Continuous quality improvement

39. For **TQM programs** to be effective, two crucial issues must be addressed. What are they?

a. _____

b. _____

40. As managers move up the corporate ladder, describe how their **workload and lives change**.

41. Why are **personal skills** important in today's competitive business environment?

PERSONAL SKILLS	WHY ARE THE SKILLS IMPORTANT?
Oral communication skills	
Written communication skills	
Computer skills	
Critical-thinking skills	

CHAPTER 8

CREATING A FLEXIBLE ORGANIZATION

Key Terms

Define each term briefly. Writing down the definition and giving an example will help you learn the term.

organization (p. 211)

organization chart (p. 212)

chain of command (p. 212)

job specialization (p. 214)

job rotation (p. 215)

departmentalization (p. 215)

departmentalization by function (p. 215)

departmentalization by product (p. 216)

departmentalization by location (p. 216)

departmentalization by customer (p. 216)

delegation (p. 217)

responsibility (p. 217)

authority (p. 217)

accountability (p. 217)

decentralized organization (p. 218)

centralized organization (p. 218)

span of management (or span of control) (p. 220)

organizational height (p. 221)

line management position (p. 221)

staff management position (p. 221)

bureaucratic structure (p. 223)

matrix structure (p. 224)

cross-functional team (p. 224)

cluster structure (p. 225)

network structure (p. 225)

corporate culture (p. 226)

intrapreneur (p. 228)

ad hoc committee (p. 229)

standing committee (p. 229)

task force (p. 229)

managerial hierarchy (p. 229)

informal organization (p. 230)

informal group (p. 230)

grapevine (p. 230)

PRACTICE EXAMINATION A

Matching Questions (A)

Match each term with a statement.

a. organization
b. cluster structure
c. bureaucratic structure
d. organization chart
e. chain of command
f. job specialization
g. job rotation
h. matrix structure

i. managerial hierarchy
j. departmentalization
k. task force
l. departmentalization by function
m. departmentalization by product
n. departmentalization by location
o. departmentalization by customer

_____ 1. Works best with projects.
_____ 2. Grouping by retailers and wholesalers is an example.
_____ 3. Two or more people working toward a common goal.
_____ 4. It is a way to organize the flow of authority.
_____ 5. A diagram that shows the positions and relationships in a firm.
_____ 6. Grouping together all activities related to a product group.
_____ 7. It consists primarily of teams.
_____ 8. Involves assigning workers to different work stations every week.
_____ 9. The Northwest region is an example.
_____ 10. The line of authority from highest to lowest levels.
_____ 11. It investigates problems.
_____ 12. Line and staff positions are clearly defined.
_____ 13. Employees repeating a particular task.
_____ 14. The process of grouping similar things together.
_____ 15. A scheme that groups all marketing activities.

True-False Questions (A)

Select the correct answer.

T F 16. United Airlines is an example of an organization.

T F 17. Most small firms find little use for organization charts.

T F 18. A benefit of specialization is improved efficiency and increased productivity.

T F 19. The more specialized a job, the more difficult it is to train new employees.

T F 20. Job rotation involves assigning an employee more tasks and greater control.

T F 21. Most smaller and newer firms base their departmentalization on function.

T F 22. Accountability is created, not delegated.

T F 23. The riskier the decision, the greater the tendency to use decentralized decision making.

T F 24. If the span of control is narrow, the organization tends to be tall.

T F 25. The corporate culture of Southwest Airlines can be described as a "process culture."

T F 26. Bureaucratic structures possess a high degree of centralization.

T F 27. Many firms find that by using matrix organization, the motivation level is lowered and personal growth of employees is limited.

T F 28. Network structured firms perform all basic functions of a business.

T F 29. Bureaucratic structures are based on cooperation and knowledge-based authority.

Multiple-Choice Questions (A)

Circle the letter before the most accurate answer.

30. An organization chart
    a. involves two or more people working together.
    b. creates a picture of an organization.
    c. defines job duties.
    d. shows position responsibilities.
    e. All of the above are true.

31. Which process separates organizational activities into distinct tasks and assigns different people to each task?
    a. Departmentalization
    b. Functionalization
    c. Specialization
    d. Communications
    e. Decentralization

32. Which departmentalization process groups activities according to hospitals, schools, and churches?
    a. Location
    b. Function
    c. Basis
    d. Product
    e. Customer

33. McDonald's Corporation practices
    a. decentralization.
    b. delegation.
    c. a combination of authority.
    d. centralization.
    e. None of the above.

34. If a firm was contemplating a merger with another firm, it might form a
    a. standing committee.
    b. task force.
    c. matrix organization.
    d. managerial hierarchy.
    e. project team.

35. The last step in the organization process is called
    a. job design.
    b. departmentalization.
    c. span of management.
    d. chain of command.
    e. delegation.

36. A firm that groups all marketing activities together and all production activities together is *most likely* using departmentalization by
    a. product.
    b. location.
    c. worker skill level.
    d. customer.
    e. function.

37. For employees to be accountable for tasks delegated to them, they must be given
    a. responsibility.
    b. power.
    c. authority.
    d. training.
    e. control.

38. When firms are decentralized, they are *more likely* to use
    a. authority.
    b. delegation.
    c. control.
    d. segmentation.
    e. power.

39. Managers often find they have too much to do in too little time, but they fail to use delegation. Why do managers fail to delegate?
    a. Subordinates already have too much to do.
    b. Managers feel they will be viewed as incapable by their supervisor.
    c. Successful managers are well-organized and can get all the work done.
    d. Subordinates may do the job too well and gain attention of upper management.
    e. Subordinates feel used when delegated tasks.

40. Committees and task forces represent _____ groups within an organization, whereas employee bowling teams represent _____ groups.
    a. staff; line
    b. formal; informal
    c. staff; staff
    d. line; staff
    e. informal; formal

Short-Answer Questions (A)

Complete each question.

41. Use the following words to describe an **organization**: (Complete on next page.)

organization	group	two or more
people	working	together
achieve	common set	goals

Description of an organization: _____

_____

42. How do **organization charts** create a picture of a business?

43. What is the **chain of command** in an organization?

44. The **organizing process** involves five basic steps. Describe what is involved in each step.

STEPS IN ORGANIZING	DESCRIPTION OF EACH STEP
1. Job design	
2. Departmentalization	
3. Delegation	
4. Span of Management	
5. Chain of Command	

45. Identify the **advantages** that each type of **departmentalization** offers.

TYPE OF DEPARTMENTALIZATION	ADVANTAGES
By function	
By product	
By location	
By customer groups	

46. Describe how **job rotation** can be used to combat the problems caused by **job specialization**.

PRACTICE EXAMINATION B

Matching Questions (B)

Match each term with a statement.

a. delegation
b. responsibility
c. authority
d. accountability
e. decentralized organization
f. centralized organization
g. span of management

h. organizational height
i. line management position
j. staff management position
k. line authority
l. advisory authority
m. functional authority
n. intrapreneurship

_____ 1. Directly responsible for accomplishing objectives of the firm.
_____ 2. Obligation to accomplish an assigned job.
_____ 3. Allows staff positions to make decisions and give directives.
_____ 4. The process of giving authority to subordinates.
_____ 5. Gives advice to line management positions.
_____ 6. Lower-level managers are allowed to make important decisions.
_____ 7. Reflects the number of subordinates.
_____ 8. Held by staff positions.
_____ 9. The duty to do a job or perform a task.
_____ 10. All decisions are made by top management.
_____ 11. Makes decisions and issues directives.
_____ 12. The power to do an assigned task.
_____ 13. Indicates the number of levels of management.
_____ 14. Uses a firm's resources to develop employees' ideas.

True-False Questions (B)

Select the correct answer.

T F 15. Staff positions are often shown on organization charts by broken lines.
T F 16. Dividing the work into units is a process called span of management.
T F 17. Canadian Life practices job rotation.
T F 18. The power to make decisions is granted through authority.
T F 19. When top-level managers allow lower-level managers to make important decisions, they are attempting to centralize authority.

T F 20. Staff managers use functional authority to make decisions and issue directives.

T F 21. A local Chevrolet dealership may use departmentalization by customer.

T F 22. Being responsible for accomplishing an assigned job is the task of authority.

T F 23. Research shows that six is the optimum number of subordinates a manager can supervise effectively.

T F 24. Line positions support staff positions in decision making.

T F 25. Ad hoc committees can be used effectively to review a firm's employee benefits plan.

T F 26. A problem with the bureaucratic structure is its lack of flexibility.

T F 27. The grapevine is the system line managers use to issue directives or assign tasks to workers.

T F 28. An advantage for using both line managers and staff managers is to reduce conflict within the organization.

Multiple-Choice Questions (B)

Circle the letter before the most accurate answer.

29. Which of the following did the 3M company use in developing Post-it Notes?
    - a. Intrapreneurship
    - b. Ad hoc committees
    - c. Task force
    - d. Entrepreneurship
    - e. Organic organization

30. A benefit of job specialization is that it
    - a. is more difficult to design equipment.
    - b. is easier to train new employees.
    - c. is more time-consuming.
    - d. eliminates boredom.
    - e. enriches the job.

31. Assigning tasks to subordinates is the process of
    - a. authority.
    - b. accountability.
    - c. control.
    - d. responsibility.
    - e. delegation.

32. A narrow span of control works best when
    - a. subordinates are located close together.
    - b. the manager has few responsibilities outside of supervision.
    - c. little interaction is required between the manager and the worker.
    - d. new problems arise frequently.
    - e. few problems arise on a daily basis.

33. The process of dividing work to be done by an entire organization into separate parts and assigning the parts to positions within the organization is called
    - a. departmentalization.
    - b. delegation.
    - c. job design.
    - d. specialization.
    - e. organizing.

34. Which statement *best* represents a viable reason for a firm to use job specialization?
    a.   Employees who learn only specialized tasks become inefficient at doing that task.
    b.   The job of most organizations is simply too large for one person to handle.
    c.   Continuously repeating the same tasks decreases employee productivity.
    d.   The more specialized the job, the harder it is to train new employees.
    e.   Job design is more difficult to implement with job specialization.

35. Since Procter & Gamble manufacturers a variety of items, which type of departmentalization would the company likely use?
    a.   Function   d.   Product
    b.   Location   e.   Model
    c.   Customer

36. Authority is
    a.   the power to accomplish an assigned job.
    b.   an obligation to perform an assigned task.
    c.   giving others the right to perform a task.
    d.   being responsible for all work completed.
    e.   a duty to perform at the highest level.

37. Which groups of people assist line management positions by providing support, advice, and expertise?
    a.   Task force committees   d.   Informal groups
    b.   Ad hoc committees   e.   Standing committees
    c.   Staff management positions

38. A budget review committee is an example of a(n) _____ committee.
    a.   ad hoc   d.   unnecessary
    b.   informal   e.   standing
    c.   task force

39. How should managers treat the grapevine?
    a.   Recognize the existence of the grapevine as part of the organization.
    b.   Try to eliminate it to minimize any damage it can cause.
    c.   Ignore the information that flows within the grapevine.
    d.   Reprimand employees involved in the grapevine.
    e.   Refrain from using the grapevine.

40. A committee is organized to review applications for scholarships. The group will award two scholarships to recent high school graduates. What type of committee would work *best*?
    a.   Ad hoc committee   d.   Standing committee
    b.   Task force   e.   Self-managed team
    c.   Liaison committee

Short-Answer Questions (B)

Complete each question.

41. What are the steps in the **delegation process**? Identify each step.

    a. _____

    b. _____

    c. _____

42. How does **accountability** differ from **responsibility**?

43. Why do some managers **fail to delegate**? Discuss three reasons.

    a. _____

    b. _____

    c. _____

44. Select the type of organization—**centralized vs. decentralized**—a firm might use based on the factors listed.

FACTORS	CENTRALIZED OR DECENTRALIZED?
Complex and unpredictable external environment	
Riskier and more important decisions	
Abilities of lower-level managers	
Structure traditionally practiced	

45. Identify factors that influence **narrow** or **wide spans of control** in firms.

NARROW SPAN OF CONTROL	WIDE SPAN OF CONTROL

46. Compare a **line management position** with a **staff management position**. How are they similar and how are they different?

SIMILARITIES	DIFFERENCES

PRACTICE EXAMINATION C

Matching Questions (C)

Match each term with a statement.

a. intrapreneur
b. corporate culture
c. wide span of control
d. ad hoc committee
e. standing committee
f. task force
g. managerial hierarchy

h. bureaucratic structure
i. network structure
j. matrix structure
k. project manager
l. informal organization
m. cross-functional team
n. grapevine

_____ 1. Structure used by the grapevine.
_____ 2. Based on a formal framework of authority.
_____ 3. One who works within a firm to develop ideas.
_____ 4. Useful in reviewing a company's recognition program.
_____ 5. An informal communications network.
_____ 6. A system that interfaces product and functional departmentalization.
_____ 7. Committee established to investigate a problem.
_____ 8. Values and rituals are key components.
_____ 9. Coordinates a special team of workers.
_____ 10. Primary functions are contracted.
_____ 11. A large number of subordinates are supervised.
_____ 12. A permanent committee.
_____ 13. Authority is increased at higher levels.
_____ 14. Employees from different departments work on a project.

True-False Questions (C)

Select the correct answer.

T F 15. The line of authority follows the chain of command.
T F 16. Adam Smith, in his book, *The Wealth of Nations*, emphasized the power of specialization.
T F 17. The results of job rotation are boredom and dissatisfaction.
T F 18. Departmentalization by function is best used by older, larger firms producing a variety of products.
T F 19. Departmentalization is the process of grouping jobs into manageable units.
T F 20. Delegation of authority is reserved for top management.
T F 21. Managers often fail to delegate because they are afraid the quality of work will be unacceptable.
T F 22. The span of management should be wide when a great deal of interaction is required between the supervisor and worker.
T F 23. Functional authority is being practiced when staff managers exercise the authority to make decisions and issue directives.
T F 24. An ad hoc committee is a permanent committee.
T F 25. In a cluster organization, the operating unit is the team.
T F 26. Groups performing multiple and difficult tasks are more likely to have smaller spans of control.
T F 27. The span of control is wide when the organization has a well-established set of standard operating procedures.
T F 28. Using a task force committee is an excellent way to research the pros and cons of establishing a day-care center for employees.

Multiple-Choice Questions (C)

Circle the letter before the most accurate answer.

29. Delegation of authority
    a. follows the chain of command.
    b. flows in an upward motion.
    c. is inherent in lower-level managers.
    d. is essential to a centralized organization.
    e. is the power to do a task.

30. The line of authority that extends from the highest to the lowest levels in an organization is called
    a. the span of control.
    b. decentralization.
    c. the chain of command.
    d. a network.
    e. communications.

31. A firm in which authority is concentrated at the top is a(n) _____ organization.
    a. centralized
    b. decentralized
    c. formal
    d. informal
    e. matrix

32. The human resources manager and the public-relations person are
    a. line personnel.
    b. staff personnel.
    c. informal leaders.
    d. a standing committee.
    e. middle managers.

33. When determining the extent to which decentralization will occur, which factor should be considered?
    a. External environment of the firm
    b. Nature of the decision
    c. Abilities of lower-level managers
    d. Traditional practice of the firm
    e. All of the above should be considered.

34. Which position would a public affairs manager hold?
    a. Line
    b. Authority
    c. Functional
    d. Responsible
    e. Staff

35. Informal groups are created
    a. by top level managers.
    b. to promote growth.
    c. to accomplish goals of its members.
    d. as ad hoc committees.
    e. to divert the grapevine.

36. A pattern of delegation in which management systematically works to concentrate authority at the upper levels of the organization is known as
    a. centralization of authority.
    b. decentralization of authority.
    c. managerial hierarchy.
    d. a wide span of control.
    e. accountability.

37. When staff managers have more formal education than line managers, it can lead to
    a. more stability within the work unit.
    b. conflicts between line and staff managers.
    c. higher levels of motivation.
    d. a reduced need for training.
    e. an increased concern for total quality management.

38. This type of organizational structure uses no or very few underlying departments.
    a. Formal
    b. Matrix
    c. Bureaucratic
    d. Cluster
    e. Informal

39. The corporate culture that characterizes feelings of passion, energy, sense of purpose, and excitement is embodied in a _____ culture.
    a. network
    b. basic
    c. fragmented
    d. communal
    e. mercenary

40. Which situation might indicate a need for culture change in an organization?
    a. When the industry is becoming more competitive
    b. When the company is meeting its goals
    c. When the firm is stable
    d. When the firm is growing at a normal rate
    e. When the economy has small fluctuations

Short-Answer Questions (C)

Complete each question.

41. Compare the **organizational structures**. Give a brief description of each type.

ORGANIZATIONAL STRUCTURE	DESCRIPTION
Bureaucratic	
Matrix	
Cluster	
Network	

42. How does a **cross-functional team** work?

43. How do the types of **corporate cultures** differ? Give an example for each type.

TYPES OF CORPORATE CULTURE	EXAMPLE
Networked Culture	
Mercenary Culture	
Fragmented Culture	
Communal Culture	

44. How does an **intrapreneur** differ from an **entrepreneur**?

45. How can each **type of committee** be used most effectively. Give an example.

COMMITTEE	EXAMPLE
Ad hoc committee	
Standing committee	
Task force committee	

46. List three **advantages** for using **committees**.

a. _____

b. _____

c. _____

47. What is a **liaison**, and when should a liaison be used?

48. How should managers treat the **grapevine**?

CHAPTER 9

PRODUCING QUALITY GOODS AND SERVICES

Key Terms

Define each term briefly. Writing down the definition and giving an example will help you learn the term.

operations management (p. 239)

analytic process (p. 240)

synthetic process (p. 240)

utility (p. 242)

form utility (p. 242)

service economy (p. 243)

research and development (R&D) (p. 244)

design planning (p. 246)

product line (p. 246)

product design (p. 246)

capacity (p. 246)

labor-intensive technology (p. 246)

capital-intensive technology (p. 246)

plant layout (p. 248)

planning horizon (p. 250)

purchasing (p. 251)

inventory control (p. 253)

materials requirement planning (MRP) (p. 253)

just-in-time inventory system (p. 253)

scheduling (p. 253)

Gantt chart (p. 254)

PERT (Program Evaluation and Review Technique) (p. 254)

critical path (p. 254)

quality control (p. 255)

statistical process control (SPC) (p. 255)

statistical quality control (SQC) (p. 255)

inspection (p. 255)

quality circle (p. 255)

robotics (p. 257)

computer-aided design (CAD) (p. 258)

computer-aided manufacturing (CAM) (p. 258)

computer-integrated manufacturing (CIM) (p. 258)

flexible manufacturing system (FMS) (p. 259)

productivity (p. 259)

PRACTICE EXAMINATION A

Matching Questions (A)

Match each term with a statement.

a. operations management
b. fixed-position layout
c. plant layout
d. service economy
e. research and development
f. basic research
g. applied research

h. design planning
i. product line
j. product design
k. materials requirement planning
l. critical path
m. analytic process
n. synthetic process

_____ 1. A group of similar products.
_____ 2. The process of discovering and implementing new ideas.
_____ 3. Managing the creation of goods and services.
_____ 4. Method used to build a 777 jet aircraft.
_____ 5. Discovering new knowledge for scientific advancement.
_____ 6. Involves creating different product variations.
_____ 7. An arrangement of machinery and personnel.
_____ 8. Activities are geared to discovering knowledge that has potential.
_____ 9. Plan for converting a product idea into an actual commodity.
_____ 10. More effort is directed at producing services than goods.
_____ 11. Breaks raw materials into different components.
_____ 12. Production activities take the longest time from start to finish.
_____ 13. Combines raw materials to create a finished product.
_____ 14. A system integrating production planning and inventory control.

True-False Questions (A)

Select the correct answer.

T F 15. A quality circle is a group of workers who give input on quality-related problems.

T F 16. Capacity is the degree to which input resources are physically changed by the conversion process.

T F 17. Basic research discovers new knowledge that has some potential use.

T F 18. In considering a product line, a business should put customers' preferences first.

T F 19. Product extension and refinement are expected results of a firm's development implementation effort.

T F 20. Operations management is the process of creating a set of specifications from which the product can be produced.

T F 21. Purchasing personnel need not worry about a tiny difference in price when a large quantity is being bought.

T F 22. The availability of skilled and unskilled labor in various geographic areas is a factor in determining plant location.

T F 23. One month is a common planning horizon for operational plans.

T F 24. ISO 9000 is used to determine when reorders should be placed for merchandise.

T F 25. The critical path is the shortest path through the sequence of activities in a PERT diagram.

T F 26. The change in the work force composition is one cause for the decline in productivity in recent years.

Multiple-Choice Questions (A)

Circle the letter before the most accurate answer.

27. Activities that create goods and services are known as
    a. capacity.
    b. operations management.
    c. capital-intensive technology.
    d. market demand.
    e. operational planning.

28. When the 3M Company combined paper with a special type of adhesive, it used
    a. basic research.
    b. applied research.
    c. development and implementation.
    d. product design.
    e. capacity.

29. The process of creating a set of specifications from which a product can be produced is called
    a. capacity.
    b. productivity.
    c. robotics.
    d. automation.
    e. product design.

30. The production of services differs from the production of manufactured goods in all ways *except* services are
    a. consumed immediately and cannot be stored.
    b. produced to satisfy customer needs.
    c. provided when and where the customer desires the service.
    d. usually labor intensive.
    e. intangible, and it's more difficult to evaluate customer service.

31. The goal of basic research is to
    a. uncover new knowledge without regard for its potential use.
    b. discover new knowledge, with regard for potential use in development.
    c. discover knowledge for potential use.
    d. put new or existing knowledge to use.
    e. combine ideas.

32. The first step in operational planning is to
    a. estimate market demand.
    b. compare demand with capacity.
    c. adjust output to match demand.
    d. select a planning horizon.
    e. control the logistics.

33. Both place and time are important factors in
    a. scheduling.
    b. market demand.
    c. applied research.
    d. horizons.
    e. layout.

34. When a firm decides to develop and market a new line of products, it must consider the required capacity, use of technology, number and location of facilities, and personnel. Making decisions about these items is part of
    a. operational planning.
    b. basic research.
    c. scheduling.
    d. design planning.
    e. applied research.

35. General Motors' automated assembly plants are termed
    a. labor-intensive.
    b. capital-intensive.
    c. logical.
    d. planned horizontally.
    e. market demanded.

36. A major objective of Mercedes-Benz's quality control program is to
    a. adopt a strategy for emphasizing lower prices.
    b. see that the firm lives up to its standards.
    c. keep track of the inventory.
    d. control operations with PERT charts.
    e. find the critical path in the production process.

Short-Answer Questions (A)

Complete each question.

37. **Operations management** consists of all the activities that managers engage in to produce goods and services. Describe what happens in each major activity of producing the goods and services.

ACTIVITIES OF OPERATIONS MANAGEMENT	DESCRIPTIONS
Product development (Research & Development)	
Planning for production	
Operations control	

38. U.S. firms are currently focusing on improving quality and meeting the needs of their customers. Identify four things firms are doing to give them a **competitive edge**.

a. _____   b. _____

c. _____   d. _____

39. What is the difference between an **analytic process** and a **synthetic process**? Give an example of each type of process.

PROCESS	EXAMPLE
Analytic	
Synthetic	

40. **Form utility** is created by converting _____

_____

41. Tell how each component of the **conversion process** is used by a local pizza parlor to create pizzas and by a dry cleaning establishment to provide cleaning services.

CONVERSION PROCESS	PIZZA PARLOR	DRY CLEANING COMPANY
Focus		
Magnitude		
No. of Production Processes		

42. How is the **production of services** different from the **production of manufactured goods**? Identify four ways.

a. _____

b. _____

c. _____

d. _____

43. Differentiate among three general types of **R&D activities**.

BASIC RESEARCH	APPLIED RESEARCH	DEVELOPMENT & IMPLEMENTATION

PRACTICE EXAMINATION B

Matching Questions (B)

Match each term with a statement.

a. process layout
b. product layout
c. operational planning
d. planning horizon
e. form utility
f. purchasing

g. utility
h. inventories
i. inventory control
j. scheduling
k. statistical process control
l. statistical quality control

_____ 1. Acquiring materials, supplies, and parts from other firms.
_____ 2. Concerned with holding costs and potential stock-out costs.
_____ 3. Grouping similar manufacturing operations together.
_____ 4. Ability of a product to satisfy a human need.
_____ 5. The process of ensuring that materials are at the right place.
_____ 6. An assembly line is an example.
_____ 7. Consist of stockpiles of materials and finished goods.
_____ 8. Plans for utilizing production facilities.
_____ 9. Created by converting production inputs into finished goods.
_____ 10. Involves a period of time.
_____ 11. It plots data on charts to help identify problems.
_____ 12. It samples work in progress.

True-False Questions (B)

Select the correct answer.

T F 13. Operations managers must understand the relationship between the customer, the marketing of a product, and the production of a product.
T F 14. The majority of American workers are employed in service organizations.
T F 15. A fixed-position layout uses an assembly line arrangement.
T F 16. Capacity is more important in a production business than in a service business.
T F 17. Marketing managers play an important role in making product-line decisions.
T F 18. In medical clinics, the capacity is the number of patients it can handle in one hour.
T F 19. When work stations are arranged to match the sequence of operations, a process layout is being used.
T F 20. Materials that will become part of a product during the conversion process are called raw materials.
T F 21. To accomplish the major objective of purchasing, managers must carefully select suppliers to ensure that required materials are available when needed in the proper amounts and at a minimum cost.
T F 22. Work-in-process inventories are completed goods awaiting shipment to customers.

T   F   23. The major objective of quality control is to ensure the organization lives up to its standard of quality.

T   F   24. In the past decade, the increase in spending for R&D has contributed to the decline in productivity growth.

Multiple-Choice Questions (B)

Circle the letter before the most accurate answer.

25. Operations management activities include
    a. product development.
    b. production planning.
    c. monitoring the production process.
    d. ensuring that goals are achieved.
    e. All of the above.

26. Developing a plan for production is called
    a. a planning horizon.
    b. product design.
    c. production planning.
    d. a process layout.
    e. design planning.

27. One worker in Department A produces 45 units of work per day on a computer while a coworker produces only 40 units of work per day on a computer. Since the first worker produces more units, that worker has a
    a. lower capacity to use technology.
    b. higher productivity rate.
    c. desire to help the coworker.
    d. computer-integrated system.
    e. computer-aided system.

28. Design planning involves decisions about
    a. the number of facilities to be used.
    b. locations of facilities.
    c. the plant layout.
    d. the capacity of the facility.
    e. All of the above.

29. When a product reaches the end of the rise-and-decline pattern in its product life cycle, the business offering only one product will die unless the firm finds ways to
    a. extend or refine the want-satisfying capability of its products.
    b. encourage existing customers to buy more of its products.
    c. reduce the cost of its products.
    d. market the products in another geographic area of the United States.
    e. increase the price of the products.

30. All of the following are advantages of the computer-integrated manufacturing system *except*
    a. lower operating costs.
    b. improved flexibility.
    c. more efficient scheduling.
    d. higher product quality.
    e. it helps design products.

31. An ISO 9000 certification is evidence that a company meets the standards for quality control procedures in
    a. manufacturing design.
    b. product testing.
    c. training of employees.
    d. record keeping.
    e. All of the above.

32. The completion of each activity on a PERT diagram is called a(n)
    a. activity.
    b. control.
    c. process.
    d. event.
    e. path.

33. When raw materials are delivered to production facilities as they are needed and in the required amounts, the method of inventory control used is known as
    a. materials requirements planning.
    b. supplier-based inventory control.
    c. just-in-time inventory control.
    d. purchasing planning.
    e. the critical path.

34. When automobile workers meet as a group on company time to solve problems about product quality, they are engaging in a quality control strategy called
    a. quality teams.
    b. quality circles.
    c. inspections.
    d. meetings.
    e. problem solving.

35. It combines robotics and computer-integrated manufacturing in a single-production system.
    a. Computer-aided design
    b. Computer-aided manufacturing
    c. Flexible manufacturing system
    d. Computer-integrated manufacturing
    e. Materials requirement planning

Short-Answer Questions (B)

Complete each question.

36. **Design planning** is the development of a plan for converting a product idea into an actual product. Define its major elements.

ELEMENTS	DEFINITION
Product line	
Required capacity	
Use of technology	

37. Describe an example for each of the following:

    a. Product line

    b. Product design

38. How does **labor-intensive technology** differ from **capital-intensive technology?**

39. What factors should be considered when **selecting a site** for a new manufacturing facility? List at least six factors.

   a. _____

   b. _____

   c. _____

   d. _____

   e. _____

   f. _____

40. Describe each type of **plant layout** and give an example for each.

PLANT LAYOUT	DESCRIPTION	EXAMPLE
Process layout		
Product layout		
Fixed-position layout		

41. What is the objective of **operational planning**?

42. Explain what happens in each step of **operational planning.**

STEPS	EXPLANATION
1. Selecting a planning horizon	
2. Estimating market demand	
3. Comparing market demand with capacity	
4. Adjusting products or services to demand	

PRACTICE EXAMINATION C

Matching Questions (C)

Match each term with a statement.

a. capacity
b. labor-intensive technology
c. capital-intensive technology
d. plant layout
e. PERT
f. quality control

g. inspection
h. quality circles
i. productivity
j. robotics
k. computer-aided design
l. computer-aided manufacturing

_____ 1. Arrangement of machinery, equipment, and personnel within a firm.
_____ 2. The work is accomplished mostly by equipment.
_____ 3. People must do most of the work.
_____ 4. Amount of production in a given period.
_____ 5. A process to ensure that goods and services meet specifications.
_____ 6. Uses programmable machines.
_____ 7. An examination of product output.
_____ 8. Technique for scheduling and maintaining control of a project.
_____ 9. Utilizes input from workers.
_____ 10. Measures output per unit of time per worker.
_____ 11. Computers aid in the development of products.
_____ 12. The manufacturing process is controlled by computers.

True-False Questions (C)

Select the correct answer.

T F 13. The focus of a conversion process is finished goods.
T F 14. The purpose of research and development is to identify new ideas.
T F 15. Design planning precedes production-facility adaptation.
T F 16. Productivity measures output per unit of time worked per employee.
T F 17. A car rolling off the assembly line every 55 seconds is an example of capacity for an automobile plant.
T F 18. Labor-intensive technology requires an owner to invest heavily to continue making a profit.
T F 19. Robots exemplify labor-intensive technology.
T F 20. The objective of operational planning is to decide the level of output for the facility.
T F 21. A Gantt chart is a follow-up technique used for monitoring production schedules.
T F 22. The choice of suppliers should be determined on the basis of price, quality, and reliability.
T F 23. PERT identifies major activities and time requirements for completing a product.
T F 24. Productivity rates in Italy, Sweden, and Japan exceed those in the United States.

Multiple-Choice Questions (C)

Circle the letter before the most accurate answer.

25. New ideas and technical advances come through
    a. research and development.
    b. design planning.
    c. productivity.
    d. capacity.
    e. market demand.

26. The amount of input that a facility can process or output that it can produce in a given time is called
    a. production.
    b. product design.
    c. logistics.
    d. capacity.
    e. scheduling.

27. A cause for the decline in productivity in the United States is that
    a. the composition of the work force is stable.
    b. government regulation has increased.
    c. businesses have increased their capital investments.
    d. unions and management are working closer together.
    e. employees are being rewarded for their contributions.

28. The conversion of resources into products and services can be described by its focus, magnitude, and
    a. the number of production processes.
    b. its integration system.
    c. the number of customers.
    d. the operations manager.
    e. the finished product.

29. When all products undergo the same operations in the same sequence, _____ is used.
    a. quota layout
    b. process layout
    c. product layout
    d. product design
    e. output layout

30. Two important components of scheduling are
    a. lead-time and planning.
    b. designing and arranging.
    c. monitoring and controlling.
    d. place and time.
    e. logistics and flow.

31. A local Toys 'R' Us store received its shipment of recently released videos. The entire stock of videos was depleted within two hours after they went on sale. The manager was delighted, but failed to understand the significance of the cost resulting from losing sales by not having more inventory. What type of inventory cost did the store suffer?
    a. Holding
    b. Storage
    c. Stock-out
    d. Variable
    e. Fixed

32. Over the past decade, the United States has experienced a decline in its rate of productivity as compared to other countries in the world. Which of the following is *not* a cause for this decline?
    a. Increased government regulation
    b. Decrease in spending for research and development
    c. Slowing down of investment dollars into equipment
    d. Major changes in the composition of the work force
    e. Increased tax credits

33. In determining where to locate a production facility, management must consider a number of variables. Which variable would have the *least* impact on the decision?
    a. Availability of skilled and unskilled labor
    b. Quantity discounts offered to mass distributors
    c. Geographic locations of suppliers for parts and raw materials
    d. Transportation costs to deliver finished products to customers
    e. The energy or water resources required

34. A scheduling device displaying tasks on the vertical axis and required on the horizontal axis is called
    a. a PERT chart.   d. an inventory control chart.
    b. a Gantt chart.   e. quality control.
    c. scheduling.

35. Automation is increasing productivity by
    a. cutting manufacturing costs.
    b. simplifying retooling procedures.
    c. reducing errors.
    d. using robots.
    e. All of the above.

Short-Answer Questions (C)

Complete each question.

36. The objective of **purchasing** is to:

    a. _____ b. _____ c. _____

37. What is involved in each area of **operations control**?

AREAS OF OPERATIONS CONTROL	DESCRIPTION
Purchasing	
Inventory control	
Scheduling	
Quality control	

38. Explain why each factor is critical when **selecting a supplier**.

FACTORS	IMPORTANCE
Price	
Quality	
Reliability	
Credit terms	
Shipping costs	

39. Give an example for each type of **inventory**.

INVENTORIES	EXAMPLES
Raw materials	
Work-in process	
Finished goods	

40. What is the major difference between **manufacturing resource planning** and **enterprise resource planning**?

41. What is the **just-in-time inventory** system designed to do?

42. Graphically illustrate each scheduling technique.

PERT CHART	GANTT CHART

43. What is the major objective of **quality control**?

44. What is the **purpose** of each type of **quality control**?

TYPE OF QUALITY CONTROL	PURPOSE
Statistical process control (SPC)	
Statistical quality control (SQC)	
Inspection	
Quality Circle	

45. What is **ISO 9000**?

46. Identify six areas of **ISO 9000** certification.

a. _____ b. _____

c. _____ d. _____

e. _____ f. _____

47. Where can **robots** be most effectively used in business?

48. Compare the **computer manufacturing systems**. Write out the name of the system and tell its purpose.

SYSTEM	NAME IN FULL	PURPOSE
CAD		
CAM		
CIM		
FMS		

49. How is **productivity** measured?

50. Identify three strategies for improving **productivity** in the United States.

a. _____

b. _____

c. _____

CHAPTER 10

ATTRACTING AND RETAINING THE BEST EMPLOYEES

Key Terms

Define each term briefly. Writing down the definition and giving an example will help you learn the term.

human resources management (HRM) (p. 272)

human resources planning (p. 273)

replacement chart (p. 274)

skills inventory (p. 274)

cultural (workplace) diversity (p. 275)

job analysis (p. 277)

job description (p. 277)

job specification (p. 277)

recruiting (p. 277)

external recruiting (p. 278)

internal recruiting (p. 279)

selection (p. 280)

orientation (p. 282)

compensation (p. 283)

compensation system (p. 283)

wage survey (p. 283)

job evaluation (p. 283)

comparable worth (p. 284)

hourly wage (p. 285)

salary (p. 285)

commission (p. 285)

incentive payment (p. 285)

lump-sum salary increase (p. 285)

profit sharing (p. 285)

employee benefits (p. 286)

flexible benefit plan (p. 286)

employee training (p. 287)

management development (p. 287)

performance appraisal (p. 289)

PRACTICE EXAMINATION A

Matching Questions (A)

Match each term with a statement.

a. human resources management
b. human resources planning
c. replacement chart
d. skills inventory
e. job analysis
f. job description

g. job specification
h. recruiting
i. external recruiting
j. internal recruiting
k. selection
l. orientation

_____   1. Jobs are studied to determine the tasks.
_____   2. Newspaper advertising is an example.
_____   3. New employees are introduced to company operations.
_____   4. People are acquired, maintained, and developed for the firm.
_____   5. The duties and responsibilities are described.
_____   6. Promotions and transfers are examples of this method of acquiring employees.
_____   7. It involves determining a firm's future personnel needs.
_____   8. Personal qualifications required in a job are described.
_____   9. The process involves choosing the best-qualified applicants for positions.
_____ 10. It lists employees who may be replaced within a certain period of time.
_____ 11. Potential applicants are made aware of available positions.
_____ 12. A computerized data bank is involved.

True-False Questions (A)

Select the correct answer.

T F 13. HRM begins with getting people to work for the organization.
T F 14. Recruiting is an activity of human resources acquisition.
T F 15. In most large firms, the human resources manager's position is classified as a staff position.
T F 16. The Age Discrimination in Employment Act covers people in the age bracket of 20 to 50 years.
T F 17. OSHA investigates employee complaints regarding unsafe working conditions.
T F 18. A skills inventory is a list of key personnel and their replacements.
T F 19. Job specifications include personal skills, abilities, education, and experience.
T F 20. Transfers involve moving employees into higher-level positions.
T F 21. In a structured interview, the interviewer uses a prepared set of questions.
T F 22. Hourly workers receive bonuses as compensation.
T F 23. In the maintaining phase of human resources management, employees' skills are improved.
T F 24. The most widely used selection technique is the employment test.

T F   25. Employees have no input into the tell-and-sell performance feedback approach.

Multiple-Choice Questions (A)

Circle the letter before the most accurate answer.

26. The human resources manager is not directly responsible for
    a. acquiring suitable applicants.
    b. maintaining a happy work force.
    c. developing a productive work force.
    d. planning for personnel needs.
    e. supervising the work force.

27. Required retirement before age 70 was outlawed in the _____ Act.
    a. Age Discrimination in Employment
    b. Equal Pay
    c. Fair Labor Standards
    d. Employee Retirement Income Security
    e. Civil Rights

28. Developing a training program involves all of the following *except*
    a. conducting an analysis of needs.
    b. determining training methods.
    c. supervising workers.
    d. selecting development methods.
    e. creating an evaluation system.

29. A one-page summary of an applicant's qualifications is known as a(n)
    a. application form.
    b. data sheet.
    c. summary sheet.
    d. résumé.
    e. qualification sheet.

30. Which item is generally *not* considered to be an employee benefit?
    a. Pay for time not worked
    b. Performance appraisals
    c. Insurance packages
    d. Pension and retirement programs
    e. Social Security

31. A method of training using experienced employees is known as
    a. role playing.
    b. on-the-job training.
    c. vestibule training.
    d. lectures.
    e. conferences.

32. Which item is *not* considered to be a main objective of a performance appraisal process?
    a. Learning how well employees are performing their jobs
    b. Guaranteeing life-time employment with the firm
    c. Rewarding employees with pay raises and/or promotions
    d. Helping monitor the employee selection process
    e. Providing input into training and development activities

33. The starting point for developing an evaluation of a training program is to
    a. select the people to be trained.
    b. use a replacement chart.
    c. set verifiable objectives.
    d. reward the most productive workers.
    e. prepare a job description.

34. Melinda walked into the ABC Company to pick up an application for an administrative assistant position. When she asked about the duties and working conditions, the busy receptionist handed her a job
    a. description.
    b. inventory.
    c. analysis.
    d. orientation.
    e. specification.

35. When firms use private employment agencies to find qualified employees, they are using
    a. a skills inventory.
    b. internal recruiting.
    c. vestibule selection.
    d. external recruiting.
    e. external replacement.

36. The type of interview that *best* allows employers to compare candidates' qualifications is a(n) _____ interview.
    a. stress
    b. open-ended
    c. in-depth
    d. closed
    e. structured

37. In designing an effective employee reward system, managers should strive to meet all of the following objectives *except*
    a. enabling employees to satisfy their basic needs.
    b. providing rewards comparable to those offered by other firms.
    c. maximizing the amount spent on compensation.
    d. distributing rewards fairly within the organization.
    e. recognizing that different people have different needs.

38. When a firm promotes a qualified female, but fails to compensate her at the same rate as men in the same position, the firm may be guilty of violating the concept of
    a. comparable worth.
    b. wage structure.
    c. compensation.
    d. flexible benefit plans.
    e. lump-sum salary plan.

39. Which training method is an effective way to help managers understand and cope with employees' problems?
    a. Vestibule training
    b. Role playing
    c. On-the-job training
    d. Seminar training
    e. Classroom training

40. A performance feedback appraisal approach that collects reviews from peers, subordinates, and supervisors and compiles the data in a feedback report is called a
    a. problem solving approach.
    b. tell-and-listen approach.
    c. 360-degree evaluation.
    d. tell-and-sell method.
    e. feedback approach.

Short-Answer Questions (A)

Complete each question.

41. What are the three main **phases of HRM**? What happens in each phase? Give a description.

HRM PHASES	DESCRIPTION
Acquiring human resources	
Maintaining human resources	
Developing human resources	

42. What major activities are required in the **acquisition phase**? Give a description.

ACTIVITIES RELATED TO ACQUIRING HUMAN RESOURCES	DESCRIPTION

43. What major activities occur in the **maintaining human resources phase**. Give a description.

ACTIVITIES RELATED TO MAINTAINING HUMAN RESOURCES	DESCRIPTION

44. List and describe the major activities that occur in **developing human resources.** Give descriptions.

ACTIVITIES RELATED TO DEVELOPING HUMAN RESOURCES	DESCRIPTION

45. Identify the steps in **human resources planning.**

a. _____

b. _____

c. _____

46. How is a **replacement chart** different from a **skills inventory**? How is each primarily used?

47. What steps can a firm take to match **supply of workers** with its **demand for workers**?

a. _____   b. _____

c. _____   d. _____

48. What are the major **benefits** associated with a **culturally diverse** work force?

a. _____

b. _____

c. _____

d. _____

e. _____

f. _____

g. _____

49. What can a firm do to help employees cope with the challenges of cultural diversity?

a. _____

b. _____

c. _____

d. _____

e. _____

PRACTICE EXAMINATION B

Matching Questions (B)

Match each term with a statement.

a. compensation
b. compensation system
c. wage survey
d. wage structure

e. job evaluation
f. hourly wage
g. salary
h. commission

_____ 1. Pay is based on a percentage of sales revenue.
_____ 2. The policies and strategies are outlined for determining wage levels, wage structure, and individual wages.
_____ 3. The process determines the relative value of various jobs within a firm.
_____ 4. The reward that employees receive for their labor.
_____ 5. It establishes pay levels for all positions within a firm.
_____ 6. This technique collects data on wage rates within an industry.
_____ 7. The rate of pay is based on hours worked.
_____ 8. Pay is based on the period of time worked.

True-False Questions (B)

Select the correct answer.

T F   9. Staffing, personnel management, and human resources management are synonymous terms.
T F 10. Job analysis is the process of rewarding employees for their effort.
T F 11. Legislation regarding personnel practices have been passed mainly to protect the rights of employers.
T F 12. Minimum wages and overtime pay rates are covered in the Equal Pay Act.

T F 13. Forecasting the supply of human resources involves both the present work force and future changes in that work force.

T F 14. Attrition is the process of acquiring information on applicants.

T F 15. The selection process matches the right candidate with each job.

T F 16. An application form can identify candidates who are worthy of further scrutiny.

T F 17. Assessment centers are used most often to evaluate applicants.

T F 18. Employee benefits such as vacation and sick leave are required by law.

T F 19. The three phases of human resources management are acquiring, maintaining, and developing.

T F 20. Managers should view cultural diversity as an opportunity rather than a limitation.

T F 21. Employment applications collect factual information about an applicant's education and work experience.

Multiple-Choice Questions (B)

Circle the letter before the most accurate answer.

22. Developing a productive work force involves
    a. recruiting.
    b. orientation.
    c. staffing.
    d. compensation.
    e. training and development.

23. Human resources planning begins with
    a. forecasting the supply of applicants.
    b. matching the supply with the demand.
    c. the organization's overall strategic plan.
    d. forecasting the demand for personnel.
    e. evaluating work performance.

24. An example of internal recruiting is
    a. job posting.
    b. private agencies.
    c. newspaper ads.
    d. union hiring.
    e. public agencies.

25. A selection tool that benefits both the applicant and the firm is the
    a. application form.
    b. interview.
    c. physical exam.
    d. testing process.
    e. résumé.

26. The process of positioning the firm's general pay level relative to the pay levels of comparable firms involves _____ decisions.
    a. wage-structure
    b. individual-wage
    c. wage-level
    d. equitable
    e. bonus

27. An objective appraisal method uses _____ to assess performance.
    a. units of output
    b. rating scales
    c. subjective analysis
    d. employee feedback
    e. judgmental estimates

28. Human resources planning requires the following steps *except*
    a. using the firm's strategic plan.
    b. forecasting the firm's future demand.
    c. determining availability of human resources.
    d. acquiring funds for implementation.
    e. matching supply with demand.

29. One responsibility of the human resources manager is to fill positions with qualified people. To do this successfully, what must a manager do first to determine the qualifications needed for the position?
    a. Draft job descriptions.
    b. Write job specifications.
    c. Conduct job analyses.
    d. Set up job orientations.
    e. Prepare a skills inventory.

30. The primary advantages for using external recruiting include all *except*
    a. bringing in people with new perspectives.
    b. being an inexpensive way to recruit candidates.
    c. attracting applicants with the required skills.
    d. encouraging people with varied backgrounds to apply.
    e. attracting applicants from outside the organization.

31. The process to introduce new employees to the location of the cafeteria and to career paths within the organization is called
    a. pre-employment testing.
    b. recruitment.
    c. compensation.
    d. internal recruitment.
    e. an orientation.

32. If the firm where you work wanted to determine the relative worth of the various jobs within the firm, it would
    a. develop job descriptions.
    b. conduct a job analysis.
    c. conduct a wage survey.
    d. develop a job evaluation.
    e. develop job specifications.

33. To prepare managers to assume increased responsibility in both their present and future positions, human resources should implement
    a. an employee training program.
    b. a management development program.
    c. vestibule training.
    d. an orientation program.
    e. skills inventorying.

34. If an employee who processes an average of 18 units of work per week is given a higher evaluation than an employee who processes an average of 14 units of work per week, which method of performance appraisal is being used?
    a. Judgmental
    b. Rating scale
    c. Performance feedback
    d. Objective
    e. Subjective

35. The Americans with Disabilities Act prohibits discrimination against qualified individuals with disabilities in all employment practices *except*

    a. application procedures.
    b. hiring and firing.
    c. transportation to work.
    d. training and advancement.
    e. compensation.

36. Employers must provide *reasonable accommodation* for disabled employees as defined under the ADA. Which activity is *not* required under this law?

    a. Providing adequate home medical care
    b. Making existing facilities accessible
    c. Modifying work schedules
    d. Providing qualified readers
    e. Changing examinations

Short-Answer Questions (B)

Complete each question.

37. Describe each term and tell why each is important in the **selection** process.

TERM	DEFINITION	IMPORTANCE
Job analysis		
Job description		
Job specifications		

38. What is the role of **recruiting**, **selection**, and **orientation** in HRM?

RECRUITING	SELECTION	ORIENTATION

39. Identify several **external** and several **internal sources** for recruiting potential applicants for available positions.

EXTERNAL RECRUITING SOURCES	INTERNAL RECRUITING SOURCES

40. What are the **advantages** and **disadvantages** of both external and internal recruiting?

EXTERNAL RECRUITING	INTERNAL RECRUITING
Advantages	Advantages
Disadvantages	Disadvantages

41. What information can each **assessment tool** reveal about an applicant?

ASSESSMENT TOOL	TYPE OF INFORMATION
Employment applications	
Employment tests	
Interviews	
References	
Assessment Centers	

42. What are the requirements of an effective **reward system**? List them.

    a. _____

    b. _____

    c. _____

    d. _____

43. Explain why **wage-related decisions** are important in designing an effective compensation system.

WAGE-RELATED DECISIONS	WHY ARE EACH IMPORTANT?
Wage level	
Wage structure	
Individual wages	

44. Explain the concept of **comparable worth**. Give an example.

45. Compare the types of **compensation**. How does each work?

TYPES OF COMPENSATION	EXPLANATION
Hourly wage	
Weekly or monthly salary	
Commissions	
Incentive payments	
Lump-sum salary increases	
Profit sharing	

46. Identify as many **types of benefits** as you can.

a. _____   b. _____

c. _____   d. _____

e. _____   f. _____

47. How do **flexible benefit plans** work?

PRACTICE EXAMINATION C

Matching Questions (C)

Match each term with a statement.

a. bonus   e. management development
b. profit sharing   f. incentive payment
c. employee benefits   g. performance appraisal
d. employee training   h. cultural diversity

_____ 1. The process includes teaching employees to do their job more efficiently.
_____ 2. Employees receive nonmonetary rewards.
_____ 3. An employee's work performance is evaluated.
_____ 4. It rewards work performance above the expected level.
_____ 5. It prepares managers to handle increased responsibilities.
_____ 6. Gain sharing is an example.
_____ 7. Employees receive a percentage of the firm's profits.
_____ 8. Managers are challenged by differences in ethnicity among employees.

True-False Questions (C)

Select the correct answer.

T   F   9. Human resources management begins by developing employees within the firm.
T   F   10. Training and development are considered a part of the acquisition phase of human resources management.
T   F   11. The purpose of Title VII is to ensure that employers make personnel decisions on the basis of employee qualifications.
T   F   12. The Employee Retirement Income Security Act requires firms to provide a retirement plan for their employees.

T F 13. A replacement chart ensures that top management positions can be filled fairly quickly.

T F 14. A systematic procedure for studying jobs is the process of job descriptions.

T F 15. A lump-sum salary increase, if given at the beginning of the year, is treated as an interest-free loan that must be repaid if the employee leaves.

T F 16. Intelligence tests are used primarily to predict specific job performance.

T F 17. Orientation is the process of acquainting new employees with the organization.

T F 18. Flexible benefit plans provide employees with benefit options.

T F 19. Employees are required by law to take lump-sum salary increases in one pay check at the end of the year.

T F 20. By the year 2005, approximately 75 percent of the women entering the work force will be minorities.

T F 21. Wage structures provide pay levels for positions within firms.

Multiple-Choice Questions (C)

Circle the letter before the most accurate answer.

22. The Equal Employment Opportunity Commission is charged with enforcing
    a. the Fair Labor Standards Act.
    b. the Civil Rights Act.
    c. the Occupational Safety and Health Act.
    d. the National Labor Relations Act.
    e. None of the above.

23. The *most* humane method of making personnel cutbacks is through
    a. attrition.
    b. firings.
    c. transfers.
    d. early retirement.
    e. layoffs.

24. The process of hiring the most qualified applicants is called
    a. interviewing.
    b. selection.
    c. recruitment.
    d. orientation.
    e. evaluating.

25. People who can verify an applicant's background information are called
    a. references.
    b. candidates.
    c. interviewers.
    d. interviewees.
    e. applicants.

26. A specific amount of money paid for a set calendar period of time is called
    a. commissions.
    b. wages.
    c. a salary.
    d. bonuses.
    e. benefits.

27. During reorganization many firms find that they have too many employees on the payroll. All methods are appropriate for reducing the size of the work force *except*
    a. lay-off.
    b. attrition.
    c. early retirement.
    d. confinement.
    e. firing.

28. A replacement chart shows
    a. key personnel scheduled to be replaced for poor performance reviews.
    b. key personnel, along with possible replacements within the firm.
    c. the skills and experience of key personnel.
    d. the key items of capital equipment due for replacement within the next year.
    e. time intervals for replacing current product items with new product items.

29. Flexible benefit plans can help a firm accomplish all *except*
    a. meet a great number of specific employee needs.
    b. help the firm seem more employee-friendly.
    c. attract and retain qualified employees.
    d. guarantee higher profits for the shareholders.
    e. help contain costs.

30. Some employee benefits are required by law. Which benefit is *not* required by law?
    a. Social security
    b. Health insurance
    c. Unemployment insurance
    d. Workers' compensation insurance for paying medical bills
    e. Workers' compensation insurance for providing income

31. A way to verify the reasons why a job candidate left a previous job is to obtain the information by
    a. asking for a résumé.
    b. administering an employment test.
    c. using a lie detector device.
    d. processing the application.
    e. conducting a reference check.

32. Rewards that are given to employees for doing outstanding work or for exceeding specific sales or production goals are called
    a. bonuses.
    b. benefits.
    c. tax shelters.
    d. profit sharing.
    e. remunerations.

33. All are examples of reasonable accommodation under ADA *except*
    a. restructuring a job.
    b. modifying work schedules.
    c. standardizing all procedures.
    d. providing interpreters.
    e. changing training programs.

34. The local bank uses an employee rating scale that consists of a number of statements, such as "This employee is always courteous." Each statement can be scored based on a range of 5 to 1, with 5 corresponding with the highest rating. This is an example of which type of appraisal method?
    a. Objective
    b. Judgmental
    c. Internal
    d. External
    e. Standardized

35. Since older people tend to have more medical problems with circulation in their legs, a national retail store recently implemented a new policy that no salesperson would be hired over the age of 40. This is illegal under the
    a. Civil Rights Act of 1964.
    b. Occupational Safety and Health Act.
    c. Age Discrimination in Employment Act.
    d. Equal Pay Act.
    e. Older Workers Equal Employment Opportunity Act.

36. Under affirmative action, all employers holding contracts with the federal government must
    a. actively encourage job applications from members of minority groups.
    b. hire qualified employees from the industry that it represents.
    c. refrain from discrimination on the basis of color.
    d. hire employees between ages 40 and 70.
    e. accommodate individuals with physical disabilities.

Short-Answer Questions (C)

Complete each question.

37. Identify six major types of **employee benefits**.

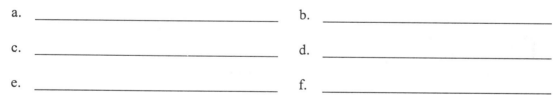

    a. _____   b. _____

    c. _____   d. _____

    e. _____   f. _____

38. What is the difference between **employee training** and **management development**?

39. What is the purpose of each **training and development method**?

METHOD	PURPOSE
On-the-job method	
Simulations	
Classroom	
Conferences Seminars	
Role playing	

40. **Performance appraisal** has three main objectives. What are the objectives?

a. _____

b. _____

c. _____

41. How do the **approaches to performance feedback** differ?

FEEDBACK APPROACHES	DIFFERENCES
Tell-and-sell	
Tell-and-listen	
Problem-solving	
360-degree evaluation	

42. What are the consequences for failing to discuss **negative aspects of a performance appraisal** with employees?

43. How does each **law** affect human resources management?

LAWS	AFFECT ON HRM
National Labor Relations Act	
Labor-Management Relations Act	
Fair Labor Standards Act	
Equal Pay Act	
Civil Rights Act	
Age Discrimination in Employment Act	
Occupational Safety and Health Act	
Employee Retirement Income Security Act	
Affirmative Action	
Americans with Disabilities Act	

44. Give several examples of how a firm can provide disabled employees with **reasonable accommodation**.

a. _____

b. _____

c. _____

d. _____

e. _____

CHAPTER 11

MOTIVATING AND SATISFYING EMPLOYEES

Key Terms

Define each term briefly. Writing down the definition and giving an example will help you learn the term.

motivation (p. 303)

morale (p. 303)

scientific management (p. 304)

piece-rate system (p. 305)

need (p. 306)

Maslow's hierarchy of needs (p. 306)

physiological needs (p. 306)

safety needs (p. 306)

social needs (p. 306)

esteem needs (p. 306)

self-actualization needs (p. 306)

motivation-hygiene theory (p. 307)

motivation factors (p. 307)

hygiene factors (p. 307)

Theory X (p. 308)

Theory Y (p. 308)

Theory Z (p. 309)

reinforcement theory (p. 309)

equity theory (p. 311)

expectancy theory (p. 312)

goal-setting theory (p. 313)

management by objectives (MBO) (p. 314)

job enrichment (p. 315)

job enlargement (p. 315)

job redesign (p. 315)

behavior modification (p. 316)

flextime (p. 317)

part-time work (p. 318)

job sharing (p. 318)

telecommuting (p. 318)

empowerment (p. 318)

self-managed work teams (p. 319)

employee ownership (p. 320)

PRACTICE EXAMINATION A

Matching Questions (A)

Match each term with a statement.

a. motivation
b. morale
c. scientific management
d. piece-rate system
e. Theory X
f. Theory Y

g. Theory Z
h. need
i. hierarchy of needs
j. goal-setting theory
k. expectancy theory
l. equity theory

_____ 1. Concept developed by Frederick W. Taylor.
_____ 2. Based on an assumption that work is important.
_____ 3. A force that causes people to behave in a particular way.
_____ 4. Developed by Abraham Maslow.
_____ 5. Involves an attitude toward a particular thing.
_____ 6. Wages paid on a per-unit rate.
_____ 7. A personal motivating drive.
_____ 8. Based on an assumption that people dislike work.
_____ 9. Employees believe they will receive the rewards.
_____ 10. Employees are motivated to achieve goals.
_____ 11. Rewards are in direct proportion to contributions.
_____ 12. It fosters participative decision making.

True-False Questions (A)

Select the correct answer.

T   F   13. Motivation is an internal drive that causes people to act.
T   F   14. Taylor created the piece-rate system.
T   F   15. Giving an employee recognition builds employee morale.

T F 16. The Hawthorne Studies concluded that human factors were responsible for the results.

T F 17. A Theory X environment is one in which managers delegate authority.

T F 18. Taylor's assumption that most people work only to earn money is compatible with the assumptions of Theory X.

T F 19. Providing a pension plan is a way to satisfy safety needs.

T F 20. Maslow's higher-level needs are the easiest to satisfy.

T F 21. The equity theory of motivation is based on the premise that everyone need not receive the same rewards, but the rewards should be in accordance with individual contributions.

T F 22. The goal-setting theory suggests that rewards should be directly tied to goal achievement.

T F 23. The expectancy theory depends on how much we want something and on how likely we think we are to get it.

T F 24. ESOPs are a highly effective way to motivate employees.

T F 25. MBO is an inflexible system that requires all goals to be met; if not, the employee is fired.

Multiple-Choice (A)

Circle the letter before the most accurate answer.

26. The process of activating an internal force within employees is
    a. morale.
    b. motivation.
    c. reinforcement.
    d. expectancy.
    e. equity.

27. It is an assumption of Theory X.
    a. People seek out responsibility.
    b. People are committed to goals.
    c. Work is important to people.
    d. People have little ambition.
    e. People enjoy coming to work.

28. To determine how the work environment affects productivity was the original objective of
    a. Taylor's scientific management.
    b. the Hawthorne Studies.
    c. McGregor's Theory X and Theory Y.
    d. Maslow's hierarchy of needs.
    e. Herzberg's theory.

29. Herzberg cited _____ as a cause of dissatisfaction.
    a. working conditions
    b. promotions
    c. pay for special projects
    d. rewards
    e. challenging work

30. According to Theory Y, which type of behavior would a supervisor expect from an employee?
    a. Delegate most of the work to others.
    b. Avoid working too hard.
    c. Spend time discussing job security.
    d. Ask to leave early several times a month.
    e. Seek opportunities to learn new skills.

31. Randi Wood wants to become the best manager in the firm. She takes every available opportunity to learn new skills and improve her knowledge about management. Which need is Randi attempting to satisfy?
    a. Social
    b. Esteem
    c. Self-actualization
    d. Physiological
    e. Safety

32. Which of the following is one of Herzberg's hygiene factors?
    a. Achievement
    b. Recognition
    c. Advancement and growth
    d. Supervision
    e. Responsibility

33. Under the equity theory, when a worker feels under-rewarded, he or she may take all but which of the following actions?
    a. Forget about it.
    b. Ask for a raise.
    c. Leave the work situation.
    d. Reduce input by working less.
    e. Do a new comparison to verify the other one.

34. If Delta Airlines ticket agents discovered they were being paid a lot less per ticket sold than a Northwest Airline ticket agent, we might expect the Delta ticket agents to
    a. increase their sales so that they will make as much as their Northwest Airlines peers.
    b. think their outcome-to-input ratios are lower than those of the Northwest ticket agents.
    c. as a group have very different personal needs than Northwest ticket agents.
    d. be very satisfied because they work for a great airline.
    e. feel that rewards are being distributed fairly and equitably.

35. The first step in the MBO process is that
    a. the manager assigns certain goals to subordinates.
    b. the manager and subordinates meet to review progress.
    c. top management endorses the program.
    d. preliminary goals must be established.
    e. each employee is surveyed to determine his or her needs.

36. The expectancy theory is based on all of the following assumptions *except*
    a. employees work for a variety of reasons.
    b. the reasons for working may change over time.
    c. employees are motivated by control.
    d. employees should be shown how to attain the outcomes they desire.
    e. employees must believe they have a chance of reaching their outcomes.

Short-Answer Questions (A)

Complete each question.

37. How can **morale** be improved through recognition and financial security?

    a. Recognition

    b. Financial security

38. What significant contributions did **Taylor** make to the **scientific management movement**?

    a. _____

    b. _____

    c. _____

    d. _____

39. Why did Taylor create the **piece-rate system**?

40. How did the results of the **Hawthorne Studies** influence researchers' thinking about employee motivation?

41. According to **Maslow's Hierarchy of Needs Theory**, how can employees be motivated on the job? Give examples of work-related activities that can motivate employees to meet each need.

NEEDS	WORK-RELATED ACTIVITIES
Physiological	
Safety	
Social	
Esteem	
Self-actualization	

42. What kinds of factors affect each dimension of **Herzberg's Motivation-Hygiene Theory**?

DIMENSION	FACTORS
Hygiene	
Motivation	

43. Compare the **assumptions** of **Theory X** and **Theory Y**.

THEORY X ASSUMPTIONS	THEORY Y ASSUMPTIONS

44. List **characteristics** of each type of firm.

TYPE J (JAPAN)	TYPE A (AMERICAN)	TYPE Z

45. What is the fundamental premise of **reinforcement theory**?

46. How can the following forms of **reinforcement** be used effectively?

FORMS OF REINFORCEMENT	EFFECTIVE USE OF REINFORCEMENT
Positive reinforcement	
Negative reinforcement	
Punishment	
Extinction	

PRACTICE EXAMINATION B

Matching Questions (B)

Match the term with the statement.

a. physiological needs
b. safety needs
c. social needs
d. esteem needs

e. self-actualization needs
f. motivation-hygiene theory
g. motivation factors
h. hygiene factors

_____ 1. Needs that are satisfied by food and shelter.
_____ 2. When not provided, they become dissatisfiers.
_____ 3. It is considered the highest level of human needs.
_____ 4. Needs that can be met partially by the informal organization.
_____ 5. Achievement, recognition, and advancement are examples of Herzberg's motivation factors.
_____ 6. Needs that can be met by health care benefits.
_____ 7. Satisfaction and dissatisfaction are separate and distinct dimensions.
_____ 8. Promotions and rewards can fulfill these needs.

True-False Questions (B)

Select the correct answer.

T F   9. Absenteeism is a result of high morale.
T F 10. The Hawthorne Studies were conducted at Bethlehem Steel.

T F 11. Social acceptance of the group played a big role in the Hawthorne Studies' results.

T F 12. Theory Y is a set of assumptions that are consistent with the human relations movement.

T F 13. Esteem needs are best met through personal accomplishment.

T F 14. Frederick W. Taylor made his most significant contribution to management practice by his involvement with the Hawthorne Studies.

T F 15. Job enrichment is a way to provide motivational factors such as achievement, recognition, and responsibility.

T F 16. According to the expectancy theory, motivation depends on how much we want something and on how likely we think we are to get it.

T F 17. Douglas McGregor first presented the concepts of Theory Z in his 1960 book, *The Human Side of Enterprise.*

T F 18. Under the piece-rate system, Frederick W. Taylor allowed each employee to decide the number of units to produce.

T F 19. Typically under flextime, employees can work whatever number of hours they desire each day.

T F 20. Job enlargement gives employees more responsibility and control over their jobs.

T F 21. When two people share one full-time position, management is using a strategy called job sharing.

Multiple-Choice Questions (B)

Circle the letter before the most accurate answer.

22. Frederick W. Taylor suggested that management should
    a. choose the best person for each job.
    b. train employees to do their jobs properly.
    c. cooperate with workers to ensure that jobs are done.
    d. use incentive pay for extra work.
    e. do all of the above.

23. Job security is an example of a(n) _____ need.
    a. safety
    b. physiological
    c. self-actualization
    d. social
    e. esteem

24. Developing an outcome-to-input ratio is the basis of the _____ theory.
    a. equity
    b. expectancy
    c. reward
    d. reinforcement
    e. quality circles

25. Motivation is the internal process that _____ , directs, and sustains behavior.
    a. irritates
    b. manages
    c. energizes
    d. inspects
    e. satisfies

26. A supervisor who constantly reminds employees of the consequences for failing to do a good job is making assumptions underlying
    a. the equity theory.
    b. Theory X.
    c. Theory Y.
    d. Theory Z.
    e. Theory J.

27. Studies show that when effectively implemented, empowerment often leads to
    a. decreased organizational commitment.
    b. higher turnover.
    c. decreased job satisfaction.
    d. improved job performance.
    e. lower quality output.

28. The need for self-actualization concerns an employee's desire for
    a. safety.
    b. a sense of belonging.
    c. becoming the best there is.
    d. self-worth.
    e. survival.

29. To make the most effective use of teams, it is essential that organizations implement all strategies *except*
    a. be committed to the team approach as an organization.
    b. establish clear team objectives.
    c. provide ongoing training and education.
    d. use compensation to reward team-based goals.
    e. reward individual accomplishments.

30. The theory stating that rewarded behavior is likely to be repeated and punished behavior is less likely to recur is called
    a. reinforcement theory.
    b. equity theory.
    c. expectancy theory.
    d. Theory X.
    e. Theory Y.

31. For a reward system to be effective, it must accomplish all of the following *except*
    a. allowing people to satisfy their basic needs.
    b. including a promotion with each reward.
    c. rewarding comparably with other organizations.
    d. distributing rewards fairly and accurately within the organization.
    e. allowing people to follow different paths to fulfill their needs.

32. Firms often use job sharing to fill positions instead of hiring full-time employees. Which reason is *not* a good reason for a firm to use job sharing?
    a. To attract highly skilled employees
    b. To save on expenses
    c. To reduce the cost of benefits
    d. To avoid the disruptions of employee turnover
    e. To reduce conflicts among employees

Short-Answer Questions (B)

Complete each question.

33. According to **equity theory**, how does an employee determine whether he or she is being treated equitably?

34. When an employee feels he or she is not being treated **equitably**, what might the employee do? List the changes.

    a. _____

    b. _____

    c. _____

    d. _____

    e. _____

35. According to **expectancy theory**, what two variables determine motivation?

    a. _____

    b. _____

36. What is the major benefit of the **goal-setting theory**?

37. Identify advantages and disadvantages of **MBO**.

ADVANTAGES OF MBO	DISADVANTAGES OF MBO

38. Explain what happens in each step of the **management by objective** process.

STEPS	EXPLANATION
1. Set up the MBO Program	
2. Establish goals	
3. Meet with employees	
4. Review progress	
5. Evaluate the process	

PRACTICE EXAMINATION C

Matching Questions (C-1)

Match each term with a statement.

a. equity theory
b. expectancy theory
c. reinforcement theory
d. reward system

e. piece-rate system
f. incentive system
g. management by objectives
h. behavior modification

_____ 1. A process of setting goals.
_____ 2. Behavior that is rewarded is likely to be repeated.
_____ 3. Employees are encouraged to produce more than a set amount.
_____ 4. Reinforcement is used to change behavior.
_____ 5. Our level of motivation depends on how much we want something.
_____ 6. Pay is tied directly to output.
_____ 7. It is aimed at motivating employees to work effectively.
_____ 8. Employees compare their rewards to the rewards received by other employees.

Matching Questions (C-2)

Match each term with a statement.

a. job enrichment
b. job enlargement
c. job redesign
d. flextime
e. part-time work

f. job sharing
g. telecommuting
h. empowerment
i. self-managed work teams
j. employee ownership

_____ 9. Groups of employees who manage themselves.
_____ 10. Computers, modems, and fax machines have advanced this practice.
_____ 11. Employees work less than a standard workweek.
_____ 12. Forming work teams may be the answer.
_____ 13. Employees have more control over their jobs.
_____ 14. It is the basis of ESOP.
_____ 15. Employees are allowed greater involvement in their jobs.
_____ 16. Two part-time employees do the work required in one full-time position.
_____ 17. A specific number of hours must be worked each day, regardless of starting time.
_____ 18. More tasks are assigned, but the routine stays the same.

True-False Questions (C)

Select the correct answer.

T   F   19. Taylor advocated that management determine the best way to perform tasks.
T   F   20. In the lighting experiments in the Hawthorne Studies, the control group outperformed the other group every time.
T   F   21. Douglas McGregor started the human relations movement in management.
T   F   22. Self-actualization needs are the most basic needs that Maslow discovered.
T   F   23. Of all Maslow's needs, the physiological needs are the most difficult to satisfy.
T   F   24. Herzberg's theory suggests that pay is a strong motivator.
T   F   25. Telecommuters report an increase in their productivity.
T   F   26. Negative reinforcement strengthens desired behavior by eliminating an undesirable task or situation.
T   F   27. Empowered employees have a voice in what they do and how and when they do it.
T   F   28. Herzberg thought that a state of complete satisfaction was common among employees.
T   F   29. MBO involves subordinates in goal setting and performance evaluations.
T   F   30. A systematic program of reinforcement that encourages desirable behavior is called behavior modification.
T   F   31. Behavior modification begins by identifying target behaviors that are to be changed.

Multiple-Choice Questions (C)

Circle the letter before the most accurate answer.

32. The Hawthorne Studies were conducted at
    a. Western Electric Company.
    b. Bethlehem Steel.
    c. Midvale Steel Company.
    d. United States Steel.
    e. IBM.

33. Which need is satisfied by a promotion to a more responsible job?
    a. Social
    b. Physiological
    c. Self-realization
    d. Esteem
    e. Safety

34. When Bethlehem Steel tied pay directly to output and paid employees a stated amount for each unit of output produced, it was using
    a. the soldiering system.
    b. an illegal system.
    c. a piece-rate system.
    d. the Mayo system.
    e. a flexible system.

35. When supervisors assume that employees accept responsibility and work toward company goals, they are relying on
    a. Maslow's Hierarachy of Needs.
    b. scientific management theory.
    c. Herzberg's theory of reinforcement.
    d. Theory X.
    e. Theory Y.

36. Which level of need does sleep satisfy?
    a. Esteem
    b. Physiological
    c. Self-realization
    d. Social
    e. Safety

37. The idea that satisfaction and dissatisfaction are distinct dimensions is part of
    a. Maslow's Hierarchy of Needs theory.
    b. Theory X and Theory Y.
    c. scientific management.
    d. the reinforcement theory.
    e. the motivation-hygiene theory.

38. A problem that self-managed work teams face is
    a. lower morale.
    b. more job specialization.
    c. insufficient training in the team approach.
    d. decreased productivity.
    e. less innovation.

39. Giving public recognition to an employee, who has done an excellent job on a project, is an example of
    a. scientific management.
    b. piece-rate scaling.
    c. an ineffective reward system.
    d. positive reinforcement.
    e. Theory X.

40. Five basic steps are required in setting up an MBO program. Which step is out of order?
    a. Review employee's progress and modify goals, if necessary.
    b. Secure an endorsement from top management.
    c. Preliminary goals are established by management.
    d. Goals are established between the manager and subordinate.
    e. The MBO process is evaluated; rewards are issued.

41. What does employee ownership provide employees?
    a. Direct financial rewards for success
    b. Motivation to make the company succeed
    c. An incentive to get involved in decisions
    d. A reason for commitment
    e. All of the above are provided.

42. Which of the following is a behavior-modification technique?
    a. Identifying target behavior
    b. Measuring existing level of behavior
    c. Providing positive reinforcement when the desired behavior is exhibited
    d. Remeasuring levels to determine any improvement
    e. All of the above

Short-Answer Questions (C)

Complete each question.

43. Compare two types of **job enrichment**.

JOB ENLARGEMENT	JOB DESIGN

44. Identify several reasons **job enrichment** programs fail.

    a. _____   b. _____

    c. _____   d. _____

45. Identify the four steps in the process of applying the technique of **behavior modification**.

    a. _____

    b. _____

c. _____

d. _____

46. How does **flextime** work?

47. How is **job sharing** different from **part-time work**?

48. What are the benefits and disadvantages of **telecommuting**?

BENEFITS	DISADVANTAGES

49. What are the benefits and obstacles of **empowerment**?

BENEFITS OF EMPOWERMENT	OBSTACLES TO EMPOWERMENT

50. What are the major benefits and most common problems associated with the use of **self-managed work teams**?

BENEFITS	PROBLEMS

51. What is the objective of **gain sharing**?

52. How do **ESOPs** motivate employees?

CHAPTER 12

ENHANCING UNION-MANAGEMENT RELATIONS

Key Terms

Define each term briefly. Writing down the definition and giving an example will help you learn the term.

labor union (p. 327)

union-management (labor) relations (p. 327)

craft union (p. 327)

strike (p. 328)

industrial union (p. 329)

National Labor Relations Board (NLRB) (p. 333)

injunction (p. 334)

bargaining unit (p. 336)

jurisdiction (p. 336)

collective bargaining (p. 337)

ratification (p. 338)

seniority (p. 340)

overtime (p. 340)

job security (p. 340)

union security (p. 341)

closed shop (p. 341)

union shop (p. 341)

agency shop (p. 341)

maintenance shop (p. 341)

grievance procedure (p. 342)

shop steward (p. 342)

arbitration (p. 343)

picketing (p. 343)

wildcat strike (p. 344)

slowdown (p. 344)

boycott (p. 344)

lockout (p. 344)

strikebreaker (p. 345)

mediation (p. 345)

PRACTICE EXAMINATION A

Matching Questions (A-1)

Match each term with a statement.

a. labor union
b. labor contract
c. labor relations
d. craft union

e. Knights of Labor
f. American Federation of Labor
g. strike
h. Industrial Workers of the World

_____ 1. It is an organization of skilled workers.
_____ 2. Its purpose is to negotiate wages and working conditions for employees.
_____ 3. The group formed in 1905 to overthrow capitalism.
_____ 4. The process involves dealings between labor unions and business management.
_____ 5. It strongly believed that striking was an effective weapon.
_____ 6. It was the first national labor union to organize workers.
_____ 7. This document covers points of agreement between labor and management.
_____ 8. A technique that temporarily stops work.

Matching Questions (A-2)

Match each term with a statement.

a. industrial union
b. National Labor Relations Board
c. injunction
d. union shop

e. bargaining unit
f. jurisdiction
g. seniority
h. overtime

_____ 9. One of its functions is to supervise union elections.
_____ 10. The work requires more than 40 hours per week to complete.
_____ 11. A union is given the right to organize a particular group of workers.
_____ 12. It is a court order.
_____ 13. It has to do with the length of time an employee has worked for a firm.
_____ 14. After a probationary period, new employees must join a union.
_____ 15. All workers in a single industry are eligible to join the union.
_____ 16. The group of employees the union represents.

True-False Questions (A)

Select the correct answer.

T F 17. A labor union is a group of organized workers.
T F 18. The first known strike in the United States involved railroad workers who demanded higher wages.

T   F   19.   The AFL believed that organized labor had no business in politics.
T   F   20.   The AFL-CIO merger occurred in 1925.
T   F   21.   The Teamsters are the largest group within the AFL-CIO.
T   F   22.   Currently the UAW has about 748,000 members.
T   F   23.   The Taft-Hartley Act lists unfair labor practices that unions are forbidden to use.
T   F   24.   The Landrum-Griffin Act provides safeguards for union funds.
T   F   25.   Under the law, employees can freely sign authorization cards while on the job.
T   F   26.   The primary form of pay in most labor contracts is direct compensation.
T   F   27.   The first step in the grievance process involves securing a mediator.
T   F   28.   The collective bargaining process begins by getting ratification from the union's membership.
T   F   29.   The first president of the AFL-CIO was George Meany.
T   F   30.   To ensure fairness, the EEOC supervises the process of forming a union.

Multiple-Choice Questions (A)

Circle the letter before the most accurate answer.

31. A written agreement that sets forth issues between labor and management is called
    a. a labor union.
    b. an injunction.
    c. collective bargaining.
    d. a jurisdiction.
    e. a labor contract.

32. The first leader of the American Federation of Labor, formed in 1886, was
    a. Uriah Stephens.
    b. George Meany.
    c. Patrick Henry.
    d. Samuel Gompers.
    e. Douglas Fraser.

33. The downward trend in union membership is caused in part by
    a. firms moving to the Sunbelt.
    b. management providing more benefits.
    c. cutbacks in major production industries.
    d. growth occurring in high-tech industries.
    e. All of the above.

34. Unfair labor practices that unions are forbidden to use include
    a. charging excessive membership dues.
    b. using a minimum-wage scale.
    c. firing a drunk worker.
    d. bargaining with management.
    e. approving strikes.

35. Authorization cards are used to
    a. make the final decision concerning the formation of a union.
    b. determine employee interest in forming a union.
    c. give management authority to promote employees.
    d. give management authority to conduct the union election.
    e. notify employees that a union has been approved.

36. Issues concerning pay include the
    a. forms of pay.
    b. determination of pay.
    c. cost-of-living clause.
    d. magnitude of pay.
    e. All of these.

37. The union representative who works directly with the workers is the
    a. mediator.
    b. bargainer.
    c. shop steward.
    d. arbitrator.
    e. negotiator.

38. Which point does The National Labor Relations Act (Wagner Act) *not* cover?
    a. Requires management to negotiate with union representatives
    b. Gives the U.S. president the power to obtain an injunction to prevent a strike
    c. Establishes procedures for employees to follow in deciding if they want a union
    d. Forbids management to fire or punish workers because they are pro-union
    e. Established the NLRB

39. The NLRB is primarily concerned with
    a. establishing procedures for obtaining an injunction.
    b. setting a minimum wage policy.
    c. monitoring the process for preparing a union's annual report.
    d. overseeing the process for creating a union.
    e. providing safeguards governing union funds.

40. Which labor law authorized states to enact "right-to-work" laws that allow employees to work in a unionized firm without joining the union?
    a. Taft-Hartley Act
    b. Wagner Act
    c. Fair Labor Standards Act
    d. Norris-LaGuardia Act
    e. Landrum-Griffin Act

41. What is the main objective of a strike?
    a. To show support to the community
    b. To gain sympathy for management
    c. To put financial pressure on the firm
    d. To promote the firm's products
    e. To allow employees time off from work

42. The *most* potent tool that management can use against labor during contract negotiations is
    a. a strike.
    b. a slowdown.
    c. a lockout.
    d. a boycott.
    e. picketing.

Short-Answer Questions (A)

Complete each question.

43. How does a **labor union** differ from **labor relations**?

44. In the early history of **labor unions**, what did each group contribute to the movement?

GROUP	CONTRIBUTION
Knights of Labor	
American Federation of Labor	
Industrial Workers of the World	
CIO	
AFL-CIO	

45. How does a **craft union** differ from an **industrial union**?

CRAFT UNION	INDUSTRIAL UNION

46. Identify the two sources from which **unions derive power** to negotiate.

a. _____

b. _____

47. What **percent** of the American work force **belongs to unions today**? _____%

48. **Union memberships** have dropped since 1980. Discuss reasons for this decline:

49. Why are unions becoming **partners with management**? Give several reasons:

a. _____ b _____

c. _____ d. _____

e. _____

50. How do **limited partnerships** differ from **long-range strategic partnerships**?

51. **Union-management partnerships** have several **benefits** for management, workers, and unions. What are the benefits?

a. _____ b _____

c. _____ d. _____

PRACTICE EXAMINATION B

Matching Questions (B)

Match each term with a statement.

a. job security
b. union security
c. closed shop
d. agency shop
e. maintenance shop

f. grievance procedure
g. shop steward
h. arbitration
i. collective bargaining
j. ratification

_____ 1. It gives the union protection as a bargaining unit.
_____ 2. An employee must remain a union member while employed within a firm.
_____ 3. It is the final step in the grievance procedure.
_____ 4. Employees are protected against the loss of employment.
_____ 5. The process helps employees resolve work-related complaints.
_____ 6. A process to negotiate labor contracts.
_____ 7. The Taft-Hartley Act declared it illegal.
_____ 8. It is the union's representative.
_____ 9. It is the final phase in collective bargaining.
_____ 10. Employees pay union dues but are not union members.

True-False Questions (B)

Select the correct answer.

T   F   11.   A labor contract is the result of the bargaining process.

T   F   12.   One major goal of the Knights of Labor was to eliminate the depersonalization of the worker that resulted from mass-production technology.

T   F   13.   The Industrial Workers of the World wanted to eliminate the existing economic system.

T   F   14.   Today, union members account for a large proportion of the total American work force.

T   F   15.   Currently, union organizers are concentrating their efforts in production industries.

T   F   16.   The Wagner Act made it difficult for businesses to ban strikes, picketing, or union membership drives.

T   F   17.   The Taft-Hartley Act gives the president the power to obtain a temporary injunction to stop a strike.

T   F   18.   The Wagner Act requires management to negotiate with union representatives.

T   F   19.   At least 50 percent of a company's workers must sign authorization cards before an official election can be held by the NLRB.

T   F   20.   The union has the responsibility to ensure that pay is equitable with that received by other employees in the same or similar industries.

T   F   21.   Arbitrators sit in the capacity of a judge who has final authority.

T   F   22.   Hiring strikebreakers is an effective way to calm down upset union members.

T   F   23.   Ratification is the first step in the collective bargaining process.

T   F   24.   Job security and union security are interchangeable terms.

Multiple-Choice Questions (B)

Circle the letter before the most accurate answer.

25. Electricians belong to
   a.   industrial unions.
   b.   craft unions.
   c.   the AFL-CIO.
   d.   independent unions.
   e.   the Knights of Labor.

26. The UAW is an example of
   a.   an industrial union.
   b.   an independent union.
   c.   the Teamsters.
   d.   a craft union.
   e.   the AFL-CIO.

27. The labor act that is considered a landmark in labor-management relations is the _____ Act.
   a.   Wagner
   b.   Landrum-Griffin
   c.   Norris-LaGuardia
   d.   Taft-Hartley
   e.   National Labor Relations

28. The act that requires unions to file annual reports with the U.S. Department of Labor regarding their finances and election proceedings is the _____ Act.
    a. Norris-LaGuardia
    b. Wagner
    c. National Labor Relations
    d. Landrum-Griffin
    e. Taft-Hartley

29. The group of employees that unions represent is called a
    a. bargaining unit.
    b. work group.
    c. management unit.
    d. steward group.
    e. union group.

30. Job security under union contracts is based on
    a. working hours.
    b. seniority.
    c. the shop steward.
    d. the job itself.
    e. the pay.

31. For a contract to be binding on labor and management, it must be
    a. approved by all shop stewards.
    b. notarized by NLRB.
    c. approved by the mediator.
    d. ratified by the union members.
    e. voted on by management.

32. Which factor is *not* a valid reason for declining union memberships?
    a. Management is providing better wages.
    b. Working conditions are improving in the workplace.
    c. Growth in employment is occurring in production industries.
    d. Reductions have occurred in the steel and auto industries.
    e. Relocated plants tend to hire nonunion workers.

33. Which of the following is a valid reason for joining a union?
    a. Employees feel alienated within the firm.
    b. A perception exists that unions provide job security.
    c. Employees are unhappy about company benefits.
    d. Employees join to keep their job.
    e. All of the above are valid reasons for joining a union.

34. The practice of requiring employees to join a union after a probation period might violate
    a. the right-to-work laws in that state.
    b. the minimum wage part of the Fair Labor Standards Act.
    c. an injunction.
    d. unfair labor practices under the Wagner Act.
    e. the provisions of the law establishing the NLRB.

35. Which statement is *not* true about the Fair Labor Standards Act?
    a. The minimum wage is $5.15 per hour.
    b. All employees are covered under the minimum wage provision.
    c. Child labor is prohibited.
    d. Overtime rates must be paid for work over 40 hours per week.
    e. This act was passed in 1938.

36. During a strike, new workers hired to replace striking employees are called
    a. strikers.
    b. representatives.
    c. managers.
    d. strikebreakers.
    e. consultants.

Short-Answer Questions (B)

Complete each question.

37. How does each piece of **legislation** affect labor and management?

LEGISLATION	PURPOSE
Norris-LaGuardia Act	
National Labor Relations Act	
Fair Labor Standards Act	
Labor-Management Relations Act	
Landrum-Griffin Act	

38. Why do employees **join unions**? List several reasons.

    a. _____   b. _____

    c. _____   d. _____

    e. _____

39. Describe what happens in each step in **forming a union**.

STEPS	DESCRIPTION
Organizing campaign	
Authorization cards	
Formal election	
NLRB certification	

40. Explain the **role of the NLRB** in the unionization process.

41. Describe what happens in each step of the **collective bargaining process.**

STEP	DESCRIPTION
Prepare for negotiations	
Negotiations and bargaining	
Ratification	

PRACTICE EXAMINATION C

Matching Questions (C)

Match the each with a statement.

a. picketing
b. strike fund
c. wildcat strike
d. slowdown

e. boycott
f. lockout
g. strikebreaker
h. mediation

_____ 1. Workers carry signs outside their place of employment.
_____ 2. Work is completed at a slower than normal pace.
_____ 3. A nonunion person is hired to replace a striking employee.
_____ 4. The money is used to support striking union members.
_____ 5. People refuse to buy goods from a particular firm.
_____ 6. A neutral third party offers suggestions for settling a dispute.
_____ 7. Action that has not been approved.
_____ 8. A firm refuses to allow its employees into the building to work.

True-False Questions (C)

Select the correct answer.

T   F   9. A craft union is one composed of both skilled and unskilled workers.

T F   10. The goal of the AFL was to improve its members' living standards within the business system.

T F   11. The Congress of Industrial Organizations (CIO) was created to organize skilled workers.

T F   12. Approximately 40 percent of the nation's workers belong to unions.

T F   13. Currently, unions are increasing the pace of their organizing activities in the eastern part of the United States.

T F   14. The NLRB is charged with investigating complaints lodged by unions or employers.

T F   15. The Norris-LaGuardia Act was designed to regulate the internal functioning of labor unions.

T F   16. In the union shop, new employees are required to join the union.

T F   17. Where jurisdictions overlap, the employees themselves may decide who will represent them.

T F   18. Federal law specifies that overtime pay must be at least one and one-half times the normal hourly wage.

T F   19. The process of collective bargaining is carried out by the negotiating committee.

T F   20. Job security is based on seniority.

T F   21. The first step in forming a union is to organize a campaign.

T F   22. The role of the mediator is to make binding decisions in labor-management disputes.

Multiple-Choice Questions (C)

Circle the letter before the most accurate answer.

23. The Haymarket riot of 1886 contributed to the downfall of the
    a. American Federation of Labor.   d. Knights of Columbus.
    b. Congress of Industrial Organizations.   e. Industrial Workers of the World.
    c. Knights of Labor.

24. Which is *not* true about arbitration?
    a. Both sides must accept the arbitrator's decision.
    b. The arbitrator hears both sides of the unresolved issue.
    c. The arbitrator makes the final decision.
    d. Arbitration is the final step in the grievance process.
    e. The final decision in arbitration can be overturned by mediation.

25. The act that requires management to negotiate with union representatives is the _____ Act.
    a. Taft-Hartley   d. Norris-LaGuardia
    b. National Labor Relations   e. Landrum-Griffin
    c. Labor-Management Relations

26. The process of promoting widespread interest among employees in having a union is called
    a. internal communications.   d. jurisdiction.
    b. injunction.   e. a boycott.
    c. an organizing campaign.

190

27. After authorization cards are submitted, the NLRB generally conducts an election within _____ days.
    a. ten
    b. fifteen
    c. thirty
    d. forty-five
    e. sixty

28. When workers must join a union before they are hired, which type of shop is in existence?
    a. Union shop
    b. Maintenance shop
    c. Required shop
    d. Open shop
    e. Closed shop

29. Caterpillar has a long history of conflicts between labor and management. What is the term used for dealing with this situation?
    a. Labor unions
    b. Rights administration
    c. Union-management relations
    d. Labor and management goals
    e. Work procedures

30. The benefits of union-management partnerships include
    a. increased revenue.
    b. improved product quality.
    c. greater customer satisfaction.
    d. less supervision.
    e. All of the above.

31. Magnitude of pay involves
    a. cost-of-living clauses.
    b. direct compensation.
    c. benefits.
    d. disability.
    e. a strike vote.

32. Which issue is paramount to union contracts?
    a. Working hours
    b. Security
    c. Grievance procedures
    d. Management rights
    e. Employee pay

33. Where does the grievance procedure process begin?
    a. An employee believes that he or she has been treated unfairly.
    b. The employee explains the situation to the shop steward.
    c. The employee, shop steward, and supervisor discuss the grievance.
    d. The grievance is discussed with higher level union and management people.
    e. The employee takes the grievance to arbitration.

34. After unsuccessful mediation, the air traffic controllers threaten a strike that would close down air transportation in the United States. The next step would be to
    a. set up a picket.
    b. secure an injunction.
    c. prepare for a lot of confusion.
    d. call for a wildcat strike.
    e. call in the NLRB.

Short-Answer Questions (C)

Complete each question.

35. What is the **role of an arbitrator** in the grievance procedure process?

36. Several issues associated with **employee pay** are generally addressed in union contracts. Discuss the essence of each issue.

EMPLOYEE PAY ISSUES	EXPLANATION OF EACH ISSUE
Forms of pay	
Magnitude of pay	
Pay determinants	

37. **Union contracts** address the following issues. What is the union's major concern with each issue?

CONTRACT ISSUES	CONCERNS
Employee pay	
Working hours	
Security	
Management rights	
Grievance procedures	

38. What is the job of a **shop steward**?

39. Describe what happens in each step of the **grievance procedure**.

STEPS	EXPLANATION
Original grievance	
Broader discussion	
Full-scale discussion	
Arbitration	

40. Describe each **negotiating tool**. Tell who uses it and why.

NEGOTIATION TOOL/TECHNIQUE	EXPLANATION
Strike	
Picketing	
Slowdown	
Boycott	
Lockout	
Strikebreaker	
Mediation	
Arbitration	

CHAPTER 13

BUILDING CUSTOMER RELATIONSHIPS THROUGH EFFECTIVE MARKETING

Key Terms

Define each term briefly. Writing down the definition and giving an example will help you learn the term.

marketing (p. 356)

utility (p. 356)

form utility (p. 356)

place utility (p. 357)

time utility (p. 357)

possession utility (p. 357)

marketing concept (p. 358)

relationship marketing (p. 358)

market (p. 359)

marketing strategy (p. 360)

marketing mix (p. 360)

target market (p. 360)

undifferentiated approach (p. 361)

market segment (p. 363)

market segmentation (p. 363)

marketing plan (p. 366)

sales forecast (p. 368)

marketing information system (p. 368)

marketing research (p. 368)

buying behavior (p. 370)

consumer buying behavior (p. 370)

business buying behavior (p. 370)

personal income (p. 373)

disposable income (p. 373)

discretionary income (p. 373)

PRACTICE EXAMINATION A

Matching Questions (A)

Match each term with a statement.

a. marketing
b. utility
c. form utility
d. place utility
e. time utility
f. possession utility

g. marketing concept
h. marketing information system
i. marketing research
j. market
k. market segment
l. market segmentation

_____ 1. The process of dividing a market into concentrated and differentiated markets.

_____ 2. The process of planning and executing the conception, pricing, promotion, and distribution of ideas, goods, and services.

_____ 3. A business philosophy that involves the satisfying of customer's needs while achieving a firm's goals.

_____ 4. A place where sellers and buyers meet.

_____ 5. Value added through converting raw materials into finished goods.

_____ 6. It manages market information gathered from external and internal sources.

_____ 7. The ability to satisfy a human need.

_____ 8. Individuals in a market who share common characteristics.

_____ 9. Having goods available when needed adds value.

_____ 10. Systematically gathering, recording, and analyzing data about products and markets.

_____ 11. It is created through the transfer of title to goods.

_____ 12. Availability of goods where customers want them adds value.

True-False Questions (A)

Select the correct answer.

T F 13. Marketing is a process that fulfills consumers' needs.

T F 14. The right to use a product is part of possession utility.

T F 15. Form utility is created directly by marketing activities.

T F 16. Determining what customers need is the essence of customer orientation.

T F 17. The first step in implementing marketing is to provide a product that satisfies customers.

T F 18. Sales figures are examples of external data in the marketing information system.

T F 19. Income, sex, and ethnic origin are ways to segment markets.

T F 20. The marketing mix is composed of product, price, distribution, and promotion.

T F 21. The total market approach assumes customers have different needs.

T F 22. Market plans are affected by competitive forces in the external environment.

T F 23. Markets are classified as consumer markets or business-to-business markets.

T F 24. Financing and risk taking are physical distribution functions of marketing.

Multiple-Choice Questions (A)

Circle the letter before the most accurate answer.

25. When fresh vegetables are shipped to Oklahoma from Mexico, which utility is added?
   a. Form
   b. Place
   c. Price
   d. Possession
   e. Time

26. Sales orientation predominated primarily during the
   a. late 1800s.
   b. 1920s.
   c. 1940s.
   d. late 1950s.
   e. 1970s.

27. The three major categories of marketing functions are
    a. place, time, and possession.
    b. form, buying, and exchange.
    c. risk taking, selling, and form.
    d. physical distribution, facilitating, and possession.
    e. exchange, physical distribution, and facilitating.

28. Which facilitating function of marketing is riddled with thefts, obsolescence, and lawsuits?
    a. Risk taking
    b. Standardizing
    c. Financing
    d. Information gathering
    e. Selling

29. Women in the market can be classified as
    a. market segmentation.
    b. a marketing mix.
    c. a market segment.
    d. an independent market.
    e. a producer market.

30. Older Americans have more discretionary income to spend than younger people. As a result, firms are focusing their attention on developing new products and services for this market. What type of market is this?
    a. Industrial
    b. Producer
    c. Governmental
    d. Consumer
    e. Institutional

31. Robin Wallace owns a frozen yogurt shop. She has decided to concentrate her marketing efforts on health-conscious customers. Robin is practicing the _____ approach.
    a. product differentiation
    b. total market
    c. market segmentation
    d. target market
    e. marketing-mix

32. What element in the market mix provides information to consumers?
    a. Product
    b. Price
    c. Promotion
    d. Distribution
    e. Quality

33. Which ingredient in the marketing mix focuses on transportation, storage, and intermediaries?
    a. Product
    b. Price
    c. Distribution
    d. Promotion
    e. Buying

34. Which environmental force influences change in consumers' attitudes, customs, and lifestyles?
    a. Legal, political, and regulatory
    b. Competitive
    c. Technological
    d. Economic
    e. Sociocultural

35. Consumers buy products because
    a. they have uses for the products.
    b. they like the convenience that products provide.
    c. they take pride in ownership of products.
    d. they believe that products will enhance their wealth.
    e. of all of the above.

36. The development of a marketing strategy begins with
    a. an assessment of the marketing environment.
    b. formulating detailed marketing objectives.
    c. selecting a target market.
    d. designing a marketing mix.
    e. evaluating the performance of its strategy.

37. What type of income is Ramona's $2,450 monthly *net* take-home amount?
    a. Ordinary
    b. Personal
    c. Disposable
    d. Gross
    e. Discretionary

Short-Answer Questions (A)

Complete each question.

38. **Utility** is the ability of a good or service to satisfy a human need. Give an example of how each type of utility helps satisfy human needs.

UTILITIES	WAYS UTILITIES SATISFY HUMAN NEEDS
Form utility	
Place utility	
Time utility	
Possession utility	

39. Identify three basic steps for **implementing** the marketing concept.

   a. _____

   b. _____

   c. _____

40. Discuss how **relationship marketing** is different from the **marketing concept**.

41. Explain how the **marketing concept** was implemented during each period in history.

   a. Industrial Revolution until the early Twentieth Century

   b. 1920s to the 1950s

   c. During the 1950s

42. What are the steps in implementing a **marketing concept**?

   a. _____

   b. _____

   c. _____

   d. _____

43. Give an example for each type of **industrial market**.

INDUSTRIAL MARKETS (BUSINESS-TO-BUSINESS MARKETS)	EXAMPLE
Producer market	
Reseller market	
Government market	
Institutional market	

PRACTICE EXAMINATION B

Matching Questions (B)

Match each term with a statement.

a. buying behavior
b. promotional ingredient
c. consumer buying behavior
d. sales forecast
e. marketing mix
f. marketing strategy

g. business buying behavior
h. personal income
i. disposable income
j. discretionary income
k. relationship marketing
l. marketing concept

_____ 1. The purchasing of products by producers and resellers.
_____ 2. An estimation of the amount of product a firm expects to sell.
_____ 3. Income less Social Security payments.
_____ 4. Income less savings, food, clothing, and housing.
_____ 5. A combination of product, price, distribution, and promotion.
_____ 6. Decisions and actions of people involved in buying and using products.
_____ 7. Focuses on providing information to target markets.
_____ 8. A plan of actions intended to accomplish a marketing goal.
_____ 9. Personal income less all personal taxes.
_____ 10. Decision process used when purchasing personal-use items.
_____ 11. A strategy for stimulating long-term customer loyalty.
_____ 12. A philosophy that involves the entire organization.

True-False Questions (B)

Select the correct answer.

T F 13. Marketing research data may indirectly influence form utility.
T F 14. The four common bases of market segmentation are demographic, strategic, geographic, and discretionary.
T F 15. The undifferentiated approach to marketing assumes that consumers have similar needs.
T F 16. Marketing is "the process of planning and executing the conception, pricing, promotion, and distribution of ideas, goods, and services to create exchanges that satisfy individual and organizational objectives," as defined by the AMA.
T F 17. An effective marketing information system provides information on a continuing basis.
T F 18. Internal sources of data include economic conditions.
T F 19. When the Ford Motor Company focuses its advertising for the Explorer on the population between the ages of 20 and 34, it is targeting a market.
T F 20. The distribution element of the marketing mix focuses on both pricing and discounts.

T F 21. Marketers must be cognizant of technological changes that may cause a product to become obsolete almost overnight.

T F 22. Decisions about product design, brand name, and packaging are part of the product ingredient of the marketing mix.

T F 23. A market consists of people with needs, money to spend, and the desire and authority to spend it.

T F 24. Understanding factors that affect buying behavior helps marketing managers predict consumer responses to marketing strategies and helps develop a market mix.

Multiple-Choice Questions (B)

Circle the letter before the most accurate answer.

25. Recording a warranty deed on a piece of real estate, adds _____ utility value to the property.
    a. possession
    b. form
    c. target
    d. time
    e. place

26. The last step in the marketing research process is
    a. defining the problem.
    b. interpreting the information.
    c. reaching a conclusion.
    d. gathering factual information.
    e. planning research strategies.

27. When Taco Bell decides on brand names, package designs, sizes of orders, and recipes, which ingredient in the marketing mix is it using?
    a. Product
    b. Pricing
    c. Place
    d. Distribution
    e. Promotion

28. Measuring the sales potential for specific types of market segments helps a firm make important decisions. All of the following are viable reasons for measuring the sales potential *except*
    a. evaluating the feasibility of entering new segments.
    b. deciding how best to allocate its marketing resources.
    c. designing the product.
    d. defining the geographic boundaries of the sales.
    e. estimating relevant time frames.

29. Computers at a local retail store are financed by manufacturers, cars are financed by banks, and discount stores receive financing from wholesalers, manufacturers, and banks. Which marketing function is performing these activities?
    a. Physical distribution function
    b. Standardization function
    c. Marketing information function
    d. Financing function
    e. Storage function

30. External factors that affect the marketing environment include _____ forces.
    a. economic
    b. societal
    c. legal and political
    d. technological
    e. All of the above

31. When customers' needs vary, which approach is more appropriate?
    a. Total approach
    b. Market systems
    c. Market segmentation
    d. Utilities approach
    e. The marketing mix

32. In selecting a target market, marketing managers should
    a. examine their present market for behaviors that are unique.
    b. ignore last year's sales and profits, if it was a bad year.
    c. determine whether the firm has the resources to produce a marketing mix.
    d. analyze the strengths and numbers of their best customers.
    e. disregard the competitors already marketing to your target market.

33. When factors such as climate, city size, rural, and urban are used as indicators, the type of market segmentation is called
    a. geographic.
    b. behavioristic.
    c. psychographic.
    d. demographic.
    e. educational.

34. The ingredients in the marketing mix are used to
    a. demonstrate the expertise of the marketing staff.
    b. meet product display requirements.
    c. encourage in-house support for marketing.
    d. fulfill trade show and other promotional commitments.
    e. reach the target market.

35. When market managers in Wal-Mart stores use surveys from buyers, executive judgments, time series analysis, and correlations analyses, they are using
    a. market analysis.
    b. sales forecasting methods.
    c. market outlook.
    d. a purchase plan.
    e. a budget analysis.

36. When marketers use data such as sales figures, product and marketing costs, inventory levels, and activities of its sales force to make marketing decisions, they are using which type of data?
    a. Internal
    b. Continual
    c. Economic
    d. External
    e. Government

37. The buying process is *least* influenced by
    a. perceptions.
    b. attitudes.
    c. productivity.
    d. peer groups.
    e. family.

Short-Answer Questions (B)

Complete each question.

38. Compare the **undifferentiated approach** with the **market segmentation approach**.

39. Explain each **ingredient** in the **marketing mix**.

MARKETING MIX INGREDIENTS	EXPLANATION
Product	
Pricing	
Distribution	
Promotion	

40. How does each **external force** in the marketing environment influence business operations?

EXTERNAL FORCES	INFLUENCE OF EACH FORCE
Economic forces	
Sociocultural forces	
Political forces	
Competitive forces	
Legal and regulatory forces	
Technological forces	

41. What is a **marketing plan**? Why is it important?

42. Briefly describe the information that comprises each component in a **marketing plan**.

COMPONENTS OF A MARKETING PLAN	DESCRIPTION OF EACH COMPONENT
Executive Summary	
Environmental Analysis	
Strengths and Weaknesses	
Opportunities and Threats	
Marketing Objectives	
Marketing Strategies	
Marketing Implementation	
Evaluation and Control	

PRACTICE EXAMINATION C

Matching Questions (C)

Match each term with a statement.

a. industrial market
b. producer market
c. reseller market
d. governmental market
e. institutional market

f. consumer market
g. target market
h. marketing plan
i. undifferentiated approach
j. market

_____   1. Hospitals, churches, and schools are examples of this market.
_____   2. Goods are purchased to use in making other products for resale.

_____ 3. Wholesalers and retailers are the primary intermediaries in this market.

_____ 4. Purchasers who intend to consume or benefit from the products make up this market.

_____ 5. A market where businesses buy goods to use in manufacturing other products.

_____ 6. Highways and education are examples of end products of this market.

_____ 7. Marketing activities focused on a particular group such as teenagers.

_____ 8. A group of individuals or organizations with the authority to purchase products.

_____ 9. It establishes the marketing objectives for a product.

_____ 10. It directs a single marketing mix to the entire market.

True-False Questions (C)

Select the correct answer.

T F 11. Form utility is created by converting inputs into outputs.

T F 12. Currently, most American businesses have a strong production orientation.

T F 13. Continual collection of data is essential to marketing information systems.

T F 14. The four kinds of utility are time, form, place, and price.

T F 15. Marketing information systems generate daily sales reports.

T F 16. Defining the problem is the first step in the market research process.

T F 17. Some firms develop different products for different target markets.

T F 18. Promotion is used to make potential customers aware of product information.

T F 19. Government regulations on packaging help decrease the cost of marketing.

T F 20. Americans save approximately 20 percent of their disposable income.

T F 21. The greatest portion of disposable income is spent on transportation and clothing.

T F 22. Consumers are spending more money on luxury items like fur and jewelry.

T F 23. An effective marketing plan includes marketing strategies for selecting the target market and for developing the marketing mix.

Multiple-Choice Questions (C)

Circle the letter before the most accurate answer.

24. Consumers buy some specific products because they
    a. have a use for the product.
    b. like the convenience a product offers.
    c. believe the product will enhance their wealth.
    d. take pride in ownership.
    e. feel any of the above may be a reason to buy.

25. The marketing concept involves a process that includes
    a. talking with potential customers about their needs.
    b. developing goods to satisfy customer needs.
    c. providing services customers want.
    d. continually seeking ways to provide customer satisfaction.
    e. All of the above.

26. What is the *most* important factor that influences a consumer's decision about where to buy a particular product?
    a. Free delivery
    b. Return privileges
    c. Perception of the store
    d. Credit terms
    e. Product assortment

27. A product is available in the store at the time a customer wants it. Which type of value does this add to the product?
    a. Form
    b. Production
    c. Place
    d. Time
    e. Possession

28. Which of the following is *not* one of the steps in implementing the marketing concept?
    a. Obtaining information about existing and potential customers
    b. Pinpointing needs and potential customers for further marketing activities
    c. Mobilizing marketing resources to provide, promote, and distribute products
    d. Obtaining new information about the effectiveness of efforts
    e. All are steps in the marketing concept.

29. What do consumers spend the largest share of their disposable income on?
    a. Housing
    b. Transportation
    c. Entertainment
    d. Food
    e. Clothing

30. When AMC built a 24-screen movie entertainment complex in Dallas, it assumed that everyone in the Metroplex area liked to go to the movies. Which market approach did they use?
    a. Marketing-mix
    b. Total market
    c. Product differentiation
    d. Target market
    e. Market segmentation

31. Discretionary income is used to buy
    a. food.
    b. clothing.
    c. automobiles.
    d. housing.
    e. government bonds.

32. Marketing research is the process of systematically gathering, recording, and analyzing data
    a. for keeping track of daily sales.
    b. for comparing each day's receipts against the previous day's sales.
    c. for monitoring the quality of the product.
    d. concerning a particular marketing problem.
    e. for ordering supplies and maintaining an adequate inventory.

33. Organizational buyers consider a product's quality, its price, and the service provided by suppliers. Which of the following should be considered in buying for an organization's needs?
    a. Plans, goals, objectives, and procedures
    b. Place, form, time, and possession utilities
    c. Price, quality, and quantity
    d. Descriptions, inspections, samples, and negotiations
    e. Price, promotion, and distribution

Short-Answer Questions (C)

Complete each question.

34. A marketing information system is a framework for managing information. Identify several **internal and external sources** for collecting marketing information.

INTERNAL SOURCE	EXTERNAL SOURCES

35. Briefly describe what is involved in each step of **marketing research**.

STEPS IN MARKETING RESEARCH	EXPLANATION OF EACH STEP
Define the problem	
Make a preliminary investigation	
Plan the research	
Gather factual information	
Interpret the information	
Reach a conclusion	

36. How can marketers use each type of **technology**?

TECHNOLOGIES	WAYS TO USE TECHNOLOGY IN MARKETING
Database	
Online information services	
Internet	

37. Contrast consumer buying behavior to organizational buying behavior.

CONSUMER BUYING BEHAVIOR	ORGANIZATIONAL BUYING BEHAVIOR

38. Identify the steps in the **consumer buying decision process**.

a. _____   b. _____

c. _____   d. _____

39. Describe how each factor influences a **consumer's buying decision**.

FACTOR	HOW IT INFLUENCES BUYING BEHAVIOR
Situational Factors	
Psychological Factors	
Social Factors	

40. Explain why **discretionary income** is of particular interest to marketers.

41. List **reasons why consumers make purchases**. What need is satisfied in each case?

REASONS CONSUMERS BUY	HUMAN NEED THAT IS SATISFIED

42. Discuss how **understanding buying behavior** helps marketers.

43. Consumers have many choices of where to buy goods and services. Discuss the major factors that influence where consumers buy goods and services.

CHAPTER 14

CREATING AND PRICING PRODUCTS THAT SATISFY CUSTOMERS

Key Terms

Define each term briefly. Writing down the definition and giving an example will help you learn the term.

product (p. 383)

consumer product (p. 383)

business product (p. 383)

convenience product (p. 384)

shopping product (p. 384)

specialty product (p. 384)

raw material (p. 384)

major equipment (p. 384)

accessory equipment (p. 384)

component part (p. 384)

process material (p. 385)

supply (p. 385)

business service (p. 385)

product life cycle (p. 385)

product line (p. 388)

product mix (p. 388)

product modification (p. 389)

product deletion (p. 389)

brand (p. 392)

brand name (p. 392)

brand mark (p. 392)

trademark (p. 392)

trade name (p. 393)

manufacturer (or producer) brand (p. 393)

store (or private) brand (p. 393)

generic product (or brand) (p. 394)

brand loyalty (p. 394)

brand equity (p. 394)

individual branding (p. 396)

family branding (p. 397)

packaging (p. 397)

labeling (p. 398)

express warranty (p. 398)

price (p. 399)

supply (p. 399)

demand (p. 399)

product differentiation (p. 400)

price competition (p. 400)

nonprice competition (p. 401)

markup (p. 403)

breakeven quantity (p. 403)

total revenue (p. 403)

fixed cost (p. 403)

variable cost (p. 403)

total cost (p. 403)

price skimming (p. 405)

penetration pricing (p. 406)

negotiating pricing (p. 406)

secondary-market pricing (p. 406)

periodic discounting (p. 406)

random discounting (p. 407)

odd-number pricing (p. 407)

multiple-unit pricing (p. 407)

reference pricing (p. 407)

bundle pricing (p. 407)

everyday low pricing (p. 407)

customary pricing (p. 408)

captive pricing (p. 408)

premium pricing (p. 408)

price lining (p. 408)

price leaders (p. 409)

special-event pricing (p. 409)

comparison discounting (p. 409)

transfer pricing (p. 410)

discount (p. 410)

PRACTICE EXAMINATION A

Matching Questions (A)

Match each term with a statement.

a. product
b. product line
c. product mix
d. product life cycle
e. brand
f. brand name
g. brand mark

h. trademark
i. manufacturer brand
j. private brand
k. generic products
l. individual branding
m. family branding
n. packaging

_____ 1. A registered brand.
_____ 2. Products labeled with only the name of the product.
_____ 3. Branding strategy used by IBM, Sony, and Dell.
_____ 4. Can be an idea or a thing received in exchange.
_____ 5. Includes all products that a firm sells.
_____ 6. A name, symbol, or design that identifies a seller's products.
_____ 7. A symbol or distinctive design of a brand.
_____ 8. Sears's Kenmore is an example.
_____ 9. A firm uses a different brand on each of its products.
_____ 10. A group of similar products.
_____ 11. A series of stages reflecting a product's sales.
_____ 12. The names IBM, Procter & Gamble, and Nike are examples.
_____ 13. It is owned by a manufacturer, such as Honda and Whirlpool.
_____ 14. The basic function is to protect the product.

True-False Questions (A)

Select the correct answer.

T F 15. An idea may be classified as a product.
T F 16. In the introduction stage of the product life cycle, consumer awareness and acceptance of the product are generally low.
T F 17. Imitations are products designed for an established market.
T F 18. Bicycles and cellular phones are examples of specialty goods.
T F 19. Preliminary sales and cost projections are prepared in the testing phase of new product development.
T F 20. Poor planning and a lack of proper testing are the main reasons products fail.
T F 21. A design or symbol that distinguishes a product from its competitor is called packaging.
T F 22. Store-branded items demand higher prices, and therefore are more profitable.
T F 23. Generic products first appeared in stores in 1982.

T F 24. A function of packaging is to offer consumer convenience.
T F 25. Price allocates goods among those who are willing and able to buy them.
T F 26. Promotions for Crest toothpaste use product differentiation.

Multiple-Choice Questions (A)

Circle the letter before the most accurate answer.

27. Prell, Head & Shoulders, and Pert Plus form a _____ for Procter and Gamble
    a. product mix
    b. product line
    c. brand name
    d. brand
    e. trademark

28. Features of a product that are designed to attract customers at the point of sale include all of the following *except*
    a. packaging.
    b. labeling.
    c. screening.
    d. branding.
    e. pricing.

29. IBM and Xerox use a strategy that helps promote all their products. This strategy is called
    a. family branding.
    b. generic brands.
    c. store brands.
    d. individual branding.
    e. None of the above.

30. A cost determined by the number of units produced is called _____ cost.
    a. variable
    b. selling
    c. differentiation
    d. fixed
    e. penetration

31. Which of the following is *not* an example of business products?
    a. A lathe in a machine shop
    b. Stereo units in a department store
    c. Supplies in an office
    d. Cleaning products used by the janitorial service
    e. Iron ore in a steel plant

32. Western Day was a special day at the office. Janice wanted to dress in the latest western fashion, but she had limited funds. She visited several shops before finding the right outfit. For Janice, what type of product is the clothing?
    a. A specialty product
    b. Major equipment
    c. An industrial product
    d. A shopping product
    e. A convenience product

33. In which stage of the product life cycle do you find sales increasing, industry profit declining, pricing strategies becoming flexible, and marketing incentives being offered?
    a. Evaluation
    b. Maturity
    c. Growth
    d. Decline
    e. Introduction

34. Procter & Gamble, with its large assortment of products, has significantly improved the firm's profitability by using an effective product mix. It has done this by
   a. implementing a product deletion program.
   b. using generic products.
   c. promoting imitation products.
   d. adapting variations in existing products.
   e. adding new products.

35. The manager of a local restaurant wants to add new desserts to the menu. Customers were asked to complete a survey about what they like. The restaurant is in which stage of the new-product development process?
   a. Test marketing
   b. Product development
   c. Idea generation
   d. Screening
   e. Business analysis

36. What is a major problem with using markup pricing?
   a. Revenue can be easily projected.
   b. It is difficult to determine an effective markup percentage.
   c. The price is dictated by the number of units sold.
   d. Markup pricing negatively affects the breakeven point.
   e. Markup pricing sets the minimum price for a product.

37. Which statement is *not* true about competition-based pricing?
   a. The seller emphasizes low price.
   b. It may set prices below competitors' prices.
   c. A firm's costs and revenue are secondary to competitors' prices.
   d. This strategy charges the highest possible price in the first stage of its life cycle.
   e. This strategy is important in markets where competing products are quite similar.

38. Before setting prices for a firm's products, management must decide what it expects to accomplish through pricing. Which of the following factors is important?
   a. Survival
   b. Profit maximization
   c. Return on investment
   d. Market share
   e. All of the above are important.

Short-Answer Questions (A)

Complete each question.

39. What is a **product**?

40. **Consumer products** are classified according to buyers' purchasing behavior. Describe the characteristics and identify several examples for each category of consumer products.

CATEGORIES OF PRODUCTS	CHARACTERISTICS OF EACH CATEGORY	EXAMPLES
Convenience products		
Shopping products		
Specialty products		

41. Describe each category of **business products** and identify several examples for each category.

CATEGORIES OF BUSINESS PRODUCTS	DESCRIPTION OF EACH CATEGORY	EXAMPLES
Raw material		
Major equipment		
Accessory equipment		
Component parts		
Process material		
Supplies		
Services		

42. What are the stages of the **product life cycle**?

   a. _____   b. _____

   c. _____   d. _____

43. How can a business determine which **stage** a product is in?

44. Compare a **product line** to a **product mix** and give an example for each.

PRODUCT LINE	PRODUCT MIX
Example	Example

45. Compare the **width** of a product mix to the **depth** of the product mix.

WIDTH OF A PRODUCT MIX	DEPTH OF THE PRODUCT MIX

PRACTICE EXAMINATION B

Matching Questions (B-1)

Match each term with a statement.

a. labeling
b. express warranty
c. price
d. supply
e. demand
f. product differentiation
g. return on investment (ROI)
h. secondary-market pricing

i. product modification
j. reference pricing
k. trade name
l. brand loyalty
m. brand equity
n. production deletion
o. consumer product
p. negotiated pricing

_____ 1. Quantities of products that producers are willing to sell.
_____ 2. A written explanation of the producer's responsibilities.
_____ 3. Quantities of products that buyers are willing to purchase.
_____ 4. Presentation of information on a package.
_____ 5. The process of promoting differences between products.
_____ 6. It is set by the seller.
_____ 7. A target for investing.
_____ 8. Changes that make a product more dependable.
_____ 9. Positioning a moderate level price product next to a more expensive product.
_____ 10. Different prices set for each market.
_____ 11. It is used to manage weak products with unfavorable images.
_____ 12. It represents the value of a brand to an organization.
_____ 13. Customers consistently choose specific brands.
_____ 14. It is the legal name of an organization.
_____ 15. Bargaining occurs between seller and buyer.
_____ 16. It satisfies personal and family needs.

Matching Questions (B-2)

Match each term with a statement.

a. periodic discounting
b. markup
c. breakeven quantity
d. total revenue
e. fixed cost
f. variable cost
g. total cost
h. random discounting
i. price competition

j. bundle pricing
k. everyday low prices
l. customary pricing
m. captive pricing
n. premium pricing
o. price leaders
p. special-event pricing
q. comparison discounting

_____ 17. A systematic temporary reduction of prices.
_____ 18. Costs that depend on the number of units produced.
_____ 19. Is used to pay overhead.
_____ 20. The sum of fixed costs and variable costs.
_____ 21. A point where revenue equals cost.
_____ 22. The total amount received from the sale of products.
_____ 23. Used to gain sales by setting prices lower than other sellers'.
_____ 24. Combining two or more products for a single price.
_____ 25. Rent is an example of this type of cost.
_____ 26. An unsystematic temporary reduction of prices.
_____ 27. It attracts customers by giving them especially low prices on a few items.
_____ 28. A product's price is compared with a higher-priced product.
_____ 29. The basic product in a product line is priced low.
_____ 30. Summer sales are an example.
_____ 31. The highest-quality product in a product line is given the highest price.

_____ 32. Candy bars and chewing gum use this type of pricing.
_____ 33. Low prices are used consistently.

True-False Questions (B)

Select the correct answer.

T   F   34. Cheerios, Wheaties, and Total cereals are considered a product mix.
T   F   35. Competition enters when new products reach the growth stage of the product life cycle.
T   F   36. Innovative products often give rise to new industries.
T   F   37. The majority of new products entering the marketplace are successful.
T   F   38. New product test marketing is limited to representative locations to determine buyers' probable reactions.
T   F   39. Producer branding offers products with national recognition and consistent quality that are widely available.
T   F   40. Sears, Ford, and IBM are examples of store brands.
T   F   41. A generic product has no brand.
T   F   42. Sony, Dell, and IBM use family branding.
T   F   43. Labels may include the brand name and the trademark.
T   F   44. In a demand relationship, the quantity demanded by purchasers increases as the price increases.
T   F   45. The equilibrium point occurs when all units of a product are sold at the highest price, meeting the expectations of both buyers and sellers.
T   F   46. Markup includes insurance costs and profits.

Multiple-Choice Questions (B)

Select the most accurate answer.

47. In what stage of the product life cycle is the price of the product generally high?
    a. Introduction
    b. Maturity
    c. Modification
    d. Growth
    e. Decline

48. Caffeine-free diet soft drinks are an example of a product
    a. innovation.
    b. adaptation.
    c. promotion.
    d. imitation.
    e. deletion.

49. For Hewlett-Packard, what do the letters *hp* inside a circle placed inside a shaded rectangle represent?
    a. Brand
    b. Generic name
    c. Label
    d. Name
    e. Trademark

50. A set of attributes and benefits that has been carefully designed to satisfy its market while earning a profit for the seller is known as a
    a. market.
    b. product.
    c. warranty.
    d. brand.
    e. label.

51. Competition-based pricing
    a. has not been used since 1985.
    b. is an unfair business practice.
    c. considers costs and revenue.
    d. is used primarily by wholesalers.
    e. is illegal at the state level.

52. Which of the following is an example of a shopping product?
    a. Process materials
    b. Cranes
    c. Bicycles
    d. Soft drinks
    e. Chewing gum

53. Pizza Inn recently replaced one of its ovens. How should this business product be classified?
    a. Major equipment
    b. Accessory equipment
    c. Raw material
    d. Process material
    e. Component part

54. When concept testing a new product, which question is of *no* real value?
    a. Which features are of little or no interest to you?
    b. What are the primary advantages of the proposed product over the one you currently use?
    c. If this product was available at an appropriate price, how often would you buy it?
    d. What is the price to earnings ratio of the company stock?
    e. How could this proposed product be improved?

55. Procter & Gamble, Kodak, and General Electric manufacture several lines of products. These lines of products are referred to as the firm's
    a. product line.
    b. product mix.
    c. product differentiation.
    d. brand name.
    e. inventory line.

56. Product modification makes changes to existing products in three primary ways. They are
    a. screening, testing, and changing.
    b. growth, maturity, and decline.
    c. quality, function, and aesthetics.
    d. quantity, description, and appearance.
    e. product, price, and service.

57. How do functional modifications affect products? Which of the following is *not* a cause for functional modification of a product?
    a. Product's versatility
    b. Effectiveness of the product
    c. Appearance of the product
    d. Convenience of the product
    e. Safety of the product

58. Before setting prices for a firm's products, management must decide what it expects to accomplish through pricing. Which factor might a firm choose?
    a. Survival
    b. Market share
    c. Status quo pricing
    d. Maximum profits
    e. Any of the above

59. Psychological pricing strategies include
    a. periodic discounting.
    b. negotiated pricing.
    c. price skimming.
    d. multiple-unit pricing.
    e. price lining.

60. Promotional pricing methods include
    a. comparison discounting.
    b. captive pricing.
    c. customer pricing.
    d. periodic discounting.
    e. None of the above.

Short-Answer Questions (B)

Complete each question.

61. Identify three ways a firm can **improve a product mix**.

    a. _____

    b. _____

    c. _____

62. How can existing products be altered using **modifications**? Give examples.

PRODUCT MODIFICATIONS	EXAMPLES
Quality modifications	
Functional modifications	
Aesthetic modifications	

63. **New products** are generally grouped into three categories. Distinguish among them.

    a. Imitations

    b. Adaptations

    c. Innovations

64. Explain what happens in each **phase of developing** a new product.

PHASES OF PRODUCT DEVELOPMENT	DESCRIPTION OF EACH PHASE
Idea generation	
Screening	
Concept testing	
Business analysis	
Product development	
Test marketing	
Commercialization	

65. Why do **products fail**?

66. Give an example for each part of a brand.

BRAND	EXAMPLES
Brand name	
Brand mark	
Trademark	
Trade name	

67. Compare a **manufacturer brand** with a **store brand** and a **generic brand**.

MANUFACTURER BRAND (Producer)	STORE BRAND (Private)	GENERIC BRAND

68. Discuss several **benefits** of branding.

a. _____

b. _____

c. _____

d. _____

e. _____

PRACTICE EXAMINATION C

Matching Questions (C)

Match each term with a statement.

a. price skimming
b. penetration pricing
c. odd-number pricing
d. multiple-unit pricing
e. transfer pricing
f. price lining

g. discount
h. negotiating pricing
i. secondary-market pricing
j. periodic discounting
k. allowance
l. reference pricing

_____ 1. Amount deducted from the price of an item.
_____ 2. A store has two seasonal sales a year.
_____ 3. Positioning a lower-priced product next to a higher-priced product.
_____ 4. A strategy that promotes more units during the early life-cycle stages.
_____ 5. Pricing two bottles at "$1.99 for both" is an example.
_____ 6. Early bird diners at restaurants receive a discount.
_____ 7. One unit in an organization sells to another unit.

_____ 8. A strategy that introduces a product at a high price.
_____ 9. Offering goods at certain predetermined prices.
_____ 10. The price of $4.99 is an example.
_____ 11. Buyer seeks a lower price.
_____ 12. Buyer trades in used equipment on the purchase of new equipment.

True-False Questions (C)

Select the correct answer.

T F 13. Tobacco products, alcoholic beverages, and Del Monte brand fruits are considered a product line.

T F 14. Weaker competition leaves the market during the maturity stage of the product life cycle.

T F 15. Screening is the first step in the evolution of a new product.

T F 16. Once established, a product mix remains effective.

T F 17. Commercialization is the final stage in the development of a new product.

T F 18. Food product labels must state only the number of calories per product.

T F 19. Product differentiation makes products more competitive with similar products.

T F 20. "Peanut Butter" written on a plain white wrapper is an example of a generic product.

T F 21. Packaging has little influence on buying decisions.

T F 22. Garments must be labeled with the name of the manufacturer, country of manufacture, fabric contents, and cleaning instructions.

T F 23. The equilibrium point is when all products produced are sold at a price that produces some profits.

T F 24. Total revenue is the selling price times the number of units sold.

T F 25. Labels may carry details of written or express warranties.

T F 26. Promoting differences between one's own product and similar products is the process of product differentiation.

T F 27. The breakeven quantity includes the desired profit level.

Multiple-Choice Questions (C)

Circle the letter before the most accurate answer.

28. In what stage does price competition increase?
    a. Growth
    b. Maturity
    c. Testing
    d. Decline
    e. Introduction

29. During which stage are the largest number of product ideas rejected?
    a. Idea generation
    b. Screening
    c. Concept testing
    d. Business analysis
    e. Test marketing

30. The process of developing and promoting differences between similar products is called
    a. product demand.
    b. market segmentation.
    c. competition pricing.
    d. product differentiation.
    e. penetration pricing.

31. A brand name should
    a. suggest the product's use.
    b. suggest special characteristics of the product.
    c. suggest the major benefits of the product.
    d. be distinctive enough to set it apart from the competition.
    e. accomplish all of the above.

32. Three classifications of consumer goods are
    a. convenience, shopping, and business.
    b. industrial, specialty, and shopping.
    c. shopping, convenience, and specialty.
    d. shopping, component, and specialty.
    e. convenience, component, and accessory.

33. A strategy of charging the highest possible price for a product during the introduction stage of its life cycle is known as
    a. penetration pricing.
    b. competition-based pricing.
    c. demand-based pricing.
    d. cost-based pricing.
    e. price skimming.

34. Which of the following is a technique for discounting the price of a product?
    a. Trade discount
    b. Quantity discount
    c. Cash discount
    d. Multiple-unit pricing
    e. All of the above are ways to reduce the cost of a product.

35. Which reason is *not* valid for rejecting a new product idea?
    a. The company lacked the expertise to develop and market the product.
    b. The product did not match organizational resources.
    c. The product would allow the company to gain a 10 percent market share.
    d. The product was not consistent with the company's objectives.
    e. The company lacked the needed human resources.

36. Ivory, Camay, Lava, Zest, and Safeguard are examples of bar soaps manufactured by Procter & Gamble. What type of branding is being used?
    a. Producer
    b. Individual
    c. Unity
    d. Family
    e. Promotion

37. A basic function of packaging is to
    a. influence pricing.
    b. communicate the product's image.
    c. make the product safer.
    d. eliminate customer theft.
    e. decrease costs.

38. Which pricing method estimates the amount of product that customers will demand at different prices?
    a. Demand-based pricing
    b. Odd-number pricing
    c. Prestige pricing
    d. Sample pricing
    e. Price skimming

39. An express warranty is a(n)
    a. statement of how the product should perform.
    b. oral agreement between the buyer and seller.
    c. regulation manufacturers must follow in making the product.
    d. written explanation of the producer's responsibilities, if the product is found defective.
    e. psychological strategy for convincing consumers to buy the product.

Short-Answer Questions (C)

Complete each question.

40. Identify two **advantages** of each branding strategy.

INDIVIDUAL BRANDING ADVANTAGES	FAMILY BRANDING ADVANTAGES

41. List three basic functions of **packaging** materials.

    a. _____

    b. _____

    c. _____

42. What are the **purposes of labeling**? What information may be included in the label?

43. What are three functions of **price as an allocator**?

    a. _____

    b. _____

    c. _____

44. Discuss how **prices** are determined by **supply and demand**?

45. Explain why a producer would be interested in **product differentiation**.

46. Contrast the marketing variables of **price competition** to **nonprice competition**.

COMPETITION	MARKETING VARIABLES
Price competition	
Nonprice competition	

47. What is the **objective** of each pricing factor?

PRICING FACTOR	OBJECTIVE OF EACH PRICING FACTOR
Survival	
Profit maximization	
Target return on investment (ROI)	
Market share goals	
Status quo pricing	

48. Distinguish among the **types of pricing**.

PRICING	CHARACTERISTICS
Cost-based pricing	
Demand-based pricing	
Competition-based pricing	

49. What is the **strategy** in each type of **differential pricing**?

DIFFERENTIAL PRICING	STRATEGY
Negotiated pricing	
Secondary-market pricing	
Periodic discounting	
Random discounting	

50. What is the **strategy** in each type of **psychological pricing**?

PSYCHOLOGICAL PRICING	STRATEGY
Odd-number pricing	
Multiple-unit pricing	
Reference pricing	
Bundle lining	
Everyday low prices	
Customary pricing	

51. What is the **strategy** in each type of **product-line pricing**?

PRODUCT-LINE PRICING	STRATEGY
Captive pricing	
Premium pricing	
Price lining	

52. What is the **strategy** in each type of **promotional pricing**?

PROMOTIONAL PRICING	STRATEGY
Price leaders	
Special-event pricing	
Comparison discounting	

53. What is the **role** of each type of each **business pricing strategy**?

BUSINESS PRICING STRATEGY	WHAT IS ITS ROLE?
Geographic pricing –FOB origin pricing –FOB destination	
Transfer pricing	
Discounting –Trade discounts –Quantity discounts –Cash discounts –Seasonal discounts –Allowances	

CHAPTER 15

WHOLESALING, RETAILING, AND PHYSICAL DISTRIBUTION

Key Terms

Define each term briefly. Writing down the definition and giving an example will help you learn the term.

channel of distribution (or marketing channel) (p. 419)

middleman (or marketing intermediary) (p. 419)

merchant middleman (p. 419)

functional middleman (p. 419)

retailer (p. 419)

wholesaler (p. 419)

intensive distribution (p. 421)

selective distribution (p. 421)

exclusive distribution (p. 422)

supply chain management (p. 422)

vertical channel integration (p. 423)

vertical marketing system (VMS) (p. 423)

merchant wholesaler (p. 426)

full-service wholesaler (p. 426)

general merchandise wholesaler (p. 426)

limited-line wholesaler (p. 426)

specialty-line wholesaler (p. 426)

limited-service wholesaler (p. 426)

commission merchant (p. 426)

agent (p. 426)

broker (p. 426)

manufacturer's sales branch (p. 426)

manufacturer's sales office (p. 427)

independent retailer (p. 428)

chain retailer (p. 428)

department store (p. 428)

discount store (p. 429)

catalog showroom (p. 429)

warehouse showroom (p. 429)

convenience store (p. 430)

supermarket (p. 430)

superstore (p. 430)

warehouse club (p. 430)

traditional specialty store (p. 431)

off-price retailer (p. 431)

category killer (p. 431)

nonstore retailing (p. 432)

direct selling (p. 432)

direct marketing (p. 432)

catalog marketing (p. 432)

direct-response marketing (p. 432)

telemarketing (p. 433)

television home shopping (p. 433)

online retailing (p. 433)

automatic vending (p. 434)

wheel of retailing (p. 434)

neighborhood shopping center (p. 435)

community shopping center (p. 436)

regional shopping center (p. 436)

physical distribution (p. 436)

inventory management (p. 437)

order processing (p. 437)

warehousing (p. 437)

materials handling (p. 438)

transportation (p. 438)

carrier (p. 438)

PRACTICE EXAMINATION A

Matching Questions (A-1)

Match each term with a statement.

a. channel of distribution
b. middleman
c. merchant wholesaler
d. functional middleman
e. retailer
f. wholesaler
g. intensive distribution

h. selective distribution
i. exclusive distribution
j. manufacturer's agent
k. broker
l. manufacturer's sales branch
m. manufacturer's sales office
n. independent retailer

_____ 1. The widest possible exposure in the marketplace.
_____ 2. It begins with the producer and ends with the user.
_____ 3. A middleman that does not take title to goods.
_____ 4. Concerned with transfer of ownership of products.
_____ 5. Type of distribution used by automobile manufacturers.
_____ 6. A middleman that actually buys and resells products.
_____ 7. A middleman that sells to consumers.
_____ 8. A middleman that sells to other firms.
_____ 9. Represents the producer but does not take title to goods.
_____ 10. It is owned by a manufacturer.
_____ 11. A type of distribution used for designer clothes.
_____ 12. A sales agent that specializes in a particular commodity.
_____ 13. A firm that operates only one retail outlet.
_____ 14. A merchant wholesaler that is owned by a manufacturer.

Matching Questions (A-2)

Match each term with a statement.

a. vertical channel integration
b. vertical marketing system
c. merchant wholesalers
d. full-service wholesalers
e. general merchandise wholesaler
f. limited-line wholesalers

g. limited-service wholesalers
h. jobbers or distributors
i. sales agent
j. specialty-line wholesaler
k. commission merchants

_____ 15. An agent representing one or more manufacturers on a commission basis.
_____ 16. It carries a select group of products within a line of products.
_____ 17. They usually operate warehouses, take title to goods, and store goods.
_____ 18. They perform the entire range of wholesaler functions.
_____ 19. They carry merchandise and negotiate sales for manufacturers.
_____ 20. They are merchant wholesalers.
_____ 21. A retailer that warehouses its own stock is an example.
_____ 22. It is a middleman that deals in a wide variety of products.
_____ 23. Cash-and-carry wholesalers are an example.
_____ 24. It is a centrally managed distribution channel that combines operations.
_____ 25. This middleman carries a few lines with many products within each line.

True-False Questions (A)

Select the correct answer.

T F 26. A functional middleman transfers ownership but does not take title to the products.
T F 27. Avon Products uses a direct channel of distribution for its products.
T F 28. A direct channel of distribution includes both wholesalers and retailers.

T F 29. Multiple channels of distribution are used to capture a larger share of the market.
T F 30. Exclusive distribution makes use of all available outlets for a product.
T F 31. A wholesaler provides retailers with an instant sales force.
T F 32. Agents who represent producers are called manufacturer's agents.
T F 33. Approximately 35 percent of retailers operate chains.
T F 34. Wal-Mart is a full-service department store.
T F 35. Supermarkets emphasize low prices and one-stop shopping for household items.
T F 36. Warehouse clubs turn their stock over on the average of 24 times each year.
T F 37. Burlington Coat Factory is an example of an off-price retailer that buys manufacturers' seconds and off-season production lines.
T F 38. Unit loading in materials handling can reduce pilferage, breakage, and spoilage.
T F 39. Piggyback service is unique to air freight.

Multiple-Choice Questions (A)

Circle the letter before the most accurate answer.

40. Which channel of distribution *most* directly moves goods from the producer to the end user?
    a. Producer to consumer
    b. Producer to retailer to consumer
    c. Producer to wholesaler to retailer to consumer
    d. Producer to agent to wholesaler to retailer to consumer
    e. Producer to broker to wholesaler to retailer to consumer

41. Which type of distribution coverage would a convenience good, like candy, *most likely* use?
    a. Intensive distribution
    b. Selective distribution
    c. Exclusive distribution
    d. Warehousing
    e. All of the above

42. Oil companies that own wells, transportation facilities, refineries, terminals, and service stations exemplify
    a. exclusive distribution.
    b. selective distribution.
    c. total vertical integration.
    d. intensive distribution.
    e. the need for intermediaries.

43. Merchant wholesalers usually
    a. operate one or more warehouses.
    b. take title to goods.
    c. store goods in warehouses.
    d. analyze market needs.
    e. do all of the above.

44. Which activity combines inventory management, order processing, warehousing, materials handling, and transportation?
    a. Marketing
    b. Merchandising
    c. Warehousing
    d. Physical distribution
    e. Transporting

45. Which statement is *not* true about regional shopping centers? Regional shopping centers
    a. carry similar merchandise as do downtown shopping districts.
    b. may include hotels and movie theaters.
    c. have influenced downtown merchants to renovate their stores.
    d. maintain a suitable mix of stores.
    e. attract small independent stores over national stores.

46. Which service is *not* provided to manufacturers by wholesalers?
    a. Assuming credit risks
    b. Providing loans
    c. Furnishing market information
    d. Reducing inventory costs
    e. Providing an instant sales force

47. Which type of retailer advertises only through direct mail, has concrete floors, stacks merchandise on pallets, and requires payments to be in cash?
    a. Warehouse club
    b. Discount store
    c. Warehouse showroom
    d. Convenience store
    e. Off-price retailer

48. Which type of stores are The Gap and Foot Locker?
    a. Warehouse
    b. Convenience
    c. Specialty
    d. Department
    e. Wholesale

49. The criteria for selecting a mode of transportation include
    a. determining the cost.
    b. calculating the speed.
    c. the dependability and the frequency.
    d. the load flexibility and accessibility.
    e. All of the above are viable criteria.

Short-Answer Questions (A)

Complete each question.

50. Compare a **merchant middleman** with a **functional middleman**. How are they similar and different?

51. What are the **channels of distribution** for **consumer** products? Give an example of a good that would use each channel.

    a. producer to _____
       Example of a good to use this channel is_____ .

    b. producer to _____ to _____
       Example of a good to use this channel is _____ .

c. producer to _____ to _____ to _____
   Example of a good to use this channel is _____ .

d. producer to _____to _____ to _____ to _____
   Example of a good to use this channel is _____ .

52. The two most commonly used **channels of distribution** for **business** products are

   a. producer to _____

   b. producer to _____ to _____ to _____

53. Describe three approaches producers use to get **market coverage** for their products. Give several examples of products in each approach.

APPROACHES	DESCRIPTION	EXAMPLES
Intensive distribution		
Selective distribution		
Exclusive distribution		

54. Identify the elements of **supply chain management**?

a.	b.	c.
d.	e.	f.
g.	h.	i.
j.	k.	l.

55. How do the three types of **vertical marketing systems** (VMSs) differ?

ADMINISTERED VMS	CONTRACTUAL VMS	CORPORATE VMS

PRACTICE EXAMINATION B

Matching Questions (B)

Match each term with a statement.

a. chain retailer
b. department store
c. discount store
d. warehouse showroom
e. catalog showroom
f. specialty store

g. supermarkets
h. convenience store
i. direct selling
j. catalog marketing
k. supply chain management
l. online retailing

_____ 1. A store that generally offers minimal customer services.
_____ 2. A store that sells a single category of merchandise.
_____ 3. Marketing approach used by Mary Kay and Amway.
_____ 4. A firm that operates more than one retail outlet.
_____ 5. Includes Safeway and Kroger grocery stores.
_____ 6. Solicits orders through catalogs.
_____ 7. Macy's in New York is an example.
_____ 8. Type of distribution used by Service Merchandise.
_____ 9. Small food stores that sell a limited variety of products.
_____ 10. Store in which customers select merchandise from cases on display.
_____ 11. Customers place orders through computers.
_____ 12. A partnership created to reduce inefficiencies, costs, and redundancies.

True-False Questions (B)

Select the correct answer.

T F 13. A retailer buys and sells merchandise.
T F 14. Bulky items, like furniture and major appliances, often go through wholesalers.
T F 15. Heavy machinery and major installations are usually distributed directly from producer to business user.
T F 16. Warehousing creates possession utility.
T F 17. Wholesalers help promote the products they sell to retailers.
T F 18. Wholesalers help retailers reduce their inventory costs.
T F 19. Manufacturers' sales branches carry stock, extend credit, deliver goods, and help promote products.
T F 20. Materials handling is the actual physical handling of goods in both warehousing and transportation.
T F 21. Neighborhood shopping centers include one to two department stores and serve consumers who live 30 minutes to an hour away.
T F 22. Wal-Mart is a catalog discount store.

T F 23. Inventory holding costs consist of money invested in inventory, cost of storage space, insurance costs, and inventory taxes.

T F 24. Community shopping centers strive to reach 150,000 or more customers in their target market.

T F 25. One problem with telemarketing is employee turnover.

T F 26. The most common product sold on television home shopping is automobiles.

Multiple-Choice Questions (B)

Circle the letter before the most accurate answer.

27. Which channel of distribution is *best* for perishable products?
    a. Producer to consumer
    b. Producer to retailer to consumer
    c. Producer to wholesaler to retailer to consumer
    d. Producer to agent to consumer
    e. Producer to wholesaler to consumer

28. Which service is provided to retailers by wholesalers?
    a. Providing an instant sales force
    b. Reducing inventory costs
    c. Assuming credit risks
    d. Promoting products
    e. Delivery of products to consumers

29. A sales agent may
    a. represent only one firm at a time.
    b. have an unlimited territory.
    c. work on a salary.
    d. represent more than one firm at a time.
    e. take title to goods.

30. Total vertical integration occurs when
    a. the goods move from the retailer to the consumer.
    b. wholesalers are eliminated from the distribution process.
    c. a single management controls all operations from production to final sale.
    d. retailers take on the financing function.
    e. intensive distribution is the goal.

31. Which type of distribution uses only one retail store in each geographic area?
    a. Exclusive
    b. Intensive
    c. Patterned
    d. Selective
    e. Intentional

32. A direct channel of distribution would *most likely* be used by
    a. IBM.
    b. Mary Kay Cosmetics.
    c. The Gap.
    d. Home Depot.
    e. McDonald's.

33. Which type of marketing intermediary takes title to goods?
    a. Functional middleman
    b. Agent
    c. Producer
    d. Merchant middleman
    e. None of the above take title.

34. What type of store is located within a mile of 70 percent of its customers?
    a. Specialty store
    b. Discount store
    c. Department store
    d. Supermarket
    e. Convenience store

35. Which of the following statements is *not* true about catalog marketing?
    a. Catalog marketing is effective for all types of products.
    b. Customers find catalog marketing efficient and convenient.
    c. Retailers do not have to invest in expensive store fixtures.
    d. Personal selling expenses are reduced.
    e. Catalog marketing provides limited services.

36. The job of a freight forwarder is to
    a. ensure that each shipment travels alone to receive the best rate.
    b. assume responsibility for the safe delivery of the shipments.
    c. ask the sender to bring the shipment to a central location.
    d. allow the shipper to supervise loading selected carriers.
    e. ensure that the shipper selects a private carrier.

Short-Answer Questions (B)

Complete each question.

37. Some people believe the **elimination of wholesalers** would bring about lower prices for consumers. What do you believe? Justify your position.

38. Identify three **services wholesalers provide to retailers** and give an example for each.

SERVICES TO RETAILERS	EXAMPLES

39. List several **services wholesalers perform for producers** (manufacturers) and give an example for each.

SERVICES TO PRODUCERS	EXAMPLES

40. Compare a **full-service wholesaler** to a **limited-service wholesaler**.

41. Describe the **role of each wholesaler**.

WHOLESALERS	DESCRIPTION
General merchandise	
Limited-line	
Specialty-line	

42. What are the major differences among three **types of wholesalers**?

TYPES OF WHOLESALERS	MAJOR DIFFERENCES
Commission merchant	
Agent	
Broker	

43. As reported in August, 2000, the top three largest retail firms in the United States were

    a. _____ b. _____ c. _____

44. Identify the advantages and/or benefits that **in-store retailers** provide to their customers.

TYPE OF RETAILERS	ADVANTAGES/BENEFITS TO CUSTOMERS
Department stores	
Discount stores	
Catalog and warehouse showrooms	
Convenience stores	
Supermarkets	
Superstores	
Warehouse clubs	
Traditional specialty stores	
Off-price retailers	
Category killers	

PRACTICE EXAMINATION C

Matching Questions (C-1)

Match each term with a statement.

a. physical distribution
b. inventory management
c. holding costs
d. stock-out costs
e. order processing

f. warehousing
g. materials handling
h. transportation
i. carriers
j. telemarketing

_____ 1. Process of managing inventories.
_____ 2. Involves receiving and filling customers' purchase orders.
_____ 3. Shipment of products to customers.
_____ 4. Costs involved in storing products.
_____ 5. Involves storing goods and preparing them for reshipment.
_____ 6. Firms that offer transportation services.
_____ 7. Involves the movement of goods from producer to consumer.
_____ 8. Insufficient inventory induce these costs.
_____ 9. Actual physical handling of goods.
_____ 10. Marketing-related activities are performed by phone.

Matching Questions (C-2)

Match each term with a statement.

a. superstore
b. warehouse club
c. traditional specialty store
d. off-price retailer
e. category killer
f. nonstore retailing
g. direct selling
h. direct marketing

i. catalog marketing
j. direct-response marketing
k. television home shopping
l. automatic vending
m. wheel of retailing
n. neighborhood shopping center
o. community shopping center
p. regional shopping center

_____ 11. Purchasers are required to have a membership.
_____ 12. Its products may be manufacturer's seconds or off-season merchandise.
_____ 13. It is a process for communicating with customers by mail, telephone, or online.
_____ 14. Its customers live less than ten minutes away.
_____ 15. Spiegel, JC Penney, L.L. Bean, and Lands' End use this type of retailing.
_____ 16. Tupperware and Sarah Coventry use this retailing method.
_____ 17. The benefits include product demonstration and customer convenience.
_____ 18. Large department stores and national chain stores are found here.
_____ 19. This establishment carries food, hardware, clothing, personal-care products, garden products, and automotive merchandise.
_____ 20. It uses machines to dispense products.
_____ 21. A hypothesis suggests that new retail operations usually begin at the bottom.
_____ 22. Sending letters, samples, brochures, or booklets to prospects on a mailing list is an example.
_____ 23. It uses direct selling, direct marketing, and vending machines.
_____ 24. It offers a deep product line, service, atmosphere, and location.
_____ 25. It is a large specialty store that takes business away from smaller stores.
_____ 26. Art exhibits, automobile shows, and other special events generate customers.

True-False Questions (C)

Select the correct answer.

T F 27. The direct channel of distribution for business products includes retailers.
T F 28. When products are carried by many retailers, the manufacturers use wholesalers.
T F 29. Agent intermediaries receive commissions from the party they represent, either the buyer or seller.
T F 30. Wholesalers gather information about consumer demand.
T F 31. Merchant wholesalers do not take title to goods.
T F 32. Wholesalers do not extend direct financial assistance to retailers.
T F 33. Discount retail stores provide maximum customer service.
T F 34. Supermarkets emphasize one-stop shopping for household needs.
T F 35. Most commodities carried by railroads could just as easily be transported by some other mode.
T F 36. In terms of total freight carried, railroads are America's least important mode of transportation.
T F 37. As a selling technique, catalog selling has failed to grow in the United States.
T F 38. Warehousing activities include sorting goods and marshaling shipments.
T F 39. The ability to handle particular kinds of shipments is an important factor in deciding on the mode of transportation.
T F 40. Private carriers are available for hire by shippers.

Multiple-Choice Questions (C)

Circle the letter before the most accurate answer.

41. Automobile parts used by General Motors assembly plants move from
    a. producer to business user.
    b. manufacturer to agent to business user.
    c. manufacturer to retailer to business user.
    d. producer to wholesaler to retailer to business user.
    e. producer to agent to user.

42. Wholesaler services to manufacturers include
    a. setting up displays.
    b. gathering information.
    c. making deliveries.
    d. extending long-term loans.
    e. handling consumer financing.

43. A broker
    a. is a sales agent.
    b. specializes in different products.
    c. is paid a salary.
    d. takes title to products.
    e. All of the above.

44. Which of the following is *not* an advantage of using telemarketing for market-related activities?
    a. Generating sales leads
    b. Improving customer service
    c. Monitoring safety regulations in the office
    d. Speeding up payments on past-due accounts
    e. Gathering marketing information

45. An electronic shopping mall is an example of which type of direct marketing?
    a. Telemarketing
    b. Direct-response marketing
    c. Catalog marketing
    d. On-line retailing
    e. Television home shopping

46. Mary Kay Cosmetics, Amway, Tupperware, and Sarah Coventry are examples of companies that use
    a. direct selling.
    b. party plan of selling.
    c. face-to-face sales presentations.
    d. nonstore retailing.
    e. All of the above.

47. Category killer stores take business away from smaller, high-cost retail stores. Which company is an example of a category killer store?
    a. Toys "R" Us
    b. Sears
    c. Macy's
    d. Neiman Marcus
    e. Ace Hardware

48. A retail store that employs 25 or more people, sells a wide range of household and apparel items, provides credit, and offers a pleasant shopping atmosphere is classified as a
    a. catalog showroom.
    b. superstore.
    c. supermarket.
    d. specialty store.
    e. department store.

49. What type of carrier is American Airlines?
    a. Freight
    b. Common
    c. Private
    d. Long-distance
    e. Contract

Short-Answer Questions (C)

Complete each question.

50. Identify five types of nonstore direct marketing activities and describe how each is special.

TYPES OF NONSTORE MARKETING	DESCRIPTION OF EACH TYPE
Direct selling	
Direct marketing	
Catalog marketing	
Direct-response marketing	
Telemarketing	
Television home shopping	
Online retailing	
Automatic vending	

51. Explain the **wheel of retailing hypothesis**. What does it suggest about new retail operations?

52. Compare and contrast **community shopping centers** with **regional shopping centers**.

53. Briefly describe each major function of **physical distribution**.

FUNCTION OF PHYSICAL DISTRIBUTION	DESCRIPTION
Inventory management	
Order processing	
Warehousing	
Materials handling	
Transportation	

54. What is involved in each **warehousing** activity?

WAREHOUSING ACTIVITY	DESCRIPTION
Receiving goods	
Identifying goods	
Sorting goods	
Dispatching goods to storage	
Holding goods	
Recalling, selecting, or picking goods	
Marshaling shipments	
Dispatching shipments	

55. Identify the six major criteria used for **selecting transportation modes**.

a. _____   b. _____

c. _____   d. _____

e. _____   f. _____

56. Identify the **modes of transportation**, and list one advantage for each mode.

MODES OF TRANSPORTATION	ADVANTAGES OF EACH MODE

CHAPTER 16

DEVELOPING INTEGRATED MARKETING COMMUNICATIONS

Key Terms

Define each term briefly. Writing down the definition and giving an example will help you learn the term.

promotion (p. 449)

promotion mix (p. 449)

integrated marketing communications (p. 449)

advertising (p. 450)

personal selling (p. 451)

sales promotion (p. 451)

public relations (p. 451)

primary-demand advertising (p. 452)

selective demand (or brand) advertising (p. 452)

institutional advertising (p. 452)

advertising media (p. 453)

direct-mail advertising (p. 453)

outdoor advertising (p. 454)

infomercial (p. 455)

advertising agency (p. 458)

order getter (p. 460)

creative selling (p. 460)

order taker (p. 460)

sales support personnel (p. 460)

missionary salesperson (p. 460)

trade salesperson (p. 460)

technical salesperson (p. 460)

consumer sales promotion method (p. 463)

trade sales promotion method (p. 463)

rebate (p. 463)

coupon (p. 463)

sample (p. 464)

premium (p. 464)

frequent-user incentive (p. 464)

point-of-purchase display (p. 464)

trade show (p. 465)

buying allowance (p. 465)

cooperative advertising (p. 465)

publicity (p. 467)

news release (p. 467)

feature article (p. 467)

captioned photograph (p. 467)

press conference (p. 467)

promotional campaign (p. 468)

positioning (p. 468)

PRACTICE EXAMINATION A

Matching Questions (A)

Match each term with a statement.

a. promotion
b. promotion mix
c. advertising
d. selective advertising
e. comparative advertising
f. institutional advertising
g. primary-demand advertising

h. advertising media
i. integrated marketing communications
j. infomercial
k. trade salesperson
l. technical salesperson
m. press conference

_____ 1. Any nonpersonal, paid form of communication.
_____ 2. Usually based on information from a study.
_____ 3. Informs, persuades, or reminds potential users.
_____ 4. Designed to sell a particular brand of product.
_____ 5. Designed to enhance a firm's image.
_____ 6. A combination of ways to inform, persuade, or remind customers.
_____ 7. Its aim is to increase demand for all brands of a product.
_____ 8. Promotes broad product categories.
_____ 9. Duties include restocking shelves and setting up displays.
_____ 10. Focuses on how to use product or to install product.
_____ 11. Ensures the maximum informational impact on customers.
_____ 12. Important news is announced.
_____ 13. Program-length televised commercial message.

True-False Questions (A)

Select the correct answer.

T F 14. The characteristics of a target market determine the promotion mix.
T F 15. Institutional advertising promotes specific brands of products and services.
T F 16. Most nationally advertised products use immediate-response advertising.
T F 17. Infomercials and radio account for 63 percent of all advertising expenditures.
T F 18. It is difficult to target markets using newspapers.
T F 19. A major disadvantage of magazines is their lack of timeliness.
T F 20. Television advertising rates are based on the estimated number of viewers at the time the commercial is aired.
T F 21. Critics argue that advertising is wasteful.
T F 22. Television and radio account for less than one-third of all media expenditures.
T F 23. Sales promotion techniques are used primarily to enhance and supplement other promotion methods.
T F 24. A report on the six o'clock news covering the opening of a new store is an example of publicity.
T F 25. Available resources and the target market affect the makeup of a promotional mix.
T F 26. Personal selling is less expensive to use than advertising.
T F 27. Network time is an effective and efficient medium for local firms.

Multiple-Choice Questions (A)

Circle the letter before the most accurate answer.

28. The process of making potential consumers aware of products is known as
    a. positioning.
    b. promotion.
    c. missionary selling.
    d. a push strategy.
    e. order taking.

29. Promotional material mailed directly to individuals is known as _____ advertising.
    a. selective
    b. primary-demand
    c. comparative
    d. direct-mail
    e. cooperative

30. Which of the following is *not* considered a major element in the promotion mix?
    a. Advertising
    b. Personal selling
    c. Sales promotion
    d. Publicity
    e. Public relations

31. A sample is an example of
    a. sales promotion.
    b. missionary selling.
    c. couponing.
    d. publicity.
    e. advertising.

32. Promotion and marketing objectives include
    a. positioning the product.
    b. stabilizing sales.
    c. increasing the market share.
    d. improving consumer attitudes.
    e. all of the above.

33. Selective advertising is *best* used to
    a. increase the demand for all brands of a product.
    b. persuade consumers to make purchases within a short time.
    c. enhance a firm's image or reputation.
    d. personally inform customers about a product.
    e. deliver a news story about a product.

34. Many large department stores and supermarkets in the community run full-page advertisements in the local newspaper. Which type of advertising are they using?
    a. Immediate response
    b. Comparative
    c. Institutional
    d. Primary-demand
    e. Reminder

35. A program-length televised commercial message resembling an entertainment or consumer affairs programs is called _____ advertising.
    a. reminder
    b. selective
    c. infomercial
    d. primary-demand
    e. institutional

36. What kind of advertising time is *best* for Honda to use for introducing and promoting nationwide its new minivan?
    a. Sponsorship
    b. Network time
    c. Local time
    d. Spot time
    e. Regional time

37. Firms that want to promote their products or services, but do not have the personnel to prepare an advertising campaign, should seek the services of a(n)
    a. merchants' association.
    b. advertising agency.
    c. public relations firm.
    d. referral agency.
    e. trade affiliation.

38. Closing the sale is considered the critical point in the selling process. Many sales people use a trial closing. Based on an assumption that the customer is going to buy, which of the following statements is an appropriate trial closing?
    a. "Will you be placing an order, Mrs. Johnston?"
    b. "Do you want the standard or the deluxe model?"
    c. "Here's my card. Give me a call if you would like to place an order."
    d. "Shall I give you a week to consider the offer?"
    e. "I'll put you down for the deluxe model. Is that your natural hair color?"

Short-Answer Questions (A)

Complete each question.

39. What is the major role of **promotion**?

40. Identify and describe the major ingredients of a **promotion mix**.

INGREDIENT	DESCRIPTION OF EACH INGREDIENT

41. Explain the **purpose** of each type of advertising and give an example for each type.

TYPE OF ADVERTISING	PURPOSE OF EACH TYPE	EXAMPLES
Primary-demand		
Institutional		
Selective		

42. List advantages and disadvantages for each **print media**.

PRINT MEDIA	ADVANTAGES	DISADVANTAGES
Newspapers		
Magazines		
Direct-mail		
Outdoor		

43. Identify who would use each **electronic medium**.

ELECTRONIC MEDIA	EXAMPLES OF USERS
Television	
Radio	
Internet	

PRACTICE EXAMINATION B

Matching Questions (B)

Match each term with a statement.

a. cooperative advertising
b. direct-mail advertising
c. outdoor advertising
d. advertising agency
e. personal selling

f. order taker
g. creative selling
h. missionary salesperson
i. frequent-user incentive
j. buying allowance

_____ 1. An arrangement by which costs are shared by producer and retailer.
_____ 2. The most adaptable of all promotional methods.
_____ 3. Explains benefits of products and creates goodwill.
_____ 4. The most selective medium for advertising products.
_____ 5. Processes the purchases of customers.
_____ 6. Billboards, signs, and skywriting are examples.
_____ 7. Determines customers' needs and matches products with those needs.
_____ 8. An independent firm that plans, produces, and places advertising.
_____ 9. An incentive to resellers to handle new products.
_____ 10. It helps build customer loyalty.

True-False Questions (B)

Select the correct answer.

T F 11. Publicity is a nonpersonal, paid form of promotion.
T F 12. The focus of primary-demand advertising is image building.
T F 13. Comparing two brands of toothpaste on television is illegal.
T F 14. Newspapers account for just over 20 percent of all advertising expenditures.
T F 15. Advertisers can reach very specific market segments through ads in special-interest magazines.
T F 16. Billboards are especially suitable for products that lend themselves to pictorial display.
T F 17. Radio advertising offers a high degree of selectivity.
T F 18. Advertising encourages competition.
T F 19. Most retail clerks are simply order getters.
T F 20. Sales promotions can effectively boost sales to current customers.
T F 21. The news release is the least used type of publicity.
T F 22. The content and timing of publicity are not controlled by the affected firm.
T F 23. Advertising and personal selling make up the entire field of promotion.
T F 24. Advertising can be broadly classified into three groups: selective, institutional, and primary-demand.

Multiple-Choice Questions (B)

Circle the letter before the most accurate answer.

25. The American Express television promotion, "Don't Leave Home Without It," is an example of
    a. creative selling.
    b. public relations.
    c. publicity.
    d. advertising.
    e. refunding.

26. Retailers use newspaper advertising extensively because
    a. it is reasonable in cost.
    b. it provides local coverage.
    c. it is timely.
    d. ads can be placed on short-term notice.
    e. of all of the above reasons.

27. One argument against advertising is that it
    a. can be deceptive.
    b. encourages competition.
    c. provides job opportunities.
    d. pays for news coverage.
    e. is too inexpensive.

28. L'eggs hosiery is generally promoted in
    a. point-of-purchase displays.
    b. promotional campaigns.
    c. cooperative advertising.
    d. push strategies.
    e. comparative advertising.

29. When a firm wants to increase sales of its products and services, what would you suggest?
    a. Select the appropriate channel of distribution.
    b. Select the best manufacturer for its products.
    c. Don't worry; intelligent people will find good products.
    d. Select the appropriate promotional activities.
    e. Avoid expensive advertising.

30. The job of a trade salesperson is to
    a. explain how a computer works.
    b. persuade retailers to buy a manufacturer's product.
    c. assist retailers by restocking shelves or setting up displays.
    d. install the equipment and test it.
    e. provide follow-up service.

31. When a college district uses the local television and radio stations to advertise the benefits of getting an education, it is using _____ advertising.
    a. institutional
    b. primary-demand
    c. immediate-response
    d. reminder
    e. comparative

32. NCR is introducing a new electronic cash register and it wants to include detailed explanations in its advertisements. NCR will *most likely* use
    a. billboards.
    b. mass transit.
    c. television.
    d. radio.
    e. magazines.

33. Which of the following is a factor in determining rates for radio advertising?
    a. The number of people expected to hear the commercial
    b. The number of people located in the geographic area
    c. The type of product or service to be promoted
    d. The type of station to be used and the time period specified
    e. How the product or service will be used

34. Creative selling involves perceiving buyers' needs, supplying information about a firm's products, and persuading customers to buy the product. Which type of salesperson does this job?
    a. Order getter
    b. Trade
    c. Missionary
    d. Order taker
    e. Technical

35. When Best Hair Products offers marketing assistance to resellers that buy its products, it is engaging in what type of promotion technique?
    a. Bribe
    b. Bait-and-switch method
    c. Consumer-product promotion technique
    d. Consumer-sales promotion technique
    e. Trade-sales promotion method

36. When the public accounting firm of Deloitte & Touche helps underwrite certain productions at the Theater Center, it is using a
    a. point-of-purchase activity.
    b. sales promotion.
    c. public-relations activity.
    d. community service activity.
    e. cooperative advertising.

Short-Answer Questions (B)

Complete each question.

37. Identify the major **steps in developing an advertising campaign**, and briefly describe what happens in each step.

STEPS IN AN ADVERTISING CAMPAIGN	DESCRIPTION OF EACH STEP
1.	
2.	
3.	
4.	
5.	
6.	
7.	
8.	

38. Critics argue that **advertising is wasteful and it can be deceptive**. Provide four arguments against their position.

a. _____

_____

b. _____

_____

c. _____

_____

d. _____

_____

39. Give an example for each **type of salesperson**.

TYPES OF SALESPEOPLE	EXAMPLES
Order getters	
Order takers	
Support personnel	

40. What is the job of each category of sales **support personnel**?

TYPES OF SALES SUPPORT PERSONNEL	DESCRIPTION OF THEIR JOB
Missionary salesperson	
Trade salesperson	
Technical salesperson	

41. List the steps in the **personal-selling process**.

STEPS IN THE PERSONAL-SELLING PROCESS	ACTIVITIES IN EACH STEP
	Research potential buyers. Choose likely customers. Concentrate on financial resources of prospects.
	Understand customer's situation. Make a good first impression. Use knowledge of prospect's needs.
	Demonstrate the product. Point out the product's features and benefits. Provide referrals of satisfied customers.
	Ask questions. Point out additional features. Mention special services the company offers.
	Ask the prospect to buy the product. Use trial closing. "When would you want delivery?"
	Ensure the product is delivered on time. Ensure product is in proper operating condition. Be available in case problems develop.

PRACTICE EXAMINATION C

Matching Questions (C)

Match each term with a statement.

a. sales promotion
b. rebate
c. cents-off coupon
d. sample
e. premium
f. news release
g. point-of-purchase display

h. trade show
i. publicity
j. public relations
k. promotional campaign
l. positioning
m. sales-support personnel
n. feature article

_____ 1. Part of the purchase price is returned to the customer.
_____ 2. A gift in return for using a product.
_____ 3. An industry-wide exhibit of products and services.
_____ 4. A plan using various promotional methods.
_____ 5. Information prepared exclusively for a particular publication.
_____ 6. Cash refunds, samples, and coupons are examples.
_____ 7. Most widely used type of publicity.
_____ 8. Free printed or broadcast information about products, employees, or a company.
_____ 9. The process of developing an image for a product.
_____ 10. Reduces the retail price at the time of purchase.
_____ 11. A device that holds merchandise for promotional purposes.
_____ 12. It involves all activities to create a favorable public image.
_____ 13. Locating prospects is a major objective.
_____ 14. A product is given to a potential customer.

True-False Questions (C)

Select the correct answer.

T F 15. The largest share of the business advertising dollar goes to magazines.
T F 16. Brand advertising is the most common type of advertising.
T F 17. AT&T uses institutional advertising.
T F 18. An advantage for using newspaper advertising is its long life span.
T F 19. When quality color reproduction is required, newspapers should be used.
T F 20. It is best to use only one type of promotion medium for selling multiple products.
T F 21. Kmart is the nation's leading advertiser.
T F 22. Advertising is a detriment to the mass communications media.
T F 23. A prospect is a potential buyer.
T F 24. Couponing has recently been declared illegal in the United States.
T F 25. A cents-off coupon increases the retail price of an item at the time of purchase.
T F 26. "Don't leave home without it" is an example of a promotional campaign theme.
T F 27. A refund is a gift that producers offer customers for using their product.
T F 28. Positioning develops a product image in buyers' minds relative to the images they have of competing products.

Multiple-Choice Questions (C)

Circle the letter before the most accurate answer.

29. A Coca-Cola advertisement on television is an example of _____ advertising.
    a. selective
    b. immediate-response
    c. reminder
    d. comparative
    e. cooperative

30. When a manufacturer and middleman share advertising expenditures, it is called
    a. cooperative advertising.
    b. institutional advertising.
    c. a promotional campaign.
    d. a promotional mix.
    e. comparative advertising.

31. Television advertising
    a. has a long life span.
    b. is inexpensive.
    c. reaches the mass market.
    d. has a short placement time.
    e. is effective for target markets.

32. After answering objections in the personal-selling process, the next step is to
    a. make the presentation.
    b. prospect.
    c. close the sale.
    d. approach the prospect.
    e. follow up on the prospect.

33. Which statement is *not* true about advertising?
    a. Most advertising is deceptive and wasteful.
    b. Advertising encourages competition.
    c. Advertising revenues support our mass communications media.
    d. Advertising is the least expensive means of communicating product information to millions of consumers.
    e. Advertising provides job opportunities in fields ranging from sales to film production.

34. When Sears advertises appliances, financial services, auto repair services, home remodeling services, and insurance products all in one ad, Sears is
    a. appealing only to market segments.
    b. confusing the consumers.
    c. using comparative advertising.
    d. communicating simultaneously different messages to different target markets.
    e. using cooperative advertising.

35. Coupons seem to work *best* for
    a. reminding customers to keep buying the product.
    b. older citizens.
    c. new and improved products.
    d. old established products.
    e. fresh food items.

36. The *most* common type of Internet ad is a(n)
    a. sponsorship ad.
    b. banner ad.
    c. button ad.
    d. publicity.
    e. infomercial.

37. What type of advertisement is used when a producer, like Revlon, and a retailer, like Macy's, share the cost of advertising a cosmetic product?
    a. Institutional
    b. Long-term
    c. Primary-demand
    d. Cooperative
    e. Comparative

38. Advertising campaigns are developed to
    a. increase product awareness.
    b. convey product information.
    c. increase sales by a stated percentage.
    d. expand the market share by a given amount.
    e. accomplish all of the above items.

Short-Answer Questions (C)

Complete each question.

39. What is the **purpose** of each sales **promotion method**?

    a. Consumer sales promotion method

    b. Trade sales promotion method

40. What is each **sales promotion method** designed to do?

SALES PROMOTION METHODS	PURPOSE OF EACH METHOD
Rebates	
Coupons	
Samples	
Premiums	
Frequent user incentives	
Point-of-purchase displays	
Trade shows	
Buying allowances	
Cooperative advertising	

41. List four types of **publicity** and give an example for each type.

TYPES OF PUBLICITY	EXAMPLES

42. What is the **purpose** of a **promotional campaign**?

43. Why is **positioning a product** important?

44. How can **promotion** help **further marketing objectives**?

MARKETING OBJECTIVES	PROMOTION ASSISTANCE
Provide information	
Increase market share	
Position the product	

CHAPTER 17

ACQUIRING, ORGANIZING, AND USING INFORMATION

Key Terms

Define each term briefly. Writing down the definition and giving an example will help you learn the term.

data (p. 481)

information (p. 482)

database (p. 482)

management information system (MIS) (p. 482)

data processing (p. 487)

statistic (p. 487)

frequency distribution (p. 488)

arithmetic mean (p. 488)

median (p. 488)

mode (p. 489)

range (p. 489)

qualitative research (p. 492)

quantitative research (p. 493)

information society (p. 494)

Internet (p. 494)

telecommunications (p. 494)

intranet (p. 495)

groupware (p. 499)

collaborative learning system (p. 499)

database management program (p. 503)

graphics program (p. 503)

spreadsheet program (p. 503)

word processing program (p. 504)

desktop publishing program (p. 504)

accounting program (p. 504)

communications program (p. 504)

PRACTICE EXAMINATION A

Matching Questions

Match each term with a statement.

a. data
b. information
c. management information system
d. database

e. data processing
f. statistic
g. frequency distribution
h. intranet

_____ 1. Data that have been processed.

_____ 2. Numerical or verbal descriptions resulting from a measurement.

_____ 3. A way of dispensing vast amounts of information to people.

_____ 4. Lists the number of times a value appears in the data set.

_____ 5. A collection of data generally stored in one place.

_____ 6. Transforms data into useful information.

_____ 7. Summarizes a particular characteristic of a group of numbers.

_____ 8. It can access a firm's policy documents.

True-False Questions (A)

Select the correct answer.

T F 9. Data include both numerical and verbal facts.

T F 10. Human resources managers need information about wage levels and benefits.

T F 11. It is crucial that an MIS be tailored to the firm's needs.

T F 12. Administrative managers are most concerned about the state of the economy.

T F 13. Content analysis may involve measuring particular items in a written publication.

T F 14. Information rules are the highest order of information organization and structure.

T F 15. The recommendation section of a business report lists the findings.

T F 16. Sales reports are a source of internal data.

T F 17. *The Wall Street Journal* and the *Monthly Labor Review* are examples of external sources of information.

T F 18. Data processing transforms information into data.

T F 19. To find the mode, add 10, 12, and 40, and divide the total by 4.

T F 20. Pie charts are useful in illustrating the importance of various items to the whole.

T F 21. Most data gathered for an MIS come from external sources.

T F 22. The purpose of an MIS is to distribute timely and useful information.

T F 23. The cost of collecting data should be weighed against the potential benefits.

Multiple-Choice Questions (A)

Circle the letter before the most accurate answer.

24. Which of the following is considered to be data?
    a. A description of an individual
    b. A report on the results of the project
    c. Numerical information only
    d. Processed numbers
    e. Projected sales figures based on last quarter's results

25. Operations managers are concerned with
    a. target markets.
    b. union activities.
    c. coordination of information.
    d. new technology.
    e. product mix.

26. A software program that allows the user to prepare and edit letters and store them on disk is called a _____ program.
    a. spreadsheet
    b. word processing
    c. graphics
    d. communications
    e. database

27. External sources of information include
    a. inventory records.
    b. production costs.
    c. bankers.
    d. sales forecasts.
    e. budgets.

28. The *most* accurate visual display is a
    a. bar chart.
    b. column.
    c. pie chart.
    d. spreadsheet.
    e. graph.

29. A work environment that allows problem-solving participation by all team members is called a
    a. word processing program.
    b. collaborative learning system.
    c. web browser.
    d. management information system.
    e. data processing system.

30. Which type of software package allows users to prepare text and graphics in high-quality, professional-looking reports, newsletters, and pamphlets?
    a. Spreadsheet programs
    b. Desktop publishing programs
    c. Word processing programs
    d. Graphics programs
    e. Database management programs

31. The goal of a management information system is to
    a. provide needed information to all managers.
    b. train the workers in their technical areas.
    c. understand the data.
    d. screen information and provide only what is needed.
    e. All of the above are correct.

32. Which of the following is an external source for data?
    a. Company records
    b. Last year's sales reports
    c. Minutes of meetings
    d. Customer service complaints
    e. Suppliers' forecasts

33. What is the mode in the following array, 8, 0, 3, 5, 8, 1, 9, 7, 6, 4, 8, 6, 2?
    a. 0
    b. 3
    c. 6
    d. 8
    e. 9

Short-Answer Questions (A)

Complete each question.

34. Discuss how information affects the **level of risk** in decision making.

35. What are **information rules**? How do they simplify the process for making decisions?

36. Compare **data** with **information**. How are they different?

DATA	INFORMATION

37. Describe the **purpose** of an **MIS**.

38. Explain why a **management information system** must be tailored to the needs of the organization it serves.

39. Identify special types of information that **managers** need to do their job.

TYPES OF MANAGERS	TYPES OF INFORMATION NEEDED BY EACH TYPE OF MANAGER
Financial managers	
Operations managers	
Marketing managers	
Human resources managers	
Administrative managers	

40. Describe what happens in each **function** of an MIS.

FUNCTIONS OF AN MIS	DESCRIPTION OF EACH FUNCTION
Collecting data	
Storing and updating data	
Processing data	
Presenting data	

PRACTICE EXAMINATION B

Matching Questions (B)

Match each term with a statement.

a. information society
b. Internet
c. telecommunications
d. groupware
e. collaborative learning system

f. accounting program
g. word processing program
h. data management program
i. qualitative research
j. quantitative research

_____ 1. Descriptive or subjective reporting of information is involved.
_____ 2. A worldwide network of computers linked through telecommunications.
_____ 3. It enables the user to record and report financial information.
_____ 4. Employees at various locations can keep track as work progresses.
_____ 5. The process involves the collection of numerical data.
_____ 6. Large groups of employees depend on information to do their job.
_____ 7. A work environment that allows groups to solve problems.
_____ 8. It is a merger of computers and telephone technologies.
_____ 9. Personalized collection letters can be designed on this program.
_____ 10. A program that transfers data into information and stores it.

True-False Questions (B)

Select the correct answer.

T F 11. Financial managers are most concerned with a firm's product mix and products offered by competitors.
T F 12. Administrative managers ensure that all employees have access to information.
T F 13. A computer can perform all functions of a management information system.
T F 14. When the amount of information is high, there is more risk.
T F 15. Information rules lengthen the time required to make decisions.
T F 16. Future forecasts should not be used in an MIS.
T F 17. Information gathered from trade journals is considered primary data.
T F 18. A statistic summarizes the characteristic for an entire group.
T F 19. A major way to conduct quantitative research is to use focus groups.
T F 20. Visual displays have less impact than tabular displays.
T F 21. MIS is defined as a system of connected computers revolving around a mainframe or minicomputer.
T F 22. Data processing transforms data into useful information.
T F 23. Pie charts are most useful for presenting comparisons between related variables.

Multiple-Choice Questions (B)

Circle the letter before the most accurate answer.

24. Who needs management information?
    a. Marketing managers
    b. Operations managers
    c. Administrative managers
    d. Financial managers
    e. All of the above need information.

25. Management information systems
    a. collect data, hire personnel, and compensate workers.
    b. store data, present data to users, and make final decisions.
    c. collect, store and update, process, and present data.
    d. supervise personnel, reprimand workers, and conduct follow-ups.
    e. collect relevant information and present useful data.

26. What is the first step in using an MIS?
    a. Analyzing data
    b. Processing data
    c. Presenting information
    d. Storing and updating data
    e. Collecting data

27. The arithmetic mean measures the
    a. value in the middle of an array.
    b. average of the numbers.
    c. number that appears the most times.
    d. difference between the numbers.
    e. total.

28. An example of a spreadsheet software program is
    a. WordPerfect.
    b. Microsoft Word.
    c. Lotus 1-2-3.
    d. Desktop Publishing.
    e. Ventura.

29. When comparing two or more related variables, it is *best* to use
    a. tabular displays.
    b. graphs.
    c. bar charts.
    d. pie charts.
    e. visual displays.

30. To connect to a site on the Internet, enter the _____ in the web browser.
    a. intranet
    b. LAN
    c. ISP
    d. URL
    e. search engine

31. A management information system must be capable of presenting the information in a usable form. Which item below is *not* appropriate for presenting the information in report format?
    a. The introduction describes the problem and techniques used to gather data.
    b. The body of the report describes the facts.
    c. The conclusions describe the findings.
    d. The recommendations present suggestions for solving the problem.
    e. A summary that rebukes the polices of the firm.

32. In the following array, 5, 8, 9, 5, 3, 4, 5, 1, 1, 3, 6, the median number is
    a. 1.
    b. 3.
    c. 5.
    d. 9.
    e. undeterminable.

33. Which visual display can effectively emphasize trends?
    a. Pie chart
    b. Graph
    c. Tabular display
    d. Bar chart
    e. Array

Short-Answer Questions (B)

Complete each question.

34. List examples of **internal** and **external** sources of information.

INTERNAL SOURCES	EXTERNAL SOURCES

35. Several **cautions** must be observed in collecting data. List them.

a. _____

b. _____

c. _____

36. Discuss several key factors that determine how often **data is updated** and whether a manual or automatic system is used.

37. Using the numbers 2, 1, 5, 1 and 6 **calculate** the following **measures**.

a. Median _____   b. Mode _____

c. Mean _____   d. Range _____

e. Frequency distribution _____

38. Identify the parts of a typical **business report** and describe each part.

PARTS OF A BUSINESS REPORT	DESCRIPTION OF EACH PART

39. Explain how each type of **visual display** can be used in a report.

TYPES OF VISUAL DISPLAYS	EXAMPLES OF HOW EACH TYPE OF VISUAL DISPLAY CAN BE USED MOST EFFECTIVELY
Graph	
Bar chart	
Pie chart	

40. Contrast **qualitative research** to **quantitative research**. Give an example for each.

QUALITATIVE RESEARCH	QUANTITATIVE RESEARCH
Example:	Example:

41. Identify three **methods** used by business researchers to conduct **qualitative** and three methods for doing **quantitative** research.

QUALITATIVE RESEARCH	QUANTITATIVE RESEARCH

42. List three factors that determine the **research method** to choose in conducting research.

a. _____

b. _____

c. _____

PRACTICE EXAMINATION C

Matching Questions (C)

Match each term with a statement.

a. arithmetic mean
b. median
c. mode
d. range
e. visual display
f. bar chart

g. pie chart
h. tabular display
i. spreadsheet program
j. graphics program
k. desktop publishing program
l. communications program

_____ 1. The value that appears the most times in a data set.
_____ 2. Display in which each value is represented as a vertical or horizontal bar.
_____ 3. The most commonly used measure.
_____ 4. The difference between the highest and lowest value in a set of data.
_____ 5. Values are depicted as a portion of a circle.
_____ 6. The middle value in an array of numbers.
_____ 7. A diagram presenting information.
_____ 8. Presents information in columns or rows.
_____ 9. Organizes numerical data in grids of rows and columns.
_____ 10. Enables users to combine text with graphics.
_____ 11. Enables users to display and print pictures.
_____ 12. E-mail is its most popular function.

True-False Questions (C)

Select the correct answer.

T F 13. A word processing program is the best software for reporting financial information.
T F 14. An MIS must collect, store, update, process, and present information.
T F 15. Concerns about security issues on the Internet are expected to decrease in the future.
T F 16. For the financial institution, online banking is often cheaper than traditional banking activities.
T F 17. Surveys typically compare two or more groups of people.
T F 18. E-business transactions have found Visa's "Next Card" to be a failure.
T F 19. America Online is an example of an Internet service provider.
T F 20. TCP/IP allow computers from all over the world to communicate with each other.
T F 21. Frequency distribution increases the number of data items.
T F 22. Graphs are useful in comparing several pieces of information.
T F 23. FrontPage can be used to develop web pages.
T F 24. Interviews are used in conducting qualitative research.
T F 25. Data entered into an MIS must be relevant, accurate, timely, and useful.

Multiple-Choice Questions (C)

Select the most accurate answer.

26. Marketing managers need detailed information about
    a. personnel.
    b. pricing strategies.
    c. logistics.
    d. inventory costs.
    e. interest rates.

27. Software that uses both a firm's server and an employee's personal computer is called
    a. a data-based management program.
    b. a browser.
    c. integrated software.
    d. a decision support system.
    e. groupware.

28. The *most* common used network for finding information on the Internet is the
    a. World Wide Web.
    b. home page.
    c. local area network.
    d. URL.
    e. intranet.

29. Three common problems associated with collecting data are
    a. costs, forecasts, and predictions.
    b. judgments, mistakes, and accuracy.
    c. storage, personnel, and completeness.
    d. costs, mistakes, and accuracy.
    e. costs, sources, and information.

30. As an administrative manager, you must ensure that
    a. information is protected.
    b. all employees have access to information.
    c. the smart group receives the data first.
    d. the promotional campaigns are aired on time.
    e. new product planning is on schedule.

31. Online recruiting web sites can
    a. help match up job seekers with businesses seeking employees.
    b. serve as a clearing house for job seekers and employers.
    c. help attract job applicants from outside the area.
    d. expand the job search for job seekers.
    e. All of the above are true.

32. Integrated software packages
    a. combine many functions in one package.
    b. allow easy linking of text, graphs, photos, and audio clips.
    c. allow dissemination electronically through a firm's MIS.
    d. can send information through the Internet.
    e. can do all the above tasks.

33. When the number of items in the set is divided into the total value of all the numbers in the set, what is the answer called?
    a. Median
    b. Mean
    c. Standard deviation
    d. Variance
    e. Mode

34. What is the range in the following array of numbers: 8, 6, 1, 3, 4, 7, 9, 5, 3?
    a. 3
    b. 9
    c. 8
    d. 7
    e. 2

35. A single collection of data stored in one place and used by employees throughout the organization is called a(n)
    a. data collection.
    b. information center.
    c. database.
    d. data center.
    e. management data center.

Short-Answer Questions (C)

Complete each question.

36. Explain the purpose of each **Internet** element.

INTERNET ELEMENT	PURPOSE
World Wide Web (www)	
Internet service provider (ISP)	
Web browser	

37. Describe how an **intranet** differs from the **Internet**.

INTRANET	INTERNET

38. What does **TCP/IP** mean? What does it do?

39. What is the role of each of the following?

    a. URL

    b. Search engine (Alta Vista, Yahoo!)

40. From a cost/benefit position, how can the **Internet** help a business with each activity?

ACTIVITY	COST/BENEFIT
Communication	
Sales	
Training	
Recruiting	
Financial services	

41. List examples of how a firm can use each type of **software program**.

SOFTWARE PROGRAMS	EXAMPLES OF USE
Database management	
Graphics	
Spreadsheets	
Word processing	
Desktop publishing	
Accounting	
Communications	
CAD, CAM, CIM	

CHAPTER 18

USING ACCOUNTING INFORMATION

Key Terms

Define each term briefly. Writing down the definition and giving an example will help you learn the term.

accounting (p. 513)

private accountant (p. 515)

public accountant (p. 515)

certified public accountant (CPA) (p. 516)

assets (p. 517)

liabilities (p. 517)

owners' equity (p. 517)

accounting equation (p. 517)

double-entry bookkeeping (p. 517)

general journal (p. 518)

general ledger (p. 518)

posting (p. 518)

trial balance (p. 518)

balance sheet (or statement of financial position) (p. 519)

liquidity (p. 519)

current assets (p. 520)

prepaid expenses (p. 521)

fixed assets (p. 522)

depreciation (p. 522)

intangible assets (p. 523)

goodwill (p. 523)

current liabilities (p. 523)

accounts payable (p. 523)

notes payable (p. 523)

long-term liabilities (p. 523)

retained earnings (p. 524)

income statement (p. 524)

revenues (p. 525)

gross sales (p. 526)

net sales (p. 526)

cost of goods sold (p. 526)

gross profit (p. 526)

operating expenses (p. 526)

net income (p. 527)

statement of cash flows (p. 527)

audit (p. 529)

financial ratio (p. 530)

return on sales (p. 531)

return on owners' equity (p. 531)

earnings per share (p. 532)

current ratio (p. 532)

acid-test ratio (p. 532)

accounts receivable turnover (p. 533)

inventory turnover (p. 533)

debt-to-owners' equity ratio (p. 533)

PRACTICE EXAMINATION A

Matching Questions (A-1)

Match each term with a statement.

a. accounting
b. double-entry bookkeeping
c. private accountant
d. public accountant
e. certified public accountant

f. assets
g. liabilities
h. owners' equity
i. accounting equation
j. audit

_____ 1. It is the process of collecting, analyzing, and reporting data.
_____ 2. It is a firm's debts.
_____ 3. Two separate accounting entries are required.
_____ 4. It is the difference between a firm's assets and its liabilities.
_____ 5. A person employed by IBM.
_____ 6. An accountant employed by PricewaterhouseCoopers.
_____ 7. An accountant who can sign an audit.
_____ 8. It shows the relationship between assets, liabilities, and owners' equity.
_____ 9. Inventories are an example.
_____ 10. Generally accepted accounting principles are involved.

Matching Questions (A-2)

Match each term with a statement.

a. accounts receivable turnover
b. fixed assets
c. general journal
d. general ledger
e. posting

f. trial balance
g. balance sheet
h. liquidity
i. retained earnings
j. statement of cash flows

_____ 11. The number of times a firm collects on its accounts receivable in one year.
_____ 12. The process of transferring journal entries to the general ledger.
_____ 13. The ease with which assets can be converted into cash.
_____ 14. It is the book for original entry.
_____ 15. It summarizes all ledger account balances.
_____ 16. It holds all the accounts for the firm.
_____ 17. This statement gives the financial position of the firm.
_____ 18. Buildings are an example.
_____ 19. Profits that are not distributed to stockholders.
_____ 20. It illustrates how operating, investing, and financing activities affect cash.

True-False Questions (A)

Select the correct answer.

T F 21. Managers are the primary users of a firm's accounting information.
T F 22. Public accountants are responsible for collecting the financial data that is processed by the accounting system.
T F 23. Accounting systems transform information into financial data.
T F 24. The accounting equation is "assets + liabilities = owners' equity."
T F 25. The trial balance summarizes the balances of all ledger accounts.
T F 26. Marketable securities are a firm's most liquid assets.
T F 27. The market value of a patent is listed as a current asset on the balance sheet.
T F 28. Revenues plus cost of goods sold plus operating expenses equals net income from operations.
T F 29. Many firms compare their financial data with those of competing firms.
T F 30. Return on equity indicates a measure of the amount earned per share.
T F 31. A firm can reduce a high debt-to-asset ratio by restricting its borrowing.
T F 32. A balance sheet is a summary of the firm's revenues and expenses.
T F 33. Posting is the process of recording transactions in the general journal.

Multiple-Choice Questions (A)

Circle the letter before the most accurate answer.

34. Deloitte Touche Tohmatsu hires
    a. bookkeepers.
    b. public accountants.
    c. ledger keepers.
    d. private accountants.
    e. recordkeepers.

35. Assets, liabilities, and owners' equity are found on the
    a. income statement.
    b. balance sheet.
    c. cash-flows statement.
    d. trial balance.
    e. earnings statement.

36. A building is considered a(n)
    a. liability.
    b. current asset.
    c. current liability.
    d. fixed asset.
    e. intangible asset.

37. Accountants generally
    a. supervise workers in operations.
    b. collect overdue payments from creditors.
    c. design accounting systems for businesses.
    d. provide credit reports to customers.
    e. coordinate the activities of MIS.

38. Which statement is *not* true about a balance sheet?
    a. It provides a "financial picture" of the firm at a particular time.
    b. It lists the current, fixed, and intangible assets.
    c. It summarizes the firm's operations during one accounting period.
    d. It gives the liabilities of the firm.
    e. It shows the owner's equity in the business.

39. The total must balance on a _____ before other financial statements can be prepared.
    a. general journal
    b. ledger
    c. balance sheet
    d. trial balance
    e. cash flows

40. What is an example of an intangible asset?
    a. Cash
    b. Goodwill
    c. Inventory
    d. Accounts receivables
    e. Securities

41. The board of directors decided to pay 50 percent of the $460,000 earnings in dividends to the stockholders. The firm has retained earnings of $680,000 on the books. After the dividends are paid, which of the following statements is true about the total owner's equity?
    a. The current value of the firm's retained earnings is $910,000.
    b. The current value of the firm's retained earnings is $450,000.
    c. The firm failed to reach its profit goal.
    d. Each shareholder will receive more than he or she received last year.
    e. The firm's retained earnings are too high.

42. A firm had gross profits from sales in the amount of $180,000, operating expenses of $90,000, and federal income taxes of $20,000. What was the firm's net income after taxes?
    a. $10,000
    b. $20,000
    c. $70,000
    d. $90,000
    e. $200,000

43. Last year a furniture store had an average inventory of $40,000, and its cost of goods sold was $200,000. How many times did the store replace its inventory last year?
    a. One time
    b. Twice
    c. Three times
    d. Four times
    e. Five times

Short-Answer Questions (A)

Complete each question.

44. Compare a **private accountant** to a **public accountant**. What are their differences?

PRIVATE ACCOUNTANT	PUBLIC ACCOUNTANT

45. Why is a firm's **accounting information** important? Identify ways each group uses a firm's financial information.

GROUPS	WAYS EACH GROUP USES ACCOUNTING INFORMATION
Managers	
Lenders	
Stockholders and potential investors	
Government	

46. Explain the requirements for becoming a **CPA**.

47. Identify the **accounting equation**.

A_____ = L_____ + O_____ E_____

48. Explain the purpose of **double-entry bookkeeping**.

49. Briefly describe what happens in each step of the **accounting cycle**.

STEPS IN THE ACCOUNTING CYCLE	DESCRIPTION
Analyzing source documents	
Recording transactions	
Posting transactions	
Preparing the trial balance	
Preparing financial statements and closing the books	

PRACTICE EXAMINATION B

Matching Questions (B-1)

Match each term with a statement.

a. current assets
b. prepaid expenses
c. fixed assets
d. depreciation

e. intangible assets
f. goodwill
g. current liabilities
h. accounts payable

_____ 1. Assets that are paid in advance.
_____ 2. Trademarks are an example.
_____ 3. Credit obligations that must be paid within a year.
_____ 4. Cash is an example.
_____ 5. The value of a firm's reputation is an example.
_____ 6. It is a category that comprises land and buildings.
_____ 7. It includes debts that must be paid within one year.
_____ 8. The cost of a fixed asset is spread over its useful life.

Matching Questions (B-2)

Match each term with a statement.

a. notes payable
b. long-term liabilities
c. income statement
d. revenues

e. gross sales
f. net sales
g. cost of goods sold
h. gross profit on sales

_____ 9. Money received by a firm.

_____ 10. The amount a firm spends on the goods it sells.

_____ 11. Debts that are paid over a long period of time.

_____ 12. The amount left after adjustment for sales returns, allowances, and discounts.

_____ 13. It shows the earnings for the company.

_____ 14. The result of net sales less cost of goods sold.

_____ 15. A long-term obligation.

_____ 16. The total dollar amount of goods and services that have been sold.

True-False Questions (B)

Select the correct answer.

T F 17. The *Occupational Outlook Quarterly* forecasts a decline in the demand for accountants between now and the year 2008.

T F 18. All public accountants may officially verify the financial contents of a corporation's annual report.

T F 19. Accounts payable are an asset of the firm.

T F 20. Sales slips and invoices are accounting source documents.

T F 21. The income statement provides a picture of what a firm owns and what it owes at a certain time.

T F 22. Insurance premiums represent prepaid expenses.

T F 23. Accounts payable are long-term financial obligations.

T F 24. Price reductions offered to customers who accept slightly damaged or soiled merchandise are called sales allowances.

T F 25. Salespersons' salaries and advertising costs are considered general expenses on the income statement.

T F 26. Working capital is the amount remaining after a firm has paid its current liabilities with cash and other current assets.

T F 27. Use the debt-to-owners' equity ratio to compare the amount of financing provided by creditors with the amount provided by owners.

T F 28. The acid-test ratio measures the number of times the firm collects its accounts receivable in one year.

T F 29. The balance sheet is the firm's statement of financial position.

Multiple-Choice Questions (B)

Circle the letter before the most accurate answer.

30. A certified public accountant is required to
    a. pass a state examination.
    b. have accounting experience.
    c. have taken accounting courses in college.
    d. do all of the above.
    e. do only "a" and "c" above.

31. In which stage of the accounting cycle is the trial balance prepared?
    a. First
    b. Second
    c. Third
    d. Fourth
    e. Fifth

32. Goodwill is considered a(n)
    a. fixed asset.
    b. intangible asset.
    c. current liability.
    d. current asset.
    e. liability.

33. The difference between $150,000 in current assets and $90,000 in current liabilities is the firm's
    a. return on equity.
    b. current ratio.
    c. working capital.
    d. net profit margin.
    e. owners' equity.

34. John Allen audits the financial statements of ABC, Inc. and issues an opinion regarding the acceptability of its accounting practices. He also consults with management about financial problems. By profession, John is probably a
    a. certified public accountant.
    b. private accountant.
    c. bookkeeper.
    d. vice president of finance.
    e. marketing manager.

35. Which ratio indicates how effectively a firm is transforming sales into profits?
    a. Return on equity ratio
    b. Earnings per share ratio
    c. Current ratio
    d. Acid-test ratio
    e. Net profit margin ratio

36. A firm has $150,000 in current assets and $50,000 in current liabilities. Which statement is true about this company?
    a. The current ratio is below the average ratio for all industries.
    b. The firm can pay off its current liabilities three times.
    c. The current assets are too high in comparison to the current liabilities.
    d. The company is near bankruptcy.
    e. The firm should reduce its dividend payments.

37. Accounts payable and salaries payable are examples of
    a. long-term liabilities.
    b. owners' equity.
    c. current liabilities.
    d. fixed assets.
    e. expenses.

38. Which statement is *not* true about the operating expenses listed on the income statement?
    a. They are the expenses directly related to the manufacture of products.
    b. They are the expenses related to the firm's marketing activities.
    c. They are the expenses incurred in managing the business.
    d. They are the expenses for salaries of office workers.
    e. They are the expenses for advertising.

39. How is working capital calculated?
    a. Current assets divided by current liabilities
    b. Current liabilities divided by current assets
    c. Current assets minus inventory
    d. Total liabilities divided by total assets
    e. Current assets minus current liabilities

40. Which ratio compares the amount of financing provided by creditors with the amount provided by owners?
    a. Acid-test ratio
    b. Current ratio
    c. Debt-to-assets ratio
    d. Debt-to-owners' equity ratio
    e. Return on equity ratio

Short-Answer Questions (B)

Complete each question.

41. Explain why fixed assets are **depreciated** on a balance sheet.

42. Contrast the differences between a **balance sheet** and an **income statement**.

BALANCE SHEET	INCOME STATEMENT

43. List examples for each type of **asset**.

ASSETS	EXAMPLES
Current assets	
Fixed assets	
Intangible assets	

44. Identify examples for each type of **liability**.

LIABILITIES	EXAMPLES
Current liabilities	
Long-term liabilities	

45. What does the **owner's equity** section of a corporation balance sheet say about the firm?

46. Explain how the **cost of goods** is calculated in an accounting period.

47. Show how **gross profit** is determined on an income statement.

48. List three ways firms generally use **net income after taxes**.

    a. _____

    b. _____

    c. _____

PRACTICE EXAMINATION C

Matching Questions (C)

Match each term with a statement.

a. operating expenses
b. selling expenses
c. general expenses
d. net income
e. financial ratio
f. return on sales
g. return on equity

h. earnings per share
i. working capital
j. current ratio
k. acid-test ratio
l. inventory turnover
m. debt-to-assets ratio
n. debt-to-owners' equity ratio

_____ 1. Selling expenses are an example.
_____ 2. It shows the relationship between sales and net profit.
_____ 3. They are the expenses related to a firm's marketing activities.
_____ 4. It is determined by dividing the net income after taxes by the net sales.
_____ 5. They include depreciation on equipment.
_____ 6. Net income after taxes is divided by owners' equity.
_____ 7. It is the profit earned after all expenses are paid.
_____ 8. It is the difference between the current assets and the current liabilities.
_____ 9. The number of times that inventory is replaced.
_____ 10. The result of dividing current assets by current liabilities.
_____ 11. It is the relationship between total liabilities and total assets.
_____ 12. Cash, marketable securities, accounts receivable, and notes receivable are divided by current liabilities.
_____ 13. Total liabilities are divided by owners' equity.
_____ 14. Net income after taxes is divided by the number of shares of common stock outstanding.

True-False Questions (C)

Select the correct answer.

T F 15. The return on equity ratio is an example of an activity ratio.
T F 16. Account information is management information.
T F 17. Merchandise inventories are the firm's owners' equity.
T F 18. The first step in the accounting cycle is to record the transaction in the general ledger.
T F 19. The ease with which an asset can be converted into cash is called liquidity.
T F 20. The process of writing off a portion of the purchase value of a piece of equipment is called depreciation.
T F 21. Owners' equity represents the total par value of a corporation's stock plus retained earnings that have accumulated to date.
T F 22. Net sales are the total dollar amount of all goods and services sold during an accounting period.
T F 23. A low net profit margin can be increased by reducing expenses.
T F 24. The acid-test ratio determines a firm's ability to pay current liabilities quickly.
T F 25. The current ratio is a measure of the firm's ability to pay current liabilities quickly.
T F 26. Owners' equity represents the owners' portion of the liabilities.
T F 27. Total assets minus owners' equity gives the amount of working capital that is available.

Multiple-Choice Questions (C)

Circle the letter before the most accurate answer.

28. Based on revenues, which certified public accounting firm is the largest?
    a. KPMG International
    b. Deloitte Touche Tohmatsu
    c. Ernst & Young International
    d. Andersen Worldwide
    e. PricewaterhouseCoopers

29. The accounting equation is
    a. assets = liabilities + owners' equity.
    b. liabilities + assets = owners' equity.
    c. owners' equity - assets = liabilities.
    d. assets = owners' equity = liabilities.
    e. owners' equity + assets = liabilities.

30. Taxes payable are
    a. long-term liabilities.
    b. current liabilities.
    c. intangible assets.
    d. fixed liabilities.
    e. owners' equity.

31. The average inventory turnover for all firms is _____ times a year.
    a. two
    b. three
    c. nine
    d. four
    e. six

32. Which group has the *least* amount of interest in a firm's accounting information?
    a. Investors
    b. Government agencies
    c. Managers
    d. Customers
    e. Creditors

33. Which statement is *not* true about the accounting equation?
    a. It forms the basis for the accounting process.
    b. It includes the resources that the firm owns.
    c. Law requires that it be used in calculating loan amounts.
    d. It includes the firm's debts and obligations.
    e. It includes the amount of owner's investment in the firm.

34. The last step in the accounting cycle is
    a. analyzing source documents.
    b. recording the transactions.
    c. posting transactions.
    d. preparing the trial balance.
    e. preparing the financial statement.

35. An income statement is sometimes called the
    a. income statement.
    b. balance statement.
    c. earnings statement.
    d. capital statement.
    e. owners' equity statement.

36. The results from taking the beginning inventory, adding the purchases and subtracting the ending inventory is
    a. net income before taxes.
    b. cost of goods sold.
    c. gross sales.
    d. net sales.
    e. gross profit on sales.

37. Which ratio measures an investor's return on common stock?
    a. Working capital ratio
    b. Debt-to-owners' equity ratio
    c. Net profit margin ratio
    d. Current ratio
    e. Earnings per share ratio

38. Which statement illustrates the effect on cash of the operating, investing, and financing activities of a company for an accounting period?
    a. Financial analysis statement
    b. Balance sheet
    c. Statement of cash flows
    d. Retained earnings statement
    e. Income statement

Short-Answer Questions (C)

Complete each question.

39. Explain the purpose of a **statement of cash flows**.

40. Explain why it is important to **compare a firm's current financial statements with those of the previous year**.

41. Explain the calculation procedure for the **profitability ratios**, and give a reason for each ratio.

PROFITABILITY RATIOS	CALCULATION PROCEDURES REASONS
Return on sales	Reason:
Return on owners' equity	Reason:
Earnings per share	Reason:

42. Give the calculation procedure for each **short-term financial ratio**, and give a reason for each ratio.

SHORT-TERM FINANCIAL RATIOS	CALCULATION PROCEDURES REASONS
Working capital	Reason:
Current ratio	Reason:
Acid-Test ratio	Reason:

43. State the calculation procedures for the **activity ratios**, and give a reason for each ratio.

ACTIVITY RATIOS	CALCULATION PROCEDURES REASONS
Accounts receivable turnover	Reason:
Inventory turnover	Reason:

44. Explain the meaning of a **debt-to-owner's equity ratio** of 48 percent.

45. Discuss what is being suggested for the future in accounting software and systems.

46. Identify problems in using outdated accounting software and systems.

CHAPTER 19

UNDERSTANDING MONEY, BANKING, AND CREDIT

Key Terms

Define each term briefly. Writing down the definition and giving an example will help you learn the term.

barter system (p. 546)

money (p. 547)

medium of exchange (p. 547)

measure of value (p. 547)

store of value (p. 547)

demand deposit (p. 549)

time deposit (p. 549)

Federal Reserve System (p. 550)

reserve requirement (p. 551)

discount rate (p. 552)

open-market operations (p. 552)

commercial bank (p. 555)

national bank (p. 556)

state bank (p. 556)

savings and loan association (S&L) (p. 556)

NOW account (p. 556)

mutual savings bank (p. 557)

credit union (p. 557)

check (p. 559)

certificate of deposit (CD) (p. 560)

line of credit (p. 560)

revolving credit agreement (p. 560)

collateral (p. 560)

debit card (p. 562)

electronic funds transfer (EFT) system (p. 564)

letter of credit (p. 565)

banker's acceptance (p. 565)

credit (p. 566)

PRACTICE EXAMINATION A

Matching Questions (A)

Match each term with a statement.

a. barter system
b. money
c. currency
d. medium of exchange
e. measure of value

f. store of value
g. demand deposits
h. time deposits
i. M_1 supply of money
j. M_2 supply of money

_____   1. Deposits in interest-bearing savings accounts.
_____   2. A system of exchanging goods and services.
_____   3. Anything acceptable as payment.
_____   4. A measure of currency and demand deposits.
_____   5. It serves as a medium of exchange.
_____   6. Money in checking accounts is an example.
_____   7. Paper money is an example.
_____   8. A standard used to assign values to products.
_____   9. A measure of currency, demand deposits, and time deposits.
_____ 10. A means of retaining and accumulating wealth.

True-False Questions (A)

Select the correct answer.

T F 11. Primitive societies used the barter system to exchange goods and services.
T F 12. Spending money on a new car is an example of how money creates a store of value.
T F 13. Paper money makes large amounts of currency easier to transport.
T F 14. The M_1 supply of money includes time deposits.
T F 15. Savings and loan associations have NOW accounts, savings accounts, and home-mortgage loans.
T F 16. The profits of savings banks are distributed to the depositors.
T F 17. Brokerage firms offer combination savings and checking accounts that pay higher-than-usual interest rates.
T F 18. NOW accounts generally restrict the number of checks that may be written each month.
T F 19. Demand deposits are called near-monies.
T F 20. Automatic teller machines are an example of an EFT system.
T F 21. The Federal Reserve System has twenty-five district banks.
T F 22. When the Fed raises the discount rate, banks begin to restrict loans.
T F 23. Margin is the amount of money an investor may borrow for purchasing stock.
T F 24. Through a process called deposit expansion, commercial banks can fund more loans.

Multiple-Choice Questions (A)

Circle the letter before he most accurate answer.

25. The process of exchanging goods for goods is called a
    a. measure of value.
    b. line of credit.
    c. medium of exchange.
    d. currency system.
    e. barter system.

26. Currency and demand deposits make up the
    a. M_1 supply of money.
    b. M_2 supply of money.
    c. M_3 supply of money.
    d. open-market operations.
    e. barter system.

27. Regular NOW accounts
    a. include unlimited check-writing privileges.
    b. charge access fees for balances that fall below a set minimum.
    c. pay interest on a maximum balance.
    d. do all of the above.
    e. do none of the above.

28. By decreasing the reserve requirement, the Fed can
    a. stifle the economy.
    b. reduce money available for lenders.
    c. stimulate a slow economy.
    d. have greater reserves.
    e. increase the inflation rate.

29. In borrowing money, lenders consider a person's
    a. character, capital, and constitution.
    b. capacity, consideration, and conditions.
    c. collateral, capacity, and character.
    d. conditions, candidacy, and capital.
    e. character, coordination, and competency.

30. When a retailer accepts money in exchange for merchandise, money is performing which function?
    a. Measure of value
    b. Medium of exchange
    c. Measurement of worth
    d. Store of value
    e. Symbol of value

31. Savings and loan associations and mutual savings banks do *not* offer their customers
    a. memberships.
    b. checking accounts.
    c. NOW accounts.
    d. savings accounts.
    e. loan privileges.

32. Terminals where you pull a bank card through a magnetic card reader and enter an identification number are often located near checkout counters in large chain grocery stores. What are these terminals called?
    a. Automated teller machines
    b. Automated clearinghouse terminals
    c. Electronic bank tellers
    d. Point-of-sale terminals (POS)
    e. Revolving credits

33. When the Fed raises the discount rate, what happens?
    a. There is more money for banks to lend.
    b. There is an increase in the overall money supply.
    c. There is increased economic activity.
    d. The banks will pay less interest to borrow from the Federal Reserve Bank.
    e. There is an economic slowdown.

34. If you have been denied credit on the basis of information provided by a credit bureau and you feel that some information in your file is inaccurate, what can you do? Which of the following is *not* an option?
    a. You have a right to know what is in the file.
    b. You can request, at no cost to you, a copy of your credit record.
    c. You can ask the credit bureau to verify any inaccurate, misleading, or vague information.
    d. You can pay to have the information removed.
    e. You can write an explanation and ask that it be made a part of your file.

Short-Answer Questions (A)

Complete each question.

35. Discuss how money solves problems associated with the **barter system**.

36. Money serves three basic functions in a society. Describe each **function.**

FUNCTIONS OF MONEY	DESCRIPTION
Medium of exchange	
Measure of value	
Store of value	

37. Explain how a **demand deposit** differs from a **time deposit**.

DEMAND DEPOSIT	TIME DEPOSIT

38. Identify the five **characteristics of money**, and tell why each characteristic is important.

CHARACTERISTICS OF MONEY	WHY EACH CHARACTERTISTIC IS IMPORTANT

39. Describe what is included in each measure of the **supply of money**.

SUPPLY OF MONEY MEASURES	COMPONENTS OF EACH MEASURE
M_1	
M_2	
M_3	

40. Explain the **mission** of the **Federal Reserve System**.

41. Explain the **basic function** of the **Fed**.

42. Discuss how the Fed is **organized**.

43. Explain how the Fed uses each **strategy to regulate the money supply**.

STRATEGIES	EXPLANATION
Reserve requirement	
Discount rate	
Open-market operations	

PRACTICE EXAMINATION B

Matching Questions (B)

Match each term with a statement.

a. credit union
b. mutual savings bank
c. check
d. NOW account
e. certificate of deposit

f. line of credit
g. collateral
h. electronic funds transfer
i. Federal Reserve System
j. reserve requirement

_____ 1. A bank that is owned by its depositors.
_____ 2. A penalty for early withdrawal of funds is imposed.
_____ 3. It uses a computer terminal or telephone hookup.
_____ 4. A financial institution created to serve its members.
_____ 5. A loan that is approved before the money is actually needed.
_____ 6. It regulates the banking industry.
_____ 7. It is a written order to pay a stated amount.
_____ 8. It is pledged as security against a loan.
_____ 9. A bank must retain a percentage of its deposits.
_____ 10. It is an interest-bearing checking account with limited privileges.

True-False Questions (B)

Select the correct answer.

T F   11. A unique feature of a bank credit card is that it extends a line of credit to the cardholder.

T F   12. Stored money is protected from inflation.

T F   13. Demand deposits are on deposit in interest-bearing savings accounts.

T F   14. The primary goal of a commercial bank is to earn a profit.

T F   15. In 1991, the federal government stopped providing deposit insurance to protect depositors in national banks.

T F   16. Insurance companies provide short-term personal loans to business firms.

T F   17. Banks charge more for business checking accounts than individual accounts.

T F   18. Depositors are not penalized for early withdrawal of funds invested in CDs in banks.

T F   19. POS terminals eliminate the need to write a check.

T F   20. The primary function of the Fed is to regulate the supply of money.

T F   21. To increase the money supply, the Fed sells government bonds.

T F   22. All national banks are required to belong to the FDIC.

T F   23. Commercial banks typically are not-for-profit organizations.

T F   24. For information concerning businesses, the most widely used credit-reporting agency in the United States is the Trans Union Credit Information Company.

Multiple-Choice Questions (B)

Circle the letter before the most accurate answer.

25. Money
    a. serves as a medium of exchange.
    b. serves as a measure of value.
    c. represents a store of value.
    d. does all of the above.
    e. does none of the above.

26. To reduce the nation's money supply, the Fed
    a. buys government bonds.
    b. borrows from foreign governments.
    c. sells government bonds.
    d. lowers the discount rate.
    e. lowers the required margin.

27. The *most* widely used credit reporting agency in the United States is
    a. the Better Business Bureau.
    b. Dun & Bradstreet.
    c. Credit Bureau, Inc.
    d. Chilton Corporation.
    e. Trans Union.

28. Which of the following is a characteristic of money?
    a. Money must be divisible into smaller units.
    b. Money must be light and easy to carry.
    c. Money should retain its value over time.
    d. Money must be durable and difficult to counterfeit.
    e. All of the above are characteristics of money.

29. Which function is created when money is invested for the purposes of accumulating wealth?
    a.   A measure of value
    b.   Medium of exchange
    c.   Store of value
    d.   Currency
    e.   Barter system

30. Which statement is *not* true about national banks?
    a.   National banks are chartered by the U.S. Comptroller of the Currency.
    b.   There are approximately 3,600 national banks in the United States.
    c.   National banks outnumber state banks by about two to one.
    d.   National banks must conform to federal banking regulations.
    e.   National banks are subject to unannounced inspections by federal auditors.

31. Sonya has $1,000 she will not need in the next year, and she wants to deposit it in a bank. Which of the following services is *best* for Sonya?
    a.   Certificate of deposit
    b.   Passbook savings account
    c.   Super NOW account
    d.   NOW account
    e.   Regular checking account

32. Banks must retain a portion of every deposit, which must be put safely into their vault or deposited with the Fed. What is this portion or percentage called?
    a.   Demand deposits
    b.   Trust fund
    c.   Collateral
    d.   Amortization
    e.   Reserve requirement

33. Which statement is true about margin requirements?
    a.   It is the portion of the selling price of stock that must be paid in cash.
    b.   The current margin requirement is $1,000.
    c.   If $4,000 of stock is purchased, $3,000 can be financed by the brokerage firm.
    d.   The current margin requirement is $2,000 or 50 percent.
    e.   The investor is required to keep a $1,000 line of credit with the broker.

34. What is the first step that a firm should take to get a customer, whose account is ten days past due, to pay his/her account?
    a.   Take legal action.
    b.   Send the customer a "Past Due" reminder.
    c.   Turn the account over to a collection agency.
    d.   Make a personal visit and stress the need to pay.
    e.   Telephone to ask when payment will be received.

Short-Answer Questions (B)

Complete each question.

35. In addition to its regulation of the money supply, the Fed has other responsibilities such as:

    a. _____

    b. _____

    c. _____

    d. _____

36. Identify what makes each financial institution special and sets it apart from other **financial institutions**.

FINANCIAL INSTITUTIONS	SPECIAL FEATURES
Savings and loan associations	
Mutual savings banks	
Credit unions	
Insurance companies	
Pension funds	
Brokerage firms	
Finance	
Investment banking firms	

37. Discuss how a **NOW account** is different from a **certificate of deposit (CD)**.

NOW ACCOUNT	CERTIFICATE OF DEPOSIT (CD)

38. Compare a **line of credit** with a **revolving credit agreement**.

LINE OF CREDIT	REVOLVING CREDIT AGREEMENT

39. Explain how a **debit card** is different from a **credit card**.

DEBIT CARD	CREDIT CARD

40. Discuss the **result** of the **Depository Institutions Deregulation and Monetary Control Act of 1980**.

41. How is **technology** impacting the banking industry? Give examples of how banks use technology.

    a. _____

    b. _____

    c. _____

    d. _____

42. Identify two **advantages** and two **disadvantages** of **electronic banking**.

ADVANTAGES OF ELECTRONIC BANKING	DISADVANTAGES OF ELECTRONIC BANKING

43. Banks can help businesses compete in the global market. Explain two services bankers provide.

BANKERS' SERVICES	EXPLANATION
Letter of credit	
Banker's acceptance	

PRACTICE EXAMINATION C

Matching Questions (C)

Match each term with a statement.

a. commercial bank
b. national bank
c. state bank
d. savings and loan association
e. discount rate
f. open-market operations
g. margin

h. credit
i. revolving credit agreement
j. pension fund
k. debit card
l. letter of credit
m. banker's acceptance
n. FDIC

_____ 1. A guaranteed line of credit from a bank.
_____ 2. Accepts deposits, makes loans, and must earn a profit.
_____ 3. Experienced vast failures in the 1980s.
_____ 4. Chartered by the U.S. Comptroller of the Currency.
_____ 5. Chartered by state banking authorities.
_____ 6. The interest rate banks pay for money they borrow from the Federal Reserve Bank.
_____ 7. Involves a promise to pay at a later date.
_____ 8. Buying or selling government bonds to control the money supply.
_____ 9. The minimum portion of the selling price of stock that must be paid in cash.
_____ 10. Established to guarantee employees a regular monthly income at retirement.
_____ 11. Its purpose is to insure deposits against bank failure.
_____ 12. A legal document guaranteeing payment for a specific time.
_____ 13. An order to pay a third party, without conditions, for a stated time.
_____ 14. It electronically transfers funds at the moment of purchase.

True-False Questions (C)

Select the correct answer.

T F 15. Money is a common denominator that is used to compare products for purchase.
T F 16. The standard unit of money must be capable of division into smaller units.
T F 17. Time deposits are immediately available to their owners.
T F 18. The Federal Reserve System has 24 Federal Reserve District Banks in the United States.
T F 19. The Fed has the responsibility for implementing the Truth-in-Lending Act.
T F 20. The Fed sets the margin requirements for stock transactions.
T F 21. The reserve requirement is the amount banks pay to their depositors.
T F 22. Collateral is generally not required for personal long-term loans.
T F 23. The Federal Reserve System was first created by Congress in 1929.
T F 24. The reserve requirement is set by each individual bank in the Federal Reserve System.

T   F   25.   The Fed has the power to establish credit terms for loans on automobiles.
T   F   26.   A person's net worth is important in getting a loan.
T   F   27.   Most POS terminals are located in banks.
T   F   28.   Debit cards are most commonly used at ATMs.

Multiple-Choice Questions (C)

Circle the letter before the most accurate answer.

29. When money retains its value over time, it has
    a. divisibility.   d. portability.
    b. stability.   e. durability.
    c. independence.

30. To lend money for home mortgages is a primary objective of
    a. national banks.   d. mutual savings banks.
    b. state banks.   e. savings and loan associations.
    c. commercial banks.

31. Interest rates paid on certificates of deposit change
    a. weekly.   d. monthly.
    b. biweekly.   e. yearly.
    c. semi-annually.

32. The FDIC insures all accounts in each member bank for up to _____ per individual at
    one bank.
    a. $100,000   d. $1,000,000
    b. $150,000   e. $10,000,000
    c. $500,000

33. If Fred has $825.45 in demand deposits at First City Bank and $1,285.98 in demand deposits
    at the Teachers Credit Union, what type of accounts does he have?
    a. Savings accounts   d. Certificates of deposits
    b. Checking accounts   e. Keogh accounts
    c. IRA accounts

34. Which statement is *not* true about the responsibilities of the Fed?
    a. The primary function of the Fed is to regulate the nation's supply of money.
    b. The Fed controls bank reserve requirements.
    c. The Fed insures deposits against bank failures.
    d. The Fed regulates the discount rate.
    e. The open-market operations are run by the Fed.

35. When lenders require that a borrower pledge real or personal property against the balance of
    the loan, what is the loan requiring?
    a. Line of credit   d. Collateral
    b. Revolving credit agreement   e. Personal loan
    c. Long-term loan

36. Credit unions are regulated by the
    a. National Credit Union Administration.
    b. Savings Association Insurance Fund.
    c. Federal Credit Union Administration.
    d. Federal Reserve System.
    e. Federal Deposit Insurance Corporation.

37. When a loan officer wants to know the loan applicant's salary and the balances on charge cards, what is the officer concerned about?
    a. Character
    b. Conditions
    c. Collateral
    d. Capital
    e. Capacity

38. Which act requires lenders to state clearly the annual percentage rate and the total finance charge on a consumer loan?
    a. Equal Pay Act
    b. Equal Employment Opportunity Act
    c. Fair Credit Reporting Act
    d. Truth-in-Lending Act
    e. Electronic Funds Transfer Act

Short-Answer Questions (C)

Complete each question:

39. Discuss the **role of credit bureaus**.

40. Identify the two major parts of the **Fair Credit Reporting Act of 1971**.

    a. _____

    b. _____

41. Identify the basic **purpose** of each organization.

ORGANIZATIONS	PURPOSES
FDIC	
SAIF	
BIF	
NCUA	

42. Assume you want to borrow $25,000. Describe the steps you would take to convince the loan officer you were a good risk.

a. _____

b. _____

c. _____

d. _____

e. _____

43. Describe the five **Cs of credit**.

CHARACTERISTICS OF CREDIT	EXPLANATION OF EACH CHARACTERISTIC
Character	
Capacity	
Capital	
Collateral	
Conditions	

44. List the steps in a sound **collection process**.

a. _____

b. _____

c. _____

d. _____

CHAPTER 20

MASTERING FINANCIAL MANAGEMENT

Key Terms

Define each term briefly. Writing down the definition and giving an example will help you learn the term.

financial management (p. 579)

short-term financing (p. 579)

cash flow (p. 579)

long-term financing (p. 580)

financial plan (p. 582)

budget (p. 584)

cash budget (p. 584)

zero-based budgeting (p. 585)

capital budget (p. 585)

equity capital (p. 585)

debt capital (p. 586)

unsecured financing (p. 587)

trade credit (p. 587)

promissory note (p. 588)

prime interest rate (p. 589)

revolving credit agreement (p. 589)

commercial paper (p. 589)

floor planning (p. 590)

accounts receivable (p. 590)

factor (p. 590)

initial public offering (p. 592)

common stock (p. 592)

preferred stock (p. 593)

par value (p. 593)

call premium (p. 594)

convertible preferred stock (p. 595)

retained earnings (p. 595)

financial leverage (p. 596)

lease (p. 597)

term-loan agreement (p. 597)

corporate bond (p. 599)

maturity date (p. 599)

registered bond (p. 599)

debenture bond (p. 599)

mortgage bond (p. 599)

convertible bond (p. 599)

bond indenture (p. 600)

serial bonds (p. 600)

sinking fund (p. 600)

trustee (p. 600)

PRACTICE EXAMINATION A

Matching Questions (A)

Match each term with a statement.

a. financial management
b. short-term financing
c. call premium
d. cash flow
e. long-term financing
f. financial plan

g. budget
h. zero-based budgeting
i. equity capital
j. debt capital
k. unsecured financing
l. trade credit

_____ 1. It is the movement of money into and out of an organization.
_____ 2. It shows projected income and expenditures.
_____ 3. Funding is from external sources.
_____ 4. One function is to determine a firm's financial needs.
_____ 5. Money that will be used longer than one year.
_____ 6. Justification of every budgeted expense is required.
_____ 7. Collateral is not required.
_____ 8. Money that is needed for less than one year.
_____ 9. It tells how money will be obtained and used.
_____ 10. Funding that comes from the sale of stock.
_____ 11. Payments are delayed until later.
_____ 12. It is the cost of redeeming preferred stock from investors.

True-False Questions (A)

Select the correct answer.

T F 13. Debt financing can be used to fund openings and operations of new businesses.
T F 14. A positive cash flow is created when more money is being spent than is coming into the firm.
T F 15. Financial management ensures that sufficient financing is available when needed, both now and in the future.
T F 16. A budget is a historical record of the previous year's financial activities.
T F 17. The sale of assets is a type of funding.
T F 18. Most lenders do not require collateral for short-term financing.
T F 19. When money is needed, most promissory notes can be sold immediately.
T F 20. A revolving credit agreement is a guaranteed line of credit.
T F 21. Cash flow is not a problem during peak selling periods, only during slow periods.
T F 22. Factoring companies buy accounts receivable for less than face value.
T F 23. Stockholders must purchase pre-emptive rights before buying shares in the company.
T F 24. Bonds are usually issued in units of $25.00.
T F 25. Most corporate bonds are backed by assets of the firm.
T F 26. By law, preferred stockholders are entitled to dividends.

Multiple-Choice Questions (A)

Circle the letter before the most accurate answer.

27. Short-term financing is money borrowed for
    a. one year or less.
    b. one year to eighteen months.
    c. less than two years.
    d. more than one year.
    e. five years.

28. Equity capital is obtained from
    a. banks.
    b. stockholders.
    c. credit unions.
    d. insurance companies.
    e. bondholders.

29. The interest rate a corporation pays when it issues commercial paper is tied to
    a. the prime rate.
    b. its accounts receivables.
    c. its credit rating.
    d. the firm's net profits.
    e. its line of credit.

30. Preferred stock
    a. has voting rights.
    b. carries residual claim on assets.
    c. represents ownership.
    d. receives interest.
    e. is considered a low-grade stock.

31. What type of bond is secured by the assets of the corporation?
    a. Mortgage
    b. Convertible
    c. Serial
    d. Debenture
    e. Callable

32. Which statement is *not* true about the need for financial management? It ensures that
    a. financing priorities are established in line with goals and objectives.
    b. spending is planned and controlled in accordance with priorities.
    c. sufficient financing is available when needed.
    d. all budgeted funds are deleted at the end of the budget period.
    e. excess cash is invested properly.

33. When a seller allows a buyer thirty days to pay for a purchase, the sales arrangement is called
    a. a bank loan.
    b. trade credit.
    c. a promissory note.
    d. equity financing.
    e. time draft.

34. What do banks often require of their line-of-credit customers?
    a. Keep a running balance in their line of credit.
    b. Keep a compensating balance on deposit at the bank.
    c. Clean up the account every five years.
    d. Guarantee continuous use for an extended period of time.
    e. Pledge collateral once a year.

35. Which assets do firms *most commonly* pledge as collateral for short-term loans?
    a. Cash and accounts receivable
    b. Accounts and notes payable
    c. Inventory and equipment
    d. Marketable securities and owners' equity
    e. Inventory and accounts receivable

36. When firms use borrowed funds to increase the return on owners' equity, what is the strategy called?
    a. Borrowing
    b. Financial leverage
    c. Long-term financing
    d. Floor planning
    e. Revolving credit

37. When a corporation sells stock to the general public for the first time, it is called
    a. unsecured financing.
    b. financial leveraging.
    c. initial public offering.
    d. floor planning.
    e. factoring.

38. A primary source of funds for a corporation includes
    a. sales revenue.
    b. equity capital.
    c. debt capital.
    d. sales of assets.
    e. All of the above.

Short-Answer Questions (A)

Complete each question.

39. Identify three steps involved in **financial planning**.

    a. _____

    b. _____

    c. _____

40. Why does a business need short-term and long-term financing? List two **reasons** for each type of financing.

SHORT-TERM FINANCING	LONG-TERM FINANCING

41. Compare a **cash budget** with a **capital budget**.

CASH BUDGET	CAPITAL BUDGET

42. Explain how **zero-base budgeting** differs from the traditional concept of budgeting.

43. Identify an example for each **primary source** of business funds.

SOURCES OF BUSINESS FUNDS	EXAMPLES
Sales revenue	
Equity capital	
Debt capital	
Sales of assets	

44. Explain how a manager **monitors and evaluates** a firm's financial performance.

PRACTICE EXAMINATION B

Matching Questions (B)

Match each term with a statement.

a. promissory note
b. prime interest rate
c. revolving credit agreement
d. commercial paper
e. cash budget
f. accounts receivable

g. factor
h. dividends
i. common stock
j. preferred stock
k. capital budget
l. par value

_____ 1. It is a guaranteed line of credit from a bank.
_____ 2. It estimates cash receipts and expenditures.
_____ 3. The distribution of earnings that stockholders receive.
_____ 4. This ownership has first claims on the profits and assets of a company.
_____ 5. It is an arbitrary dollar value printed on the stock certificate.
_____ 6. A document that promises payment at a later date.
_____ 7. A short-term promissory note issued by large corporations.
_____ 8. The money customers owe a firm.
_____ 9. An ownership that carries voting rights.
_____ 10. It estimates expenditures for major assets.
_____ 11. It is reserved for large corporations with excellent credit ratings.
_____ 12. A company specializing in buying accounts receivables.

True-False Questions (B)

Select the correct answer.

T F 13. Long-term financing is used most often for promotional campaigns.
T F 14. Short-term funds are used to finance expansions and mergers.
T F 15. Financial management begins with goal setting and planning.
T F 16. The budgeting process generally begins with preparing a sales budget.
T F 17. Equity capital is money received by borrowing.
T F 18. Trade credit is synonymous with an open-book account.
T F 19. A prearranged short-term loan is called a line of credit.
T F 20. A capital budget estimates a firm's expenditures for labor costs.
T F 21. Sole proprietorships use equity financing to raise funds for operations.
T F 22. The dividend rate is determined by the par value of stock.
T F 23. Maturity dates for bonds generally range from ten to thirty years.
T F 24. Long-term business loans are normally repaid in three to seven years.
T F 25. Most promissory notes carry a discount rate, if paid within six months.
T F 26. Par value is the portion of a corporation's profits not distributed to stockholders.

Multiple-Choice Questions (B)

Circle the letter before the most accurate answer.

27. Proper financial management can ensure that
    a. financing priorities are established.
    b. spending is planned.
    c. financial resources are obtained.
    d. the firm's financial needs are met.
    e. All of the above occur.

28. Commercial paper is short-term promissory notes
    a. issued by the federal government.
    b. paying interest rates slightly higher than most banks.
    c. issued in small denominations.
    d. issued in large denominations.
    e. used for mortgage loans.

29. A factor will buy accounts receivable for
    a. more than their face value.
    b. less than their face value.
    c. their present value.
    d. their par value.
    e. their depreciated value.

30. Corporation bonds
    a. represent ownership.
    b. pay dividends.
    c. are equity financing.
    d. pay interest.
    e. carry voting rights.

31. Which statement is true about floor planning?
    a. Title of merchandise is given to lenders in return for short-term financing.
    b. The lender controls the inventory.
    c. The borrower checks periodically to ensure the collateral is still available.
    d. As merchandise is sold, the lender repays a portion of the loan.
    e. It is a special type of financing used in the apparel industry.

32. A promissory note that requires a borrower to repay a loan in installments is called a
    a. revolving credit agreement.
    b. term-loan agreement.
    c. trade credit.
    d. lease agreement.
    e. None of the above.

33. An invoice in the amount of $200 carries cash terms of "2/10, net 30." If the buyer takes advantage of the discount terms, how much will the buyer pay?
    a. $100
    b. $120
    c. $140
    d. $160
    e. $196

34. Which statement is *not* characteristic of commercial paper?
    a. It is secured by the reputation of the issuing firm.
    b. It is issued in large denominations, ranging from $5,000 to $100,000.
    c. It pays interest rates slightly below the rates of commercial banks.
    d. It requires collateral.
    e. It is a short-term promissory note issued by a large corporation.

35. When a firm sells its accounts receivable to raise short-term cash, it is engaging in a strategy called
    a. factoring.
    b. financial planning.
    c. debt financing.
    d. drafting.
    e. retaining earnings.

36. Retained earnings, as a form of equity financing, are
    a. gross earnings.
    b. profits before taxes.
    c. profits after taxes.
    d. undistributed profits.
    e. total owner's equity.

Short-Answer Questions (B)

Complete each question.

37. Explain how **unsecured short-term financing** is different from **secured short-term financing**.

UNSECURED SHORT-TERM FINANCING	SECURED SHORT-TERM FINANCING

38. List an **advantage** and a **disadvantage** for each type of short-term financing.

SOURCES OF SHORT-TERM FINANCING	ADVANTAGES	DISADVANTAGES
Trade credit		
Promissory note		
Bank loans		
Commercial paper		

39. Explain the **prime rate,** and give an example of who gets the prime rate.

PRIME RATE	EXAMPLE

40. Describe **floor planning**, and give an example of who might use it.

FLOOR PLANNING	EXAMPLE

41. Explain how **accounts receivables** are used to secure short-term loans.

42. Discuss how **factoring** works. What benefit is factoring to the firm selling the accounts receivables?

43. Identify an **advantage** and a **disadvantage** for each **source of equity financing**.

SOURCES	ADVANTAGES	DISADVANTAGES
Selling stock		
Retained earnings		
Venture capital		

44. Describe two reasons why large corporations sell stock.

    a. _____

    b. _____

45. Contrast **common stock** with **preferred stock**.

COMMON STOCK	PREFERRED STOCK

PRACTICE EXAMINATION C

Matching Questions (C-1)

Match each term with a statement.

a. financial leverage
b. term-loan agreement
c. convertible preferred stock
d. callable preferred stock

e. retained earnings
f. corporate bond
g. maturity date
h. bond indenture

_____ 1. A promissory note that requires installment payments.
_____ 2. Stock that can be exchanged for money at the corporation's option.
_____ 3. A corporation pledges to repay a specified amount of money with interest.
_____ 4. It is a legal document.
_____ 5. Borrowed funds are used to increase ROI.
_____ 6. Profits that are reinvested in the business.
_____ 7. A time when a corporation repays the bond.
_____ 8. Preferred stock that can be exchanged for common stock at the stockholder's option.

Matching Questions (C-2)

Match each term with a statement.

a. lessee
b. serial bonds
c. sinking fund
d. trustee
e. debenture bond

f. mortgage bond
g. convertible bond
h. lease
i. registered bond
j. floor planning

_____ 9. It uses other's assets.
_____ 10. The deposits are used for redeeming a bond issue.
_____ 11. This bond is backed by the reputation of the issuing corporation.
_____ 12. A bond that can be exchanged for common stock.
_____ 13. Interest checks are mailed directly to the bondholder of record.
_____ 14. A type of financing used by automobile dealers.
_____ 15. They are bonds that mature on different dates.
_____ 16. A representative that acts for bond owners.
_____ 17. A bond that is secured by assets of the issuing firm.
_____ 18. Assets are temporarily transferred from owner to user.

True-False Questions (C)

Select the correct answer.

T F 19. Retailers use short-term financing to build inventories before peak selling periods.
T F 20. Businesses must have sufficient financing to survive.
T F 21. The first step in effective financial planning is to identify sources of funds.
T F 22. The traditional approach to budgeting requires every expense to be justified in each budget.
T F 23. A promissory note is a legally binding and enforceable document.
T F 24. The payee of a promissory note is the customer buying on credit.
T F 25. Commercial paper requires the note to be secured by collateral.
T F 26. Loans secured by inventory are more expensive than unsecured loans.
T F 27. By law every corporation must hold an annual stockholder's meeting.
T F 28. Callable preferred stock is stock a corporation may exchange at an option.
T F 29. Interest must be paid periodically on common stock.
T F 30. Part of a financial manager's job is to protect a company's credit rating.
T F 31. The discount rate is the lowest interest rate banks charge for short-term loans.
T F 32. Issuing stock is the most expensive form of long-term financing available to large firms.

Multiple-Choice Questions (C)

Circle the letter before the most accurate answer.

33. The steps in effective financial planning are
    a. establishing objectives, identifying sources, and budgeting.
    b. identifying financial resources, budgeting, and establishing goals.
    c. establishing objectives, budgeting, and identifying sources of funds.
    d. developing plans, monitoring plans, and evaluating the results.
    e. establishing goals, setting objectives, and working the plan.

34. A corporation that issues bonds must also appoint a(n)
    a. trustee.   d. maker.
    b. agent.   e. representative.
    c. maker.

35. The cost of secured loans to business owners is
    a. low.   d. high.
    b. extremely high.   e. moderate.
    c. unimportant.

36. Which legal document details all the conditions relating to a bond issue?
    a. Debenture bond   d. Registered bond
    b. Bond indenture   e. Trustee
    c. Deed

37. Some firms periodically set aside funds in hopes of accumulating enough money to pay off the bonds by their maternity date. What is the name of the account used for this purpose?
    a. Bond fund   d. Debt fund
    b. Debt fund   e. Sinking fund
    c. A trustee

38. Which of the following strategies would be the *most* economic way to eliminate problems of manipulating budgets and adding items based on personal interest?
    a. Fire the managers.   d. Use traditional budgeting.
    b. Hire an efficiency expert.   e. Hire a new accountant.
    c. Use zero-base budgeting.

39. Promissory notes are used to pay suppliers. The customer buying on credit is called the
    a. owner.   d. payee.
    b. endorser.   e. maker.
    c. cosigner.

40. Some corporate bonds carry a repayment provision that allows the issuing firm to pay a premium to buy back its bonds from the bond owners. What type of bonds are these?
    a. Discount   d. Debenture
    b. Callable   e. Convertible
    c. Registered

41. When stockholders have the right to purchase new stock before it is issued to the general public, the stockholders have
    a. presale rights.
    b. property rights.
    c. pre-emptive rights.
    d. priority rights.
    e. preferred stock.

42. To ensure that sufficient funds are available when needed to redeem bonds, the firm can issue bonds that mature on different dates. Which type of bonds would be the *best* to issue?
    a. Convertible bonds
    b. Corporate bonds
    c. Registered bonds
    d. Serial bonds
    e. Debenture bonds

Short-Answer Questions (C)

Complete each question.

43. Describe how **financial leverage** can increase the return on owner's equity.

44. Explain why **leasing** may be a viable option versus purchasing.

45. Discuss two **advantages** for **issuing corporate bonds** over using long-term loans.

    a. _____

    b. _____

46. Compare four **types of bonds.** Define each type and give a reason for issuing it.

TYPES OF BONDS	DESCRIPTION
Registered bonds	
Debenture bonds	
Mortgage bonds	
Convertible bonds	

47. Explain how each **method** ensures that **sufficient funds** will be available to redeem a bond issue.

REPAYMENT METHOD	EXPLANATION
Serial bonds	
Sinking Fund	
Sell new bonds	

CHAPTER 21

UNDERSTANDING SECURITIES MARKETS AND INVESTMENTS

Key Terms

Define each term briefly. Writing down the definition and giving an example will help you learn the term.

primary market (p. 609)

investment banking firm (p. 609)

high-risk investment (p. 610)

institutional investors (p. 610)

secondary market (p. 610)

securities exchange (p. 610)

over-the-counter (OTC) market (p. 611)

Nasdaq (p. 611)

account executive (p. 612)

market order (p. 612)

limit order (p. 612)

discretionary order (p. 613)

program trading (p. 614)

round lot (p. 614)

odd lot (p. 614)

personal investment (p. 616)

financial planner (p. 617)

blue-chip stock (p. 618)

liquidity (p. 619)

municipal bond (p. 622)

general obligation bond (p. 622)

revenue bond (p. 622)

stock dividend (p. 622)

capital gain (p. 623)

market value (p. 623)

bull market (p. 623)

bear market (p. 623)

stock split (p. 623)

mutual fund (p. 624)

net asset value (NAV) (p. 624)

family of funds (p. 626)

margin requirement (p. 627)

buying long (p. 627)

selling short (p. 628)

diversification (p. 629)

prospectus (p. 633)

security average (or security index) (p. 636)

blue-sky laws (p. 638)

Securities and Exchange Commission (SEC) (p. 638)

National Association of Securities Dealers (NASD) (p. 638)

PRACTICE EXAMINATION A

Matching Questions (A)

Match each term with a statement.

a. personal investment
b. market value
c. stock dividend
d. stock split
e. mutual fund
f. high risk investment

g. margin requirement
h. net asset value
i. buying long
j. selling short
k. financial planners
l. family of funds

_____ 1. The price a buyer is willing to pay for stock.
_____ 2. The advantages are professional management and diversification.
_____ 3. The share value in a mutual fund.
_____ 4. Experts who advise investors.
_____ 5. Personal funds are invested to earn a financial return.
_____ 6. The promise of quick profits lures investors to purchase.
_____ 7. It is a technique for buying stocks that are expected to increase in value.
_____ 8. A group of mutual funds managed by one company.
_____ 9. Additional stock is given in place of cash.
_____ 10. It requires part of the stock price be paid in cash.
_____ 11. This technique allows stock to be sold that is not owned.
_____ 12. Stocks are divided into more shares of stock.

True-False Questions (A)

Select the correct answer.

T F 13. An objective of investing is to earn money with money.
T F 14. An investment plan should be prepared prior to establishing investment objectives.
T F 15. Investments with a high degree of safety will give a high degree of return.
T F 16. General Electric is an excellent choice for investing in high risk stocks.
T F 17. Common stockholders are guaranteed a certain amount of dividends.
T F 18. Dividends are paid to common stockholders before preferred stockholders.
T F 19. Diversification provides a degree of safety in an investment program.
T F 20. An individual who invests in a no-load fund pays no sales charges at the time of purchase.
T F 21. Using borrowed funds to increase the return on an investment is called leverage.
T F 22. Load mutual funds require the investor to pay a commission for each purchase.
T F 23. Before a corporation can be listed on the New York Stock Exchange, it must have at least 2,000 stockholders who own 100 or more shares of its stock.
T F 24. Stocks trade in eighths of a dollar.
T F 25. The typical commission is approximately 20 percent of the investment.
T F 26. Selling short is a term used to describe a situation in which investors sell stock they do not own.
T F 27. A bull market is a market in which average stock prices are declining.
T F 28. The difference between a stock purchase price and selling price is its capital gain.
T F 29. Series EE savings bonds are purchased for half their maturity value.
T F 30. It is the responsibility of the issuer to inform the investor about the taxable status of a bond.

Multiple-Choice Questions (A)

Circle the letter before the most accurate answer.

31. Individual investment planning begins by
    a. establishing specific goals.
    b. comparing investment vehicles.
    c. investigating new investment opportunities.
    d. choosing high risk stocks.
    e. taking a friend's advice on selecting stocks.

32. People who want growth in their investment should invest in
    a. savings accounts.
    b. stocks of growth companies.
    c. speculative stock companies.
    d. NOW accounts.
    e. corporate bonds.

33. When an investor receives stock instead of cash dividends, it is called
    a. a stock split.
    b. par value.
    c. retained earnings.
    d. a call option.
    e. a stock dividend.

34. As interest rates rise, the market value of existing bonds typically
    a. increases.
    b. declines.
    c. bounces rapidly.
    d. stays the same.
    e. fluctuates.

35. Which of the following statements is true about mutual funds?
    a. They combine and invest the funds of many investors.
    b. Professional management is used.
    c. The funds are diversified in a wide variety of securities.
    d. Diversification gives an edge of safety for the investor.
    e. All of the above are true about mutual funds.

36. The Dow Jones Industrial Average was established in
    a. 1890.
    b. 1897.
    c. 1900.
    d. 1901.
    e. 1913.

37. When an investor gives a stockholder instructions to sell the stock at a price equal to or better than a certain amount, the investor has placed a(n) _____ order.
    a. market
    b. structure
    c. account
    d. executive
    e. limit

38. When a firm has a bad year, the owners of this stock would be assured that the omitted dividends will be paid.
    a. Convertible preferred stock
    b. Common stock
    c. Cumulative preferred stock
    d. Participating preferred stock
    e. Preferred stock

39. How are the values of bonds quoted?
    a. As a percentage of par value   d. As a percentage of face value
    b. In points that covert to dollars   e. The actual amount
    c. In dollars and cents

40. What information is found in the first two columns of a stock quotation listed in *The Wall Street Journal*?
    a. Name of the company
    b. Amount of the annual dividend being paid
    c. Highest and lowest the stock sold for in the past 52 weeks
    d. Highest the stock sold for on a particular day
    e. P/E ratio

41. Which act provides full disclosure of important facts about corporations issuing new securities?
    a. Securities Act of 1933   d. Federal Securities Act of 1964
    b. Maloney Act of 1938   e. Securities Exchange Act of 1934
    c. Investment Act of 1940

Short-Answer Questions (A)

Complete each question.

42. Describe the difference between the **primary market** and the **secondary market**.

PRIMARY MARKET	SECONDARY MARKET

43. Discuss the role of an **investment banking firm** for corporations that want to sell securities.

44. Compare **securities exchanges** to an **over-the-counter market**.

SECURITIES EXCHANGES	OVER-THE-COUNTER MARKET

45. Describe the job of an **account executive** (stockbroker or registered representative).

46. Identify the services of each type of **broker**.

TYPES OF BROKERS	SERVICES RENDERED
Full service	
Discount	

47. A **personal investment plan** includes investment goals. Identify four factors that make a goal useful.

a. _____

b. _____

c. _____

d. _____

48. Discuss why an **emergency fund** is important.

49. Potential investments must be matched against investment goals in terms of several factors. Explain each factor.

INVESTMENT FACTORS	EXPLANATION
Safety	
Risk	
Income	
Growth	
Liquidity	

PRACTICE EXAMINATION B

Matching Questions (B)

Match each term with a statement.

a. account executive
b. securities exchange
c. over-the-counter market
d. stockbroker
e. market order
f. limit order
g. round lot

h. odd lot
i. prospectus
j. security index
k. blue-sky laws
l. Securities & Exchange Commission
m. National Association of Securities Dealers

_____ 1. It is a marketplace for exchanging unlisted stocks.
_____ 2. A broker is requested to buy or sell at a price equal to or better than a specified price.
_____ 3. It describes a corporation and its stock issue.
_____ 4. They are state regulations that regulate securities trading.
_____ 5. It is another name for a stockbroker.
_____ 6. An agent who gets buyers and sellers together.
_____ 7. Stocks are sold in units of 100 shares.

_____ 8. It is an average of the current market price of selected stocks.
_____ 9. Securities activities are regulated by this agency.
_____ 10. This marketplace exchanges listed stocks and bonds.
_____ 11. It is a request to buy or sell stock at the current market price.
_____ 12. Stocks sold in less than 100 shares.
_____ 13. This group regulates the OTC market.

True-False Questions (B)

Select the correct answer.

T F 14. Investment objectives should focus only on the present.
T F 15. An effective investment program begins with an emergency-fund account.
T F 16. Securities issued by new corporations provide a high degree of safety for investors.
T F 17. Corporations that are growing usually pay high dividends.
T F 18. The market value of a stock is reflected in the ticker tape quotation.
T F 19. Growth and income are features of convertible preferred stock.
T F 20. Convertible bonds carry higher interest rates than nonconvertible bonds.
T F 21. Money-market funds invest in long-term corporate obligations and government securities.
T F 22. A decrease in the value of a leveraged investment is called margin.
T F 23. The Maloney Act of 1938 created the SEC.
T F 24. By law, brokerage firms are responsible for reporting transactions based on inside information.
T F 25. The prospectus for an issue of stock is prepared by the SEC.
T F 26. The Dow Jones Industrial Average is comprised of 15 leading utility stocks.
T F 27. Growth-income mutual funds invest in money markets and government bonds.

Multiple-Choice Questions (B)

Circle the letter before the most accurate answer.

28. The investment with the highest degree of safety is
    a. bonds.
    b. real estate.
    c. mutual funds.
    d. stocks.
    e. certificates of deposit.

29. To obtain a high return on an investment, investors usually give up
    a. risk.
    b. safety.
    c. dividends.
    d. growth.
    e. income.

30. Preferred stock dividends are
    a. declared by the board of directors.
    b. voted on by the stockholders.
    c. determined by top management.
    d. specified on the stock certificates.
    e. paid only in the last quarter.

31. The fund invests in common and preferred stocks that pay good dividends and are expected to increase in market value.
    a. Growth funds
    b. Growth-income funds
    c. Income funds
    d. Aggressive growth funds
    e. Balanced funds

32. Placing an order to buy IBM stock at $75 or less is called a
    a. market order.
    b. call option.
    c. odd lot order.
    d. limit order.
    e. put order.

33. The Dow Jones Industrial Average includes _____ stocks.
    a. fifteen
    b. twenty
    c. thirty
    d. sixty-five
    e. one hundred

34. When a stockbroker places an order for 300 shares of McDonald's stock, what type of order is being placed?
    a. Round lot
    b. Half lot
    c. Several lot
    d. Odd lot
    e. Mixed lot

35. With the current margin requirement at 50 percent, how much could an investor borrow to invest $5,000 in the market?
    a. $1,000
    b. $2,500
    c. $3,000
    d. $3,500
    e. $4,000

36. What would a bond cost that is quoted at 100 in *The Wall Street Journal*?
    a. $1.00
    b. $10.00
    c. $1,000.00
    d. $10,000.00
    e. $100.00

37. Which type of investment has the greatest liquidity?
    a. Savings accounts
    b. Stocks
    c. Mutual funds
    d. Bonds
    e. Real estate

38. If brokers are found guilty of insider trading, they will be fined based on the provisions of the
    a. Maloney Act.
    b. Federal Securities Act of 1964.
    c. Securities Amendments Act of 1975.
    d. Insider Trading Act and Securities Fraud Enforcement Act of 1988.
    e. Presidential Ethical Act of 1988.

Short-Answer Questions (B)

Complete each question.

39. Differentiate among the types of U.S. **government bonds**.

TYPES OF U.S. GOVERNMENT BONDS	EXPLANATION
Treasury bills	
Treasury notes	
Treasury bonds	
Savings bonds	

40. Differentiate among a **municipal bond**, a **general obligation bond,** and a **revenue bond**.

MUNICIPAL BOND	GENERAL OBLIGATION BOND	REVENUE BOND

41. List three ways to make money by **buying common stock**.

a. _____

b. _____

c. _____

42. Describe what happens when a **stock splits**. Give an example.

43. Identify the special features for each type of **preferred stock**.

PREFERRED STOCK	FEATURES
Cumulative stock	
Convertible stock	

44. Describe each type of **mutual fund**.

MUTUAL FUNDS	DESCRIPTION
Closed-end fund	
Open-end fund	
Load fund	
No-load fund	

45. Explain how **net asset value (NAV)** is calculated.

46. Identify two disadvantages of buying stock on **margin**.

a. _____

b. _____

47. Discuss why an investor would use the process of **selling short**.

48. Describe the **process for selling short**.

a. _____

b. _____

c. _____

d. _____

49. Discuss the concept of **diversification** and why it is important in financial planning.

50. Identify several **types of investments** for each category of risk.

CATEGORIES OF RISK	EXAMPLES OF TYPES OF INVESTMENTS
Financial security	
Safety and income	
Growth	
High-risk investments	

PRACTICE EXAMINATION C

Matching Questions (C)

Match each term with a statement.

a. primary market
b. investment banking firm
c. secondary market
d. discretionary order
e. liquidity
f. bull market
g. bear market
h. stock split

i. institutional investors
j. Nasdaq
k. program trading
l. capital gain
m. blue-chip stock
n. municipal bond
o. general obligation bond
p. revenue bond

_____ 1. A process that lowers the price of stock per share.
_____ 2. Purchasing stock directly from the Exxon Corporation creates this market.
_____ 3. A market situation that is reflecting rising prices.
_____ 4. The New York Stock Exchange is an example of this market.
_____ 5. The ease at which an asset can be converted into cash.
_____ 6. A market situation that reflects declining prices.
_____ 7. An organization that helps corporations raise funds.
_____ 8. Investors give stockbrokers the right to choose when to purchase stock.
_____ 9. Pension funds are an example.
_____ 10. It is a computerized electronic exchange system.
_____ 11. A computer monitors the market and generates transactions.
_____ 12. It is the difference between the purchasing and selling prices.
_____ 13. Income earned from a project repays its debt.
_____ 14. Debt is backed by the full faith and credit of issuing unit.
_____ 15. A safe investment that attracts conservative investors.
_____ 16. It is sometimes called a "muni."

True-False Questions (C)

Select the correct answer.

T F 17. "I want to be wealthy" is a measurable investment objective.
T F 18. The types of investments should be selected on the basis of a person's investment objectives.
T F 19. A general obligation bond is backed by the full faith and credit of the government that issued it.
T F 20. *Business Week* provides financial information about individual corporations.
T F 21. Stock splits help bring stock prices in line with the market value of the stock.
T F 22. Bonds are considered a higher risk investment than common stock.
T F 23. A closed-end mutual fund is sold only to a specified number of investors.
T F 24. The Federal Reserve System sets the margin requirement.
T F 25. Taking a loss on a stock investment is called selling short.
T F 26. Midwest Stock Exchange in Chicago is the largest and best-known securities exchange.
T F 27. Discount brokers provide information and advice to investors.
T F 28. Value Line is a service provided for investors.
T F 29. Financial planners agree that an amount equal to two years of living expenses is a reasonable amount for an emergency fund.
T F 30. The Dow Jones Industrial Average is the older stock index in use today.

Multiple-Choice Questions (C)

Circle the letter before the most accurate answer.

31. The investment with the highest potential for income is
    a. savings account.
    b. preferred stock.
    c. certificates of deposit.
    d. common stock.
    e. money market accounts.

32. Dividends are paid from
    a. sales.
    b. profits.
    c. revenue.
    d. stock accounts.
    e. leverage.

33. When the value of common stock increases, the value of a firm's convertible stocks
    a. increases.
    b. stays the same.
    c. varies.
    d. decreases.
    e. does none of these.

34. Which type of mutual fund invests in common stocks, preferred stocks, and bonds?
    a. Income fund
    b. Growth fund
    c. Growth income fund
    d. Balanced fund
    e. Special fund

35. Which market uses a computerized electronic exchange system called Nasdaq?
    a. Stocks market
    b. Bond market
    c. Over-the-counter market
    d. Mutual fund market
    e. All of the above

36. The regulation that requires a corporation to prepare a prospectus is the
    a. Securities Act of 1933.
    b. Securities Exchange Act of 1934.
    c. Maloney Act of 1938.
    d. Federal Securities Act of 1964.
    e. Truth in Lending Act.

37. Which statement is *not* true about Certified Financial Planners (CFP)?
    a. They charge consulting fees that range from $100 to $250 an hour.
    b. They must have two years experience in securities and insurance.
    c. Each CFP must establish an emergency fund covering two years of living expenses.
    d. Two years of experience in real estate, taxation, and estate planning are required.
    e. They are required to successfully pass a qualifying examination.

38. If the market price of the stock increases after investors sell short, what happens to the investment?
    a. It loses money.
    b. It gains in value.
    c. It neither gains nor loses money.
    d. It may be in violation of SEC regulations.
    e. It may trigger an investigation.

39. The group that helps corporations sell new issues of stocks, bonds, or other financial securities on the primary market is
    a. the Securities Exchange Commission.
    b. the National Association of Securities Dealers.
    c. an investment banking firm.
    d. an initial public offering.
    e. a Certified Financial Planner.

40. An important factor to consider when selecting an account executive is
    a. to find one who believes in churning.
    b. the financial advice and reports provided by discount brokers.
    c. the factor of compatibility.
    d. the number of transactions completed each day.
    e. the number of clients.

Short-Answer Questions (A)

Complete each question.

41. Identify the 12 columns of information given in a **stock quotation**.

    a. _____   b. _____

    c. _____   d. _____

    e. _____   f. _____

    g. _____   h. _____

    i. _____   j. _____

    k. _____   l. _____

42. Describe the role of the **Internet** in investing.

43. List several business, news, and financial **magazines** that provide information and advice about investments.

    a. _____   b. _____

    c. _____   d. _____

    e. _____   f. _____

    g. _____   h. _____

44. Explain the purpose of a **prospectus**.

45. Describe the type of information that **Moody's** and **Standard & Poor's** provide.

46. List the number of stocks that each **security index** uses in its average.

INDEXES	NUMBER OF STOCKS IN AVERAGE
Dow Jones Industrial Average	
Standard & Poor's 500 Stock Index	
New York Stock Exchange Composite Index	
American Stock Exchange (AMEX) Index	
Nasdaq Composite Index	

47. Describe the principal functions of the **Securities and Exchange Commission**.

    a. _____

    b. _____

    c. _____

Answer Key

CHAPTER 1—Exploring the World of Business

PRACTICE EXAM A

1.	i	2.	j	3.	c	4.	f	5.	a	6.	b	7.	e
8.	h	9.	d	10.	g	11.	l	12.	k	13.	T	14.	F
15.	F	16.	T	17.	F	18.	T	19.	F	20.	T	21.	T
22.	F	23.	a	24.	d	25.	b	26.	e	27.	b	28.	c
29.	e	30.	a										

PRACTICE EXAM B

1.	e	2.	h	3.	k	4.	a	5.	m	6.	c	7.	i
8.	f	9.	j	10.	g	11.	l	12.	d	13.	b	14.	n
15.	F	16.	T	17.	F	18.	T	19.	T	20.	F	21.	F
22.	F	23.	T	24.	F	25.	d	26.	a	27.	d	28.	e
29.	d	30.	c	31.	a	32.	e						

PRACTICE EXAM C

1.	e	2.	c	3.	j	4.	f	5.	a	6.	d	7.	g
8.	b	9.	l	10.	k	11.	F	12.	T	13.	T	14.	F
15.	F	16.	F	17.	T	18.	F	19.	T	20.	T	21.	a
22.	d	23.	a	24.	b	25.	e	26.	c	27.	b	28.	b
29.	d	30.	e	31.	c								

CHAPTER 2—Being Ethical and Socially Responsible

PRACTICE EXAM A

1.	e	2.	f	3.	c	4.	a	5.	d	6.	b	7.	T
8.	T	9.	F	10.	F	11.	T	12.	T	13.	F	14.	T
15.	F	16.	T	17.	F	18.	c	19.	a	20.	d	21.	e
22.	c	23.	a	24.	b	25.	b	26.	c	27.	e	28.	e
29.	a	30.	b										

PRACTICE EXAM B

1.	c	2.	f	3.	b	4.	d	5.	e	6.	a	7.	F
8.	T	9.	F	10.	T	11.	F	12.	T	13.	T	14.	F
15.	F	16.	F	17.	b	18.	d	19.	a	20.	b	21.	a
22.	e	23.	c	24.	d	25.	b	26.	e	27.	d	28.	a
29.	c												

PRACTICE EXAM C

1.	c	2.	f	3.	d	4.	b	5.	e	6.	a	7.	g
8.	F	9.	T	10.	T	11.	F	12.	T	13.	T	14.	F
15.	T	16.	T	17.	F	18.	T	19.	a	20.	b	21.	c
22.	e	23.	c	24.	e	25.	e	26.	b	27.	b	28.	a
29.	c												

CHAPTER 3—Exploring Global Business

PRACTICE EXAM A

1.	c	2.	f	3.	a	4.	d	5.	h	6.	b	7.	e
8.	g	9.	T	10.	T	11.	F	12.	T	13.	F	14.	T
15.	T	16.	T	17.	F	18.	T	19.	T	20.	T	21.	F
22.	d	23.	a	24.	d	25.	c	26.	b	27.	c	28.	b
29.	a	30.	a	31.	c	32.	b	33.	e	34.	a	35.	b
36.	c												

PRACTICE EXAM B

1.	e	2.	g	3.	j	4.	a	5.	d	6.	f	7.	i
8.	b	9.	h	10.	c	11.	F	12.	F	13.	T	14.	F
15.	T	16.	F	17.	T	18.	T	19.	T	20.	T	21.	F
22.	F	23.	F	24.	d	25.	c	26.	b	27.	b	28.	e
29.	a	30.	c	31.	b	32.	e	33.	c	34.	e	35.	a
36.	b	37.	e	38.	d								

PRACTICE EXAM C

1.	c	2.	b	3.	j	4.	d	5.	g	6.	a	7.	k
8.	f	9.	i	10.	e	11.	h	12.	l	13.	t	14.	p
15.	s	16.	m	17.	q	18.	n	19.	r	20.	o	21.	T
22.	T	23.	T	24.	F	25.	T	26.	F	27.	F	28.	T
29.	F	30.	F	31.	T	32.	F	33.	T	34.	b	35.	a
36.	c	37.	d	38.	a	39.	d	40.	c	41.	d	42.	a
43.	e	44.	a	45.	b	46.	d							

CHAPTER 4—Navigating the World of e-Business

PRACTICE EXAM A

1.	c	2.	b	3.	e	4.	d	5.	a	6.	f	7.	T
8.	T	9.	F	10.	T	11.	T	12.	F	13.	T	14.	F
15.	T	16.	T	17.	e	18.	b	19.	c	20.	a	21.	e
22.	b	23.	d	24.	a									

PRACTICE EXAM B

1.	e	2.	f	3.	a	4.	d	5.	b	6.	h	7.	c
8.	g	9.	T	10.	T	11.	F	12.	F	13.	T	14.	T
15.	T	16.	F	17.	T	18.	F	19.	b	20.	e	21.	c
22.	d	23.	d	24.	a	25.	b	26.	a				

PRACTICE EXAM C

1.	l	2.	k	3.	a	4.	c	5.	h	6.	g	7.	b
8.	d	9.	e	10.	n	11.	m	12.	j	13.	i	14.	f
15.	T	16.	F	17.	T	18.	F	19.	T	20.	F	21.	T
22.	F	23.	T	24.	F	25.	d	26.	e	27.	b	28.	a
29.	c	30.	d	31.	b	32.	a								

CHAPTER 5—Choosing a Form of Business Ownership

PRACTICE EXAM A

1.	f	2.	i	3.	c	4.	d	5.	j	6.	a	7.	e
8.	h	9.	b	10.	g	11.	T	12.	F	13.	T	14.	F
15.	F	16.	T	17.	T	18.	T	19.	F	20.	F	21.	T
22.	T	23.	a	24.	d	25.	c	26.	d	27.	e	28.	c
29.	c	30.	b	31.	d	32.	c	33.	c	34.	a	35.	d
36.	e												

PRACTICE EXAM B

1.	f	2.	b	3.	e	4.	d	5.	c	6.	a	7.	g
8.	h	9.	i	10.	j	11.	F	12.	T	13.	T	14.	T
15.	F	16.	T	17.	F	18.	F	19.	T	20.	T	21.	T
22.	F	23.	c	24.	d	25.	a	26.	c	27.	b	28.	e
29.	d	30.	b	31.	a	32.	c	33.	d	34.	b	35.	e
36.	a												

PRACTICE EXAM C

1.	a	2.	e	3.	h	4.	b	5.	j	6.	d	7.	g
8.	c	9.	i	10.	f	11.	T	12.	F	13.	T	14.	F
15.	T	16.	T	17.	T	18.	F	19.	T	20.	T	21.	F
22.	T	23.	d	24.	d	25.	b	26.	b	27.	c	28.	d
29.	d	30.	d	31.	b	32.	c	33.	a	34.	c	35.	d
36.	e												

CHAPTER 6—Small Business, Entrepreneurship, & Franchises

PRACTICE EXAM A

1.	e	2.	a	3.	f	4.	b	5.	c	6.	h	7.	d
8.	g	9.	T	10.	F	11.	T	12.	T	13.	F	14.	F
15.	F	16.	T	17.	F	18.	T	19.	b	20.	e	21.	d
22.	a	23.	c	24.	b	25.	d	26.	b	27.	e	28.	a

PRACTICE EXAM B

1.	e	2.	b	3.	a	4.	c	5.	d	6.	f	7.	T
8.	F	9.	T	10.	F	11.	T	12.	T	13.	T	14.	F
15.	T	16.	F	17.	c	18.	a	19.	b	20.	a	21.	c
22.	d	23.	b	24.	e	25.	b	26.	c				

PRACTICE EXAM C

1.	f	2.	a	3.	d	4.	b	5.	i	6.	e	7.	l
8.	j	9.	h	10.	k	11.	c	12.	g	13.	T	14.	F
15.	T	16.	T	17.	T	18.	T	19.	F	20.	T	21.	F
22.	T	23.	c	24.	e	25.	c	26.	b	27.	b	28.	a
29.	a	30.	e	31.	c	32.	b	33.	e				

CHAPTER 7—Understanding The Management Process

PRACTICE EXAM A

1.	i	2.	d	3.	l	4.	a	5.	j	6.	e	7.	b
8.	h	9.	k	10.	f	11.	c	12.	g	13.	m	14.	o
15.	n	16.	T	17.	T	18.	F	19.	T	20.	F	21.	T
22.	F	23.	T	24.	F	25.	F	26.	F	27.	T	28.	b
29.	b	30.	a	31.	e	32.	c	33.	b	34.	d	35.	e
36.	c	37.	e										

PRACTICE EXAM B

1. d	2. c	3. b	4. a	5. k	6. j	7. g
8. i	9. f	10. h	11. l	12. e	13. T	14. T
15. F	16. F	17. T	18. T	19. F	20. F	21. F
22. F	23. T	24. F	25. a	26. a	27. c	28. b
29. d	30. c	31. b	32. e	33. a	34. b	35. b

PRACTICE EXAM C

1. l	2. h	3. c	4. i	5. a	6. e	7. k
8. b	9. f	10. j	11. m	12. d	13. g	14. F
15. T	16. F	17. T	18. F	19. T	20. T	21. T
22. F	23. T	24. T	25. F	26. b	27. d	28. b
29. d	30. b	31. e	32. c	33. d	34. b	35. e

CHAPTER 8—Creating a Flexible Organization

PRACTICE EXAM A

1. h	2. o	3. a	4. i	5. d	6. m	7. b
8. g	9. n	10. e	11. k	12. c	13. f	14. j
15. l	16. T	17. F	18. T	19. F	20. F	21. T
22. T	23. F	24. T	25. F	26. T	27. F	28. F
29. F	30. b	31. c	32. e	33. d	34. b	35. d
36. e	37. c	38. b	39. d	40. b		

PRACTICE EXAM B

1. i	2. d	3. m	4. a	5. j	6. e	7. g
8. l	9. b	10. f	11. k	12. c	13. h	14. n
15. T	16. F	17. T	18. T	19. F	20. T	21. T
22. F	23. F	24. F	25. T	26. T	27. F	28. F
29. a	30. b	31. e	32. d	33. c	34. b	35. d
36. a	37. c	38. e	39. a	40. a		

PRACTICE EXAM C

1. l	2. h	3. a	4. d	5. n	6. j	7. f
8. b	9. k	10. i	11. c	12. e	13. g	14. m
15. T	16. T	17. F	18. F	19. T	20. F	21. T
22. F	23. T	24. F	25. T	26. T	27. T	28. T
29. a	30. c	31. a	32. b	33. e	34. e	35. c
36. a	37. b	38. d	39. e	40. a		

CHAPTER 9—Producing Quality Goods and Services

PRACTICE EXAM A

1.	i	2.	e	3.	a	4.	b	5.	f	6.	j	7.	c
8.	g	9.	h	10.	d	11.	m	12.	l	13.	n	14.	k
15.	T	16.	F	17.	F	18.	F	19.	T	20.	F	21.	F
22.	T	23.	F	24.	F	25.	F	26.	T	27.	b	28.	c
29.	e	30.	b	31.	a	32.	d	33.	a	34.	d	35.	b
36.	b												

PRACTICE EXAM B

1.	f	2.	i	3.	a	4.	g	5.	j	6.	b	7.	h
8.	c	9.	e	10.	d	11.	k	12.	l	13.	T	14.	T
15.	F	16.	F	17.	T	18.	T	19.	F	20.	T	21.	T
22.	F	23.	T	24.	F	25.	e	26.	e	27.	b	28.	e
29.	a	30.	a	31.	e	32.	d	33.	c	34.	b	35.	c

PRACTICE EXAM C

1.	d	2.	c	3.	b	4.	a	5.	f	6.	j	7.	g
8.	e	9.	h	10.	i	11.	k	12.	l	13.	F	14.	T
15.	T	16.	T	17.	T	18.	F	19.	F	20.	T	21.	T
22.	T	23.	T	24.	T	25.	a	26.	d	27.	b	28.	a
29.	c	30.	d	31.	c	32.	e	33.	b	34.	b	35.	e

CHAPTER 10—Attracting and Retaining the Best Employees

PRACTICE EXAM A

1.	e	2.	i	3.	l	4.	a	5.	f	6.	j	7.	b
8.	g	9.	k	10.	c	11.	h	12.	d	13.	T	14.	T
15.	T	16.	F	17.	T	18.	F	19.	T	20.	F	21.	T
22.	F	23.	F	24.	F	25.	T	26.	e	27.	a	28.	c
29.	d	30.	e	31.	b	32.	b	33.	c	34.	a	35.	d
36.	e	37.	c	38.	a	39.	b	40.	c				

PRACTICE EXAM B

1.	h	2.	b	3.	e	4.	a	5.	d	6.	c	7.	f
8.	g	9.	T	10.	F	11.	F	12.	F	13.	T	14.	F
15.	T	16.	T	17.	F	18.	F	19.	F	20.	T	21.	T
22.	e	23.	c	24.	a	25.	b	26.	c	27.	a	28.	d
29.	c	30.	b	31.	e	32.	d	33.	b	34.	d	35.	c
36.	a												

PRACTICE EXAM C

1.	d	2.	c	3.	g	4.	a	5.	e	6.	f	7.	b
8.	h	9.	F	10.	F	11.	T	12.	F	13.	T	14.	F
15.	T	16.	F	17.	T	18.	T	19.	F	20.	F	21.	T
22.	b	23.	a	24.	b	25.	a	26.	c	27.	d	28.	b
29.	d	30.	b	31.	e	32.	a	33.	c	34.	b	35.	c
36.	a												

CHAPTER 11—Motivating and Satisfying Employees

PRACTICE EXAM A

1.	c	2.	f	3.	a	4.	i	5.	b	6.	d	7.	h
8.	e	9.	k	10.	j	11.	l	12.	g	13.	T	14.	T
15.	T	16.	T	17.	F	18.	T	19.	T	20.	F	21.	T
22.	T	23.	T	24.	T	25.	F	26.	b	27.	d	28.	b
29.	a	30.	e	31.	c	32.	d	33.	a	34.	b	35.	c
36.	c												

PRACTICE EXAM B

1.	a	2.	h	3.	e	4.	c	5.	g	6.	b	7.	f
8.	d	9.	F	10.	F	11.	T	12.	T	13.	T	14.	F
15.	T	16.	T	17.	F	18.	F	19.	F	20.	F	21.	T
22.	e	23.	a	24.	a	25.	c	26.	b	27.	d	28.	c
29.	e	30.	a	31.	b	32.	d								

PRACTICE EXAM C

1.	g	2.	c	3.	f	4.	h	5.	b	6.	e	7.	d
8.	a	9.	i	10.	g	11.	e	12.	c	13.	a	14.	j
15.	h	16.	f	17.	d	18.	b	19.	T	20.	F	21.	F
22.	F	23.	F	24.	F	25.	T	26.	T	27.	T	28.	F
29.	T	30.	T	31.	T	32.	a	33.	d	34.	c	35.	e
36.	b	37.	e	38.	c	39.	d	40.	a	41.	e	42.	e

CHAPTER 12—Enhancing Union-Management Relations

PRACTICE EXAM A

1.	d	2.	a	3.	h	4.	c	5.	f	6.	e	7.	b
8.	g	9.	b	10.	h	11.	f	12.	c	13.	g	14.	d
15.	a	16.	e	17.	T	18.	F	19.	F	20.	F	21.	F
22.	T	23.	T	24.	T	25.	F	26.	T	27.	F	28.	F
29.	T	30.	F	31.	e	32.	d	33.	e	34.	a	35.	b
36.	e	37.	c	38.	b	39.	d	40.	a	41.	c	42.	c

PRACTICE EXAM B

1.	b	2.	e	3.	h	4.	a	5.	f	6.	i	7.	c
8.	g	9.	j	10.	d	11.	T	12.	T	13.	T	14.	F
15.	F	16.	F	17.	T	18.	T	19.	F	20.	T	21.	T
22.	F	23.	F	24.	F	25.	b	26.	a	27.	c	28.	d
29.	a	30.	b	31.	d	32.	c	33.	e	34.	a	35.	b
36.	d												

PRACTICE EXAM C

1.	a	2.	d	3.	g	4.	b	5.	e	6.	h	7.	c
8.	f	9.	F	10.	T	11.	F	12.	F	13.	F	14.	F
15.	F	16.	T	17.	T	18.	T	19.	T	20.	T	21.	T
22.	F	23.	c	24.	e	25.	b	26.	c	27.	d	28.	e
29.	c	30.	e	31.	a	32.	e	33.	a	34.	b		

CHAPTER 13—Building Customer Relationships Through Effective Marketing

PRACTICE EXAM A

1.	l	2.	a	3.	g	4.	j	5.	c	6.	h	7.	b
8.	k	9.	e	10.	i	11.	f	12.	d	13.	T	14.	T
15.	F	16.	T	17.	F	18.	F	19.	T	20.	T	21.	F
22.	T	23.	T	24.	F	25.	b	26.	b	27.	e	28.	a
29.	c	30.	d	31.	c	32.	c	33.	c	34.	e	35.	e
36.	a	37.	b										

PRACTICE EXAM B

1.	g	2.	d	3.	h	4.	j	5.	e	6.	a	7.	b
8.	f	9.	i	10.	c	11.	k	12.	l	13.	T	14.	F
15.	T	16.	T	17.	T	18.	F	19.	T	20.	F	21.	T
22.	T	23.	T	24.	T	25.	a	26.	c	27.	a	28.	c
29.	d	30.	e	31.	c	32.	c	33.	a	34.	e	35.	b
36.	a	37.	c										

PRACTICE EXAM C

1.	e	2.	a	3.	c	4.	f	5.	b	6.	d	7.	g
8.	j	9.	h	10.	i	11.	T	12.	F	13.	T	14.	F
15.	T	16.	T	17.	T	18.	T	19.	F	20.	F	21.	F
22.	F	23.	T	24.	b	25.	e	26.	c	27.	d	28.	e
29.	a	30.	b	31.	c	32.	d	33.	d				

CHAPTER 14—Creating and Pricing Products that Satisfy Customers

PRACTICE EXAM A

1.	h	2.	k	3.	m	4.	a	5.	c	6.	e	7.	g
8.	j	9.	l	10.	b	11.	d	12.	f	13.	i	14.	n
15.	T	16.	T	17.	F	18.	F	19.	F	20.	T	21.	F
22.	F	23.	F	24.	T	25.	T	26.	T	27.	b	28.	c
29.	a	30.	a	31.	b	32.	d	33.	b	34.	a	35.	c
36.	b	37.	d	38.	e								

PRACTICE EXAM B

1.	d	2.	b	3.	e	4.	a	5.	f	6.	c	7.	g
8.	i	9.	j	10.	h	11.	n	12.	m	13.	l	14.	k
15.	p	16.	o	17.	a	18.	f	19.	b	20.	g	21.	c
22.	d	23.	i	24.	j	25.	e	26.	h	27.	o	28.	q
29.	m	30.	p	31.	n	32.	l	33.	k	34.	F	35.	T
36.	T	37.	F	38.	T	39.	T	40.	F	41.	T	42.	F
43.	T	44.	F	45.	T	46.	T	47.	b	48.	b	49.	e
50.	b	51.	c	52.	c	53.	a	54.	d	55.	b	56.	c
57.	c	58.	e	59.	d	60.	a						

PRACTICE EXAM C

1.	g	2.	j	3.	l	4.	b	5.	d	6.	i	7.	e
8.	a	9.	f	10.	c	11.	h	12.	k	13.	F	14.	T
15.	F	16.	F	17.	T	18.	F	19.	T	20.	T	21.	F
22.	T	23.	T	24.	T	25.	T	26.	T	27.	F	28.	b
29.	b	30.	d	31.	e	32.	c	33.	e	34.	e	35.	c
36.	b	37.	b	38.	a	39.	d						

CHAPTER 15—Wholesaling, Retailing, and Physical Distribution

PRACTICE EXAM A

1.	g	2.	a	3.	d	4.	b	5.	h	6.	c	7.	e
8.	f	9.	j	10.	m	11.	i	12.	k	13.	n	14.	l
15.	i	16.	j	17.	c	18.	d	19.	k	20.	h	21.	a
22.	e	23.	g	24.	b	25.	f	26.	T	27.	T	28.	F
29.	T	30.	F	31.	F	32.	T	33.	F	34.	F	35.	T
36.	F	37.	T	38.	T	39.	F	40.	a	41.	a	42.	c
43.	e	44.	d	45.	e	46.	b	47.	a	48.	c	49.	e

PRACTICE EXAM B

1.	c	2.	f	3.	i	4.	a	5.	g	6.	j	7.	b
8.	e	9.	h	10.	d	11.	l	12.	k	13.	T	14.	F
15.	T	16.	F	17.	T	18.	T	19.	T	20.	T	21.	F
22.	F	23.	T	24.	F	25.	T	26.	F	27.	b	28.	d
29.	d	30.	c	31.	a	32.	b	33.	d	34.	e	35.	a
36.	b												

PRACTICE EXAM C

1.	b	2.	e	3.	h	4.	c	5.	f	6.	i	7.	a
8.	d	9.	g	10.	j	11.	b	12.	d	13.	h	14.	n
15.	i	16.	g	17.	k	18.	p	19.	a	20.	l	21.	m
22.	j	23.	f	24.	c	25.	e	26.	o	27.	F	28.	T
29.	T	30.	T	31.	F	32.	F	33.	F	34.	T	35.	F
36.	F	37.	F	38.	T	39.	T	40.	F	41.	a	42.	b
43.	a	44.	c	45.	d	46.	e	47.	a	48.	e	49.	b

CHAPTER 16—Developing Integrated Marketing Communications

PRACTICE EXAM A

1.	c	2.	e	3.	a	4.	d	5.	f	6.	b	7.	g
8.	h	9.	k	10.	l	11.	i	12.	m	13.	j	14.	T
15.	F	16.	F	17.	F	18.	T	19.	T	20.	T	21.	T
22.	T	23.	T	24.	T	25.	T	26.	F	27.	F	28.	b
29.	d	30.	e	31.	a	32.	e	33.	b	34.	a	35.	c
36.	b	37.	b	38.	b								

PRACTICE EXAM B

1.	a	2.	e	3.	h	4.	b	5.	f	6.	c	7.	g
8.	d	9.	j	10.	i	11.	F	12.	F	13.	F	14.	T
15.	T	16.	T	17.	T	18.	T	19.	F	20.	T	21.	F
22.	T	23.	F	24.	T	25.	d	26.	e	27.	a	28.	a
29.	d	30.	c	31.	d	32.	e	33.	d	34.	a	35.	e
36.	c												

PRACTICE EXAM C

1.	b	2.	e	3.	h	4.	k	5.	n	6.	a	7.	f
8.	i	9.	l	10.	c	11.	g	12.	j	13.	m	14.	d
15.	F	16.	T	17.	T	18.	F	19.	F	20.	F	21.	F
22.	F	23.	T	24.	F	25.	F	26.	T	27.	F	28.	T
29.	c	30.	a	31.	c	32.	c	33.	a	34.	d	35.	c
36.	b	37.	d	38.	e								

CHAPTER 17—Acquiring, Organizing, and Using Information

PRACTICE EXAM A

1.	b	2.	a	3.	c	4.	g	5.	d	6.	e	7.	f
8.	h	9.	T	10.	T	11.	T	12.	F	13.	T	14.	T
15.	F	16.	T	17.	T	18.	F	19.	F	20.	T	21.	F
22.	T	23.	T	24.	a	25.	d	26.	b	27.	c	28.	e
29.	b	30.	b	31.	a	32.	e	33.	d				

PRACTICE EXAM B

1.	i	2.	b	3.	f	4.	d	5.	j	6.	a	7.	e
8.	c	9.	g	10.	h	11.	F	12.	T	13.	T	14.	F
15.	F	16.	F	17.	F	18.	T	19.	F	20.	F	21.	F
22.	T	23.	F	24.	e	25.	c	26.	e	27.	b	28.	c
29.	a	30.	d	31.	e	32.	c	33.	b				

PRACTICE EXAM C

1.	c	2.	f	3.	a	4.	d	5.	g	6.	b	7.	e
8.	h	9.	i	10.	k	11.	j	12.	l	13.	F	14.	T
15.	F	16.	T	17.	F	18.	F	19.	T	20.	T	21.	F
22.	F	23.	T	24.	T	25.	T	26.	b	27.	e	28.	a
29.	d	30.	b	31.	e	32.	e	33.	b	34.	c	35.	c

CHAPTER 18—Using Accounting Information

PRACTICE EXAM A

1.	a	2.	g	3.	b	4.	h	5.	c	6.	d	7.	e
8.	i	9.	f	10.	j	11.	a	12.	e	13.	h	14.	c
15.	f	16.	d	17.	g	18.	b	19.	i	20.	j	21.	T
22.	F	23.	F	24.	F	25.	T	26.	F	27.	F	28.	F
29.	T	30.	F	31.	T	32.	F	33.	F	34.	b	35.	b
36.	d	37.	c	38.	c	39.	d	40.	b	41.	a	42.	c
43.	e												

PRACTICE EXAM B

1.	b	2.	e	3.	h	4.	a	5.	f	6.	c	7.	g
8.	d	9.	d	10.	g	11.	b	12.	f	13.	c	14.	h
15.	a	16.	e	17.	F	18.	F	19.	F	20.	T	21.	F
22.	T	23.	F	24.	T	25.	F	26.	T	27.	T	28.	F
29.	T	30.	d	31.	d	32.	b	33.	c	34.	a	35.	e
36.	b	37.	c	38.	a	39.	e	40.	d				

PRACTICE EXAM C

1.	a	2.	e	3.	b	4.	f	5.	c	6.	g	7.	d
8.	i	9.	l	10.	j	11.	m	12.	k	13.	n	14.	h
15.	F	16.	T	17.	F	18.	F	19.	T	20.	T	21.	T
22.	F	23.	T	24.	T	25.	F	26.	F	27.	F	28.	e
29.	a	30.	b	31.	c	32.	d	33.	c	34.	e	35.	c
36.	b	37.	e	38.	c								

CHAPTER 19—Understanding Money, Banking, and Credit

PRACTICE EXAM A

1.	h	2.	a	3.	d	4.	i	5.	b	6.	g	7.	c
8.	e	9.	j	10.	f	11.	T	12.	F	13.	T	14.	F
15.	T	16.	T	17.	T	18.	T	19.	F	20.	T	21.	F
22.	T	23.	F	24.	T	25.	e	26.	a	27.	b	28.	c
29.	c	30.	b	31.	a	32.	d	33.	e	34.	d		

PRACTICE EXAM B

1.	b	2.	e	3.	h	4.	a	5.	f	6.	i	7.	c
8.	g	9.	j	10.	d	11.	T	12.	F	13.	F	14.	T
15.	F	16.	F	17.	T	18.	F	19.	T	20.	T	21.	F
22.	T	23.	F	24.	F	25.	d	26.	c	27.	b	28.	e
29.	c	30.	b	31.	a	32.	e	33.	a	34.	b		

PRACTICE EXAM C

1.	i	2.	a	3.	d	4.	b	5.	c	6.	e	7.	h
8.	f	9.	g	10.	j	11.	n	12.	l	13.	m	14.	k
15.	T	16.	T	17.	F	18.	F	19.	T	20.	T	21.	F
22.	F	23.	F	24.	F	25.	T	26.	T	27.	F	28.	T
29.	b	30.	e	31.	a	32.	a	33.	b	34.	c	35.	d
36.	a	37.	e	38.	d								

CHAPTER 20-Mastering Financial Management

PRACTICE EXAM A

1.	d	2.	g	3.	j	4.	a	5.	e	6.	h	7.	k
8.	b	9.	f	10.	i	11.	l	12.	c	13.	T	14.	F
15.	T	16.	F	17.	T	18.	T	19.	T	20.	T	21.	F
22.	T	23.	F	24.	F	25.	F	26.	F	27.	a	28.	b
29.	c	30.	c	31.	a	32.	d	33.	b	34.	b	35.	e
36.	b	37.	c	38.	e								

PRACTICE EXAM B

1.	c	2.	e	3.	h	4.	j	5.	l	6.	a	7.	d
8.	f	9.	i	10.	k	11.	b	12.	g	13.	F	14.	F
15.	T	16.	T	17.	F	18.	T	19.	T	20.	F	21.	F
22.	F	23.	T	24.	T	25.	F	26.	F	27.	e	28.	d
29.	b	30.	d	31.	a	32.	b	33.	e	34.	d	35.	a
36.	d												

PRACTICE EXAM C

1. b	2. d	3. f	4. h	5. a	6. e	7. g
8. c	9. a	10. c	11. e	12. g	13. i	14. j
15. b	16. d	17. f	18. h	19. T	20. T	21. F
22. F	23. T	24. F	25. F	26. T	27. T	28. F
29. F	30. T	31. F	32. F	33. c	34. a	35. d
36. b	37. e	38. c	39. e	40. b	41. c	42. d

CHAPTER 21—Understanding Securities Markets and Investments

PRACTICE EXAM A

1. b	2. e	3. h	4. k	5. a	6. f	7. i
8. l	9. c	10. g	11. j	12. d	13. T	14. F
15. F	16. F	17. F	18. F	19. T	20. T	21. T
22. T	23. T	24. T	25. F	26. T	27. F	28. T
29. T	30. F	31. a	32. b	33. e	34. b	35. e
36. b	37. e	38. c	39. d	40. c	41. a	

PRACTICE EXAM B

1. c	2. f	3. i	4. k	5. a	6. d	7. g
8. j	9. l	10. b	11. e	12. h	13. m	14. F
15. T	16. F	17. F	18. T	19. T	20. F	21. F
22. F	23. F	24. T	25. F	26. F	27. F	28. e
29. b	30. d	31. b	32. d	33. c	34. a	35. b
36. c	37. a	38. d				

PRACTICE EXAM C

1. h	2. a	3. f	4. c	5. e	6. g	7. b
8. d	9. i	10. j	11. k	12. l	13. p	14. o
15. m	16. n	17. F	18. T	19. T	20. T	21. T
22. F	23. T	24. T	25. F	26. F	27. F	28. T
29. F	30. T	31. b	32. b	33. a	34. d	35. c
36. a	37. c	38. a	39. c	40. c